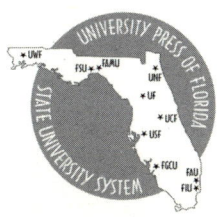

Florida A&M University, Tallahassee
Florida Atlantic University, Boca Raton
Florida Gulf Coast University, Ft. Myers
Florida International University, Miami
Florida State University, Tallahassee
University of Central Florida, Orlando
University of Florida, Gainesville
University of North Florida, Jacksonville
University of South Florida, Tampa
University of West Florida, Pensacola

Evil, Madness, and the Occult in Argentine Poetry

MELANIE NICHOLSON

University Press of Florida
Gainesville · Tallahassee · Tampa · Boca Raton
Pensacola · Orlando · Miami · Jacksonville · Ft. Myers

Copyright 2002 by Melanie Nicholson
Printed in the United States of America on acid-free, TCF (totally chlorine-free) paper
All rights reserved

07 06 05 04 03 02   6 5 4 3 2 1

Library of Congress Cataloging-in-Publication Data
Nicholson, Melanie, 1955–
Evil, madness, and the occult in Argentine poetry / Melanie Nicholson.
Includes bibliographical references and index.
ISBN 0-8130-2482-X (cloth : alk. paper)
1. Argentine poetry—20th century—History and criticism. 2. Orozco, Olga—Criticism and interpretation. 3. Pizarnik, Alejandra, 1936–1972—Criticism and interpretation. 4. Fijman, Jacobo, 1898–1970—Criticism and interpretation. 5. Occultism in literature. 6. Evil in literature. 7. Mental illness in literature. 8. French literature—20th century—Influence. I. Title.
PQ7671 .N53 2002
861'.60937—dc21   2002016591

The University Press of Florida is the scholarly publishing agency for the State University System of Florida, comprising Florida A&M University, Florida Atlantic University, Florida Gulf Coast University, Florida International University, Florida State University, University of Central Florida, University of Florida, University of North Florida, University of South Florida, and University of West Florida.

University Press of Florida
15 Northwest 15th Street
Gainesville, FL 32611–2079
http://www.upf.com

Contents

Preface   vii

Introduction   xi

1. The Esoteric Tradition in Literature   1

2. Gnostic and Hermetic Discourse in the Poetry of Olga Orozco   14

3. The Occult as Revelation and Power of Passage in Orozco's Poetry   40

4. Alejandra Pizarnik and the Literature of Evil   66

5. Poetry and Madness in Jacobo Fijman   95

6. The Dreams of Drowned Men: Jacobo Fijman and Vicente Zito Lema   123

Conclusion. A Talisman in the Darkness   149

Notes   175

Bibliography   185

Index   193

To my parents

Preface

The story of this book begins in 1978, when I first traveled to Argentina as a graduate student with a Fulbright scholarship to study contemporary women's poetry. Although I examined the work of more than 120 poets, only a few distinguished themselves as worthy of sustained study. Among these were Olga Orozco and Alejandra Pizarnik. After months of research in Buenos Aires, several observations presented themselves to me. First, it was clear that poetry was alive and well in Argentina. In spite of the economic hardships and political repression of that period, bookstores were still bustling, public poetry readings and book signings were abundant, and the act of declaring oneself a poet was not considered a sign of neurosis or social marginality (as I feared it was in my own country).

Second, women poets did not see themselves as victims of discrimination. I had done my homework in university libraries in the United States, reviewing numerous anthologies of Argentine poetry, and bore my evidence with me when I arrived in Buenos Aires: women poets appeared, on the average, in a ratio of one to twelve to their male counterparts. This "evidence" did not seem to faze most of the women I interviewed. The idea of separating female from male writers as the objects of a literary study seemed suspicious to most of them, and statistical averages meant little to individual poets, who were sure, in almost every case, that their own work had received its due recognition. The only voices opposing this general opinion were a few of the younger women (usually those without the economic means to promote their work) and one well-established older writer, María Elena Walsh, who said to me simply, "Feminism has not yet arrived in Argentina."

A third observation that arose out of my study was one that I had not gone seeking in any way but that was to define the direction of my subsequent research. It was difficult to define at first, but I knew it had to do with a certain orientation that many of the poets I was reading had in common. There seemed to be a widespread interest in the occult arts—magic, witchcraft, astrology, the tarot and other forms of divination. At the same time, there was an interest in spiritual movements only tangentially connected to orthodox Catholicism or Judaism. Finally, I noticed that a certain fairly limited coterie of literary antecedents tended to be named whenever the subject of influences arose: the Marquis de Sade, Novalis, Gérard de Nerval, Charles Baudelaire, Arthur Rimbaud, Isidore Ducasse (self-styled the Comte de Lautréamont), Stéphane Mallarmé, André Breton, and Antonin Artaud. Names could be added or subtracted from each list, but these nine seemed to form a permanent constellation in the sky over Buenos Aires.

Many years later, when I wrote my dissertation on the poetry of Olga Orozco, I saw that these recurring elements and influences fell under the rubric of "the esoteric tradition." It seemed that this was the most coherent way to approach Orozco's poetry, the best way to do justice to a poetic career that spanned five decades but that seemed to return with obsessive regularity to the same concerns: the nostalgia for a lost unity, a distrust of rational thought, the belief in an absolute but ungraspable reality, the doctrine of poetry as revelation. As my work expanded again to take in other Argentine poets, and then settled on the work of Alejandra Pizarnik and Jacobo Fijman, I began to comprehend the significance of that set of shared interests that I first noticed in the writers I had interviewed and read in 1978 and 1979. Questions arose: How can we explain the extreme attraction that figures such as Lautréamont and Rimbaud held for writers in twentieth-century Argentina? To what extent was the attraction a "purely literary" one? Why, in fact, have so many Argentine poets of the century followed a literary track—as opposed to a more directly social or political one—in their work? Why did Breton and the surrealist movement take hold so firmly in Argentine ground? What are the tenets underlying the ancient esoteric traditions that seemed to provide answers to the existential questions facing writers living under Hipólito Yrigoyen, under Perón, or under the military dictatorships of the 1960s and 1970s? Finally, what is it about the status of language in the twentieth century that made certain Argentine writers embrace (to borrow Lynn Wilkinson's phrase) "the dream of an absolute language"? These are the questions this book explores, through the work of three of Argentina's most captivating modern poets.

Acknowledgments

I wish to thank Enrique Fierro and Naomi Lindstrom of the University of Texas at Austin for their wise tutelage in the initial and middle stages of this research. I am also indebted to Naomi Lindstrom, Jacobo Sefamí, Jill Kuhnheim, and Marina van Zuylen for their careful reading of the manuscript and their insightful suggestions. In Buenos Aires, my conversations with Vicente Zito Lema were invaluable in helping me to understand the life and mind of Jacobo Fijman. My sincere thanks to Ana Prados for proofreading the manuscript and for providing me with thoughtful feedback on the translations. Finally, thanks to my family and friends for their support and encouragement at every step of the way, and to my son Isaac for smiling through it all.

A part of chapter 2 appeared in *Revista de Estudios Hispánicos* 35 (spring 2001), a part of chapter 3 appeared in *Letras Femeninas* 24 (1998), and a modified version of chapter 4 appeared in *Latin American Literary Review* 27, no. 54 (1999); I am grateful to these journals for permission to republish these pieces.

Poems and poetry extracts from the following books by Olga Orozco are reprinted by permission: *Obra poética* (Buenos Aires: Ediciones Corregidor, 1979), *Mutaciones de la realidad* (Buenos Aires: Editorial Sudamericana, 1979), *La noche a la deriva* (Mexico City: Fondo de Cultura Económica, 1983), *En el revés del cielo* (Buenos Aires: Editorial Sudamericana, 1987), *Con esta boca, en este mundo* (Buenos Aires: Editorial Sudamericana, 1994); courtesy of Alvaro Lavia. Excerpts from the interview with Olga Orozco are taken from Jacobo Sefamí, *De la imaginación poética: Conversaciones con Gonzalo Rojas, Olga Orozco, Alvaro Mutis y José Kozer* (Caracas: Monte Avila Editores Latinoamericana, 1996); reprinted by permission of Jacobo Sefamí. Poems and poetry extracts by Alejandra Pizarnik are taken from *Obras completas* (Buenos Aires: Ediciones Corregidor, 1994); reprinted by permission of Editorial Lumen, Barcelona. Poems by Jacobo Fijman are taken from *Obra poética* (Buenos Aires: La Torre Abolida, 1983); reprinted by permission of Vicente Zito Lema. Excerpts from Vicente Zito Lema, *El pensamiento de Jacobo Fijman, o El viaje hacia la otra realidad* (Buenos Aires: Rodolfo Alonso Editor, 1970), are reprinted by permission of Vicente Zito Lema.

Unless otherwise noted, all translations are mine.

Introduction

Occultism and literary theory are not comfortable bedfellows in the postmodern age. The occult or esoteric traditions are typically viewed as aberrations from the mainstream literary project and are generally held in poor regard by the scholarly community. The categories of cultural production into which most occult beliefs and practices fall are either dismissed as quaint holdovers from nineteenth-century enterprises such as the Order of the Golden Dawn, to which Irish poet William Butler Yeats belonged, or as late-twentieth-century pseudosciences and pseudoreligions collectively referred to as "New Age." Nevertheless, certain twentieth-century writers in Europe and the Americas have in fact drawn significantly from the esoteric traditions in the formation of their own worldviews; to deny this significant literary and cultural background is to fail to read these writers in the comprehensive way their work demands. In his *The Birth of Modernism: Ezra Pound, T. S. Eliot, W. B. Yeats, and the Occult* (1993), Leon Surette makes the following claim: "If we cannot expunge the occult from the history of modernism (and we cannot), then the sensible thing is to learn more about the occult so that we can not only recognize it when we meet it in a literary setting, but also have a clearer sense of what it is that mainstream literary scholarship has been avoiding for the past fifty years and more" (10). I would argue that literary scholarship has not entirely avoided the issue of esoteric thought in literature. Previous decades have seen the publication of such seminal works as Gwendolyn Bays's *The Orphic Vision: Seer Poets from Novalis to Rimbaud* (1964), Denis Saurat's *Literature and Occult Tradition: Studies in Philosophical Poetry* (1966), Octavio Paz's *Los hijos del limo: Del romanticismo a la vanguardia* [Children of the mire: Modern poetry from romanticism to the avant-garde] (1974), Harold Bloom's *Kabbalah and Criticism* (1975), and Anna Balakian's *Surrealism: The Road to the Absolute* (1986). Surette's book, as well as other recent publications such as Karl Erich Grozinger's *Kafka and*

Kabbalah (1994), Timothy Matterer's *Modernist Alchemy: Poetry and the Occult* (1995), Roger Shattuck's *Forbidden Knowledge* (1996), William Gorski's *Yeats and Alchemy* (1996), and Lynn Wilkinson's *The Dream of an Absolute Language: Emanuel Swedenborg and French Literary Culture* (1996), point to a renewed interest in the occult traditions as they have surfaced in post-Renaissance European literature.

Unfortunately, only a limited amount of scholarship has been dedicated to similar manifestations within the field of Latin American literature. Octavio Paz touches upon certain Spanish American writers in *Children of the Mire*, but his focus is on European writers, and his time frame does not extend beyond the avant-garde. In his book *Poesía y conocimiento* [Poetry and knowledge], Spanish critic Ramón Xirau has identified certain orientations relating to an esoteric worldview in the work of Paz, Jorge Luis Borges, and the Cuban poet José Lezama Lima. He traces modern Hispanic poetry to its origins in romanticism, especially to Samuel Taylor Coleridge's claim that the imagination is a primary agent in all human perception. With regard to the poetry of Paz, Xirau claims in particular that "Las palabras . . . llevan siempre una poderosa carga de contenidos mágicos" [Words . . . always carry a powerful charge of magical content] (94). The association of the poetic word with sometimes otherworldly power and knowledge is, as I will demonstrate, a foundational myth for the poets in this study. The Nicaraguan *modernista* [Hispanic Modernist] poet Rubén Darío has been the subject of two important studies based on esoteric thought: Raymond Skyrme's *Rubén Darío and the Pythagorean Tradition* (1975), and Cathy Jrade's *Rubén Darío and the Romantic Search for Unity: The Modernist Recourse to Esoteric Tradition* (1983). Jrade argues forcefully that Darío—himself credited with radically changing the direction of Spanish-language poetry in the postromantic era—was heavily influenced by occultist thought. Jrade's broad claim also lays the groundwork for the present study: "Not only does the esoteric tradition lie at the heart of Modernist poetics, but it is also the key to understanding Modernism's place in the "modern tradition"; that is, with regard to European literature that preceded it and the contemporary Hispanic literature for which it prepared the way" (3).[1] Finally, it bears mention that within the realm of Argentine literature, Saúl Sosnowski has explored esoteric influences in the work of well-known poet and fiction writer Jorge Luis Borges in his book *Borges y la Cábala: La búsqueda del verbo* (1976).

The work done by Paz, Jrade, Sosnowski, and others has initiated a discourse which I hope to broaden with the present study. To date, very little work has been devoted to examining esoteric thought in Spanish American poets beyond the *modernismo* of Darío or the *vanguardismo* of the early twentieth century.[2] In spite of the interest in Borges's incursions into the Cabala, the importance of occultist worldviews within Argentine poetry has gone virtually unnoticed by critics. With regard to literary esoterism, I believe that Argentina presents a particularly fascinating locus of critical inquiry owing to its historically close ties to European—particularly French—cultural production. Orozco, Pizarnik, and Fijman, like virtually all their literary-minded compatriots, were avid readers of the romantics, the symbolists, and the surrealists, the very writers in which esoteric thought was repeatedly incarnated. But literary influence is never a simple matter of transference over time and space. My study explores the complex, often contradictory ways in which the worldviews of writers like Charles Baudelaire or André Breton were refashioned in a world characterized by the shifting sands of the Argentine pampa or the corridors of a Buenos Aires mental hospital.

The esoteric worldview, as it appears in the best modernist writing, is not a matter of ghosts and poltergeists, witch's sabbaths and magic crystals. It is, rather, a sober and uncompromising approach to human existence, and in particular to the production of literary texts. It is a profoundly religious stance, if we take *religious* in its original sense of *religare,* meaning "to bind back." Virtually all esoteric thought begins with the principle of primordial unity, the notion that the world as we know it is the result of a fall, the shattering of an original whole. Human existence, in this view, takes on meaning only to the extent that it participates in the effort to bind back the fragmented elements, to reunite existence and essence, the contingent and the absolute. Paz's approach to the history of modern poetry reflects this view: "The revolt of the romantic poets and their modern heirs was not so much a protest against the exile from God as a search for the lost half, a descent into the region that puts us in communication with the *other*" (*Bow* 247).

In the early twentieth century, it was the French surrealists who most programmatically articulated the esoteric principles based on the notion of an essential *elsewhere.* Such an approach may seem antiquated and even misguided to those of us who, in the postmodern period, have come to view the very notions of "essence" and "absolute" with profound distrust. And yet, as Anna Balakian points out in her seminal book *Surrealism: The Road to the Absolute* (1986, 3rd ed.), these notions were far from naïve and cannot be easily dismissed:

> [C]urrent philosophers may well note extensive resignation to man's relative unimportance in the universe, which makes the notion of "absolute" vision appear derisive and anachronistic; in that context the surrealist quest may seem naïve in its revised perception of the sacred and the sublime, which is basic to the surrealist aspiration and the definition of the poet. But it must be remembered that Breton and his colleagues, most of them scientifically trained, and virtually all agnostics vis-à-vis established religions, had an acute sense of the mountain peak, i.e. the progressive and ultimate grasp of the total experience of existence: "the exceptional intensity of man before the spectacle of life" as Breton expressed it. Poetic truth was conceived as a gradation with a supreme point, unattainable but conceivable nonetheless. The apparatus of sensory coordination toward that absolute goal was the catalytic power of poetry. (6)

Naming Paz as the "sturdiest heir" of surrealism, Balakian claims that it is in the countries of Latin America where this movement has found its most fertile ground, "where the philosophy of surrealism . . . is crystallized in poetic imagery rather than in technical devices of simple wordplay and collage" (7).[3] Her point is well taken: it is the surrealist aesthetic—its conception of life and art, and not its sometimes mechanical techniques—that has informed the work of writers from Mexico to Argentina, from the 1920s to the present day. This aesthetic, as I will subsequently explain, has its deepest roots in the esoteric tradition. This is why Breton, when questioned about the significance of esoteric thought to the surrealist movement, commented: "[I]t's not really a matter of knowing whether a strict oral or written tradition has managed to stretch secretly from Antiquity to the present day . . . but rather of finding out whether the works that continue to influence us maintain appreciable—even if impure—ties with this tradition. I consider the matter beyond dispute when it comes to Hugo, Nerval, Baudelaire, Rimbaud, Lautréamont, and Jarry (and I believe it's only a matter of time for Fourier, for example, or Mallarmé)" (*Conversations* 218). By way of extrapolation, I would state that the appreciable, often impure ties that certain Argentine poets have maintained with this tradition—up to and including surrealism—is the subject of the present study.

* * *

This book examines in detail, from the perspective of the esoteric tradition in literature, several key works of three important twentieth-century Argentine poets: Jacobo Fijman (1898–1970), Olga Orozco (1920–1999), and Alejandra Pizarnik (1936–1972). I argue that by adopting certain conventions of an esoteric worldview, these writers are able to manipulate a system of tropes that posits the magical power of the poetic word; simultaneously, however, they undermine the efficacy of the word by acknowledging its failure to effect a change in the world. This fundamental tension informs the poetics of all three writers. The choice to concentrate on these writers—excluding, unfortunately, certain other worthy subjects, such as Aldo Pellegrini, Enrique Molina, and Amelia Biagioni—was made on the basis of their well-established reputations as lyric poets (particularly in the case of Orozco and Pizarnik), and of their close adherence to precepts laid out by previous writers in this highly self-conscious literary tradition. The work of these poets intersects at many points, allowing me to follow certain threads from one to the other. Orozco, for example, dedicates a poem to Pizarnik after the latter's suicide, in which she speaks of crossing a threshold into forbidden garden, a commonplace among the romantics; she also dedicates a poem to Fijman in which she alludes to him as a "hostage from another world." Notwithstanding these intersections, however, the three writers differ profoundly in their approaches to poetry. Consequently, I am able discuss their work from three perspectives: the rhetoric of the occult in Orozco, the rhetoric of evil in Pizarnik, and the rhetoric of madness in Fijman. These perspectives, as I will demonstrate, represent overlapping rather than reiterative formulations of esoterism.

For reasons of argumentative clarity, I have chosen to deviate from a strict chronological presentation of the three writers. I begin with Orozco simply because her work articulates most insistently and comprehensively the principles of literary esoterism. An analysis of her poetics provides a solid introduction to the majority of the issues that will emerge as fundamental to my approach as a whole. I then consider Pizarnik, in many ways a protegée of Orozco, who follows her lead but articulates a unique, highly subjective approach to these principles. Finally, I examine the work of Jacobo Fijman as that of a marginalized writer who explores the dynamic between reason and unreason that lies at the heart of an esoteric view of the world. Due to the strange turns of Fijman's life, his lyric voice emerges in two distinct moments (the late 1920s and again in the late 1960s), further complicating any attempt at simple chronological presentation.

Chapter 1 of this study, "The Esoteric Tradition in Literature," presents an overview of the grounding principles of this complex system of beliefs. I begin with the question "What does it mean to refer broadly to the esoteric traditions as a basis for literary analysis?" Although I trace the development of esoteric expression in literature in roughly chronological sequence from the late eighteenth century onward, my overall approach in this chapter is more conceptual than historical: I am interested in identifying certain shared assumptions—such as the notion of a transcendent reality or the analogy of poetry and magic—that reappear in different guises over the centuries. After touching briefly on Renaissance developments in esoteric thought, I focus on a nucleus of German and French writers of the past two centuries—Novalis, Gérard de Nerval, Baudelaire, Arthur Rimbaud, Stéphane Mallarmé, and, finally, the French surrealists—all of whom articulate, in varying modes, the tenets of esoteric or occult thought.

The subsequent two chapters continue to develop the basic premises outlined in the first chapter by examining the complex mythico-philosophical backgrounds of Orozco's poetry. Orozco, the 1998 recipient of the prestigious Juan Rulfo Prize for Literature, by the time of her death in 1999 had earned a reputation as one of Latin America's most respected contemporary poets. In the fifty-year span of her literary career, she published nine volumes of poetry and two collections of short stories. Her work is widely anthologized in Spanish and has appeared in translation in journals and anthologies in the United States. Generally considered a member of the "Generation of 1940," she began writing in a neoromantic vein that reflected the influence of the Austrian poet Rainer Maria Rilke and of the Chilean Pablo Neruda. But it was French surrealism (with its antecedents leading back to the German romantics) that was to have the most powerful impact on her writing. By the early 1960s, Orozco's work had fully adopted a discourse grounded in the occult traditions. The majority of my analysis is based on her 1962 collection *Los juegos peligrosos* [The dangerous games] and on three later volumes: *Mutaciones de la realidad* [Mutations of reality] (1979), *La noche a la deriva* [Night adrift] (1983), and *En el revés del cielo* [On the other side of the sky] (1987). Although her last books of poetry showed a more abstract, metaphysical orientation, Orozco's work never strayed far from the articulations of occult beliefs that are the basis of the present study.

Chapter 2 examines gnosticism and hermeticism as the major philosophico-religious foundations upon which Orozco's poetry is constructed. The gnostic worldview posited a radical dualism of good and evil, locating the human subject at an unbridgeable distance from the divine world. Both gnosticism and hermeticism developed redemptive schemes based on rituals leading toward *gnosis*, or specialized knowledge of the absolute. I show Orozco's work to be permeated with symbolism drawn from these two belief systems. For Orozco, the act of writing poetry constituted an authentic—though complex and problematic—form of gnostic practice. Chapter 3 follows with an examination of the metaphorical "dangerous games" Orozco explores in her poetry: alchemy, divination, and magic. In the literary context, each of these occult arts serves as a system of tropes the poet employs in her attempt to transcend the material world. Through a close reading of certain key poems in Orozco's oeuvre, I show that poetic language itself, that is, incantatory magic, is the basis for Orozco's most radical experiment with occultism.

In chapter 4, I establish certain links between Orozco and Pizarnik before proceeding to explore the work of the younger poet, who in many ways fashioned herself after the French *poètes maudits* of the nineteenth century. Pizarnik, the daughter of Russian Jewish immigrants, committed suicide in 1972 at the age of thirty-six. Her work has been the subject of much critical attention in the past two decades, both in Latin America and in the United States. Though her terse, epigrammatic style contrasts sharply with Orozco's liturgical, long-breathed lines, Pizarnik reflects certain aspects of the same worldview, in which poetry is a means of crossing the threshold into the absolute.[4] Unlike Orozco, however, for whom reintegration with the divine is the ultimate goal of human endeavor, Pizarnik follows the "darker path" of esoterism initiated by such nineteenth-century writers as Lautréamont and Baudelaire. In this chapter, I discuss how this orientation led her to a particular literary affiliation with the twentieth-century French writer Georges Bataille, examining traces in her work of what Bataille has identified as "the literature of evil." Through an examination of Pizarnik's evocation of childhood, death, and perverse sexuality, I show how she follows Bataille's suggestion that literature can effect a "hypermorality" by depicting certain forms of impurity or evil.

In chapter 5, my study returns to the early decades of the twentieth century. Here I direct my attention to the unusual and often disturbing poetic voice of Jacobo Fijman, whose work is currently undergoing a critical revival. Fijman was born to Jewish parents in Bessarabia, Russia, and immigrated to Argentina with his family as a young child. In the decade of the 1920s he distinguished himself as a poet of the avant-garde, moving in the literary circles that included Borges, Aldo Pellegrini, and Oliverio Girondo. However, poverty and recurrent psychological crises soon removed him from the literary and cultural mainstream. In 1942, he was placed in the state hospital where he would live out the last twenty-eight years of his life. Although his poetry has yet to be translated and he has a limited readership outside of Argentina, Fijman has become known indirectly through two sources. Leopoldo Marechal's well-known novel *Adán Buenosayres* (1948) features a Fijmanesque character in Samuel Tessler, a sarcastic and perspicacious philosopher. More recently, the Argentine film director Eliseo Subiela created a protagonist loosely based on Fijman in his widely acclaimed 1986 film *Man Facing Southeast,* shot on location at the hospital where Fijman had resided.[5] In this film, the enigmatic character known as Rantes, who voluntarily enters a mental hospital but fails to respond to psychiatric treatment, possesses supernatural abilities and an uncanny wisdom regarding human relationships and institutions. Subiela's portrayal of this character, though it has little to do with the reality of Fijman's life, does point to the messianic stance that Fijman himself adopted on occasion, as well as to the popular myth of the prophetic madman. The prophetic voice, particularly when it takes the form of irrational oracle, is another important means by which the esoteric tradition surfaces in works of literature. (Orozco explores both the potency and the dangers of the oracular voice in poems such as "La sibila de Cumas" [The Cumaean sibyl].)[6] The fascination that a figure like Fijman holds for readers and viewers alike is clearly a product of the perceived overlap between dementia (to use the poet's own term) and wisdom.[7]

Chapter 5 focuses on a nucleus of what I call "asylum poems" in *Molino rojo* in order to follow Fijman's incursions into that difficult territory where madness, mysticism, and poetry overlap. Michel Foucault's notions of the cultural degeneration of madness into mental illness, and of the survival of a language of madness in literature, informs much of my study on Fijman. In chapter 6, I examine a text called *El pensamiento de Jacobo Fijman, o El viaje hacia la otra realidad* [The thought of Jacobo Fijman; or, The journey toward the other reality] (1970), written by contemporary poet Vicente Zito Lema in conjunction with Fijman in the two years before the latter's death. Both Fijman's and Zito Lema's voices in this text attest to the viability of surrealism and of the esoteric literary aesthetic in Argentina in the latter decades of the twentieth century.

In my conclusion, I focus on the shared territory of the three poets' respective poetics, namely, the notion of poetry as revelation and power. This notion, popularized at the end of the eighteenth century by the romantic poets, exalted the poet as an occult initiate, granting him or her otherworldly powers of communication. The poet is, in Rimbaud's terms, a seer. Given the fragmented nature of the world after the mythical fall, the poet possesses the ability to comprehend mysteries that remain veiled for most humans. The act of writing poetry thus becomes a means of crossing the threshold into the absolute; armed with the knowledge that such passage affords, the poet becomes capable of changing life. In sum, Orozco, Pizarnik, and Fijman all share a sacred, magical view of poetic language. They also share a critical stance that constantly calls that view into question. The Conclusion draws inferences from the work of the three poets in order to explore the profound ambivalence each of them expresses regarding the power of the poetic word.

* * *

Certain questions arise regarding the implications of the study I have briefly outlined above. What does modern Argentina have to do with centuries-old occult traditions? What factors have drawn these writers (and others) toward a worldview that posits a dialectic of good and evil, a belief in an invisible reality, or a commitment to spiritual reintegration through unorthodox means? Why do Fijman, Orozco, and Pizarnik all begin with the premise that the poet is a type of occult initiate, a visionary or a prophet? What has led them to their profound distrust of discursive logic, and from there to a probing of "true knowledge" by embracing the occult arts, evil (in Bataille's special sense), or unreason as fundamental poetic practices? And finally, why does the notion of an absolute or sacred language define, for these writers, the role of poetry in the life of an individual or a culture?

Although I will address these questions in greater depth as I examine each of the three poets in turn, it is important to provide some initial guidelines for the consideration of these matters. My first response is a caveat. Although the current trend toward historical contextualization of literary production is a valid and necessary one, it can lead to a misguided search for exact "clues" to the interpretation of a writer's work in his or her immediate socio-political environment. There is a particular tendency, especially in the North American critical response to Latin American literature, to look for narrowly political contexts and responses. I would argue that to read Orozco, Pizarnik, or Fijman in search of specific allusions to historical situations is to risk misreading them entirely.

Certain significant factors in the national history of twentieth-century Argentina constitute some, but not all, of the story of this body of poetry. In the case of each of these writers, there is also a distinct personal and family history to be taken into account. Orozco, for instance, was profoundly influenced from an early age by the isolated landscape of a small town on the vast Argentine pampa, and by a grandmother with an idiosyncratic (largely animistic) belief system that was absorbed by the writer. For Pizarnik and Fijman, a perception of themselves as social outsiders, and a difficult interface with institutions such as the university or the psychiatric hospital frames their view of the world. In all three cases, but particularly in those of Pizarnik and Fijman, the broad factor of the culture of immigration comes to figure prominently in the personal and family story, and thus provides a link to the larger story of the nation. (An interesting parallel arises between Pizarnik and Fijman, both of whom were born into Russian Jewish families.) It is entirely possible to argue that the sense of metaphysical or spiritual exile so evident in the work of these writers is an indirect—though never a direct or allegorical—reflection of the immigrant family's sense of displacement.

All three of the writers under consideration in this study have led profoundly *literary* lives, in which there was little overt participation in the political structure. Fijman, after some initial engagement with anarchist activities in Buenos Aires, became an extremely isolated figure who dedicated himself to the study of classical and Christian scholastic texts and to poetry and painting. Orozco created, over the course of five decades, a poetic world made up of talismans, incantations, signs, sphinxes and oracles, predatory animals, and spiritual orphans; what is commonly known as the "real world" is virtually never the ostensible subject of this poetry. The case of Pizarnik is even more extreme than that of either of her two predecessors. As we shall see, Pizarnik fashioned consciously for herself a world that had much more in common with the Paris of the *poètes maudits* than with the Buenos Aires of Juan Perón or the military regimes.

To argue that these poets led inherently literary lives, however, is perhaps to beg the question. A more accurate formulation of the question might read: Why did there arise in Argentina a significant strain of poetry that was metaphysical and esoteric in nature, at the opposite end of the spectrum from Jean-Paul Sartre's ideal of engaged literature? This is a complicated question that I hope to answer more fully as I examine each poet in turn. Broadly speaking, however, there are several viable responses to this problematic. The first has to do with the country's cultural history. Argentines pride themselves on being one of the most literate nations of the continent, and poetry has historically formed a significant part of Argentine intellectual and cultural life, most notably in the capital. For the most part, this poetry has tended away from engagement with contemporary issues. As the critic Noé Jitrik puts it, in recent decades there has been a "despolitización crónica" [chronic depolitization] in Argentine literature as a whole (130).

Another factor is that, for the better part of two centuries, Argentines have considered France as the primary source of their cultural—particularly literary—inspiration.[8] (It is no coincidence that Fijman, Orozco, and Pizarnik all spent time in Paris, the undisputed mecca of Argentine intellectuals.) After the German romantics, it is the French romantic and symbolist poets of the nineteenth century and, in the twentieth century, the French surrealists who most insistently formulate a poetic theory and praxis with links to the esoteric traditions. For the most part, these influential poets detached themselves from the political realities of their respective historical periods and generated theories in which the poetic word took precedence over all other forms of language.[9] In brief, these relatively disengaged poets are those who (along with Rainer Maria Rilke and certain Spanish peninsular poets) provided the models for Fijman, Orozco, and Pizarnik.[10] Finally, lest the contextualization of these poets be presented as narrowly nationalistic, it is important to underscore the vitality of the esoteric tradition in literature in Spanish American countries other than Argentina. In addition to Rubén Darío, José Lezama Lima, and Octavio Paz, many contemporaries of the Argentine poets of the present study have manifested similar orientations in their work. A partial list of such poets would include Gilberto Owen in Mexico, Emilio Adolfo Westphalen in Perú, Juan Liscano in Venezuela, Braulio Arenas and Gonzalo Rojas in Chile, and Alvaro Mutis in Colombia. The presence of a poetics based in some degree on esoteric thought in each of these writers attests to the strength of a tradition that has found important new voices in twentieth-century Latin America.[11]

1

The Esoteric Tradition in Literature

> Ah descubrir la imagen oculta e impensable del reflejo, la palabra secreta, el bien perdido, la otra mitad que siempre fue una nube inalcanzable desde la soledad.
>
> [Oh to discover the hidden and unthinkable image of the reflection, the secret word, the lost good, the other half that was always a cloud, unreachable from this solitude.]
>
> —O. Orozco, "Catecismo animal" [Animal catechism]

What does it mean to refer broadly to the esoteric traditions as a basis for literary analysis? One could justifiably protest that such a rubric is too all-encompassing to allow for effective discussion of particular modern texts. After all, the time frame under consideration stretches back to pre-Christian Europe and even into the ancient Egyptian and Babylonian civilizations, and geographical boundaries extend from the Far East across Western Europe. Similarly, the principles involved in what has come down to us as "occultism" vary widely and in many cases contradict each other. Nevertheless, as one reads Novalis, or Rimbaud, or Orozco, one begins to identify certain shared assumptions that, taken together, do form a more or less coherent whole. In the following pages, I will trace in roughly chronological order the development of the philosophical and aesthetic principles that I take as the basis of my study. This is not meant to be an exhaustive treatment of the subject, but rather a necessary grounding for the reading of Orozco, Pizarnik, and Fijman.[1] Surette notes that "Although occultism is marginal to aesthetic culture, it is not as clearly isolated from it as might at first appear, or as one might wish. If we draw the horizons of the occult as the occultists themselves do, it possesses a long history running parallel to mainstream aesthetic culture, intersecting with it at many points" (11). I propose to redraw those horizons, locating many points of intersection in Germany and France, and taking twentieth-century Argentine poetry as one of many possible lines of development.

The attitudes and beliefs that constitute the tradition of Western occultism flourished in the mystery cults of the later centuries of the Roman Empire and, despite the dampening effect of Christian orthodoxy, continued to be widespread during the Middle Ages. Versions of these same beliefs made a strong resurgence with certain prominent thinkers of the Renaissance, survived in cults that were more or less underground during the period of Enlightenment, and rose to the surface again with the German romantics. During the nineteenth and twentieth centuries, esoteric thought and poetry were seen by many thinkers and creators as inextricably intertwined. In my overview of several aspects of this tradition, I draw heavily upon two key studies: Albert Béguin's *L'âme romantique et le rêve: Essai sur le Romantisme allemand et la Poésie française* [The romantic soul and the dream: Essay on German romanticism and French poetry] (1939) and Marcel Raymond's *From Baudelaire to Surrealism* (1933).

Without question, the essential belief upon which all esoteric thought is built is that of the primal unity of the universe. This conception of unity assumes validity only within the parameters of the fall: once human *identity* with the absolute has become impossible, *unity* is conceived in an attempt to reestablish the bonds broken when paradise was lost. "Esotericism," says Antoine Faivre, "thus permits access to a higher level of understanding where dualities of all kinds are transcended in a unity that is not to be grasped in a purely conceptual fashion but is to be experienced by one's whole being" ("Esotericism" 158). This is the common ground shared by the mystic and occult traditions. In fact, every essential component of esoteric thought, including universal analogy or correspondence, mystery and magic, and the relationship between occult knowledge and power, can be inferred from the fundamental doctrine of cosmic unity. In the history of modern thought, the reformulation of this archaic notion occurs in the Renaissance:

> Para Kepler, Paracelso, Nicolás de Cusa o Agrippa de Nettesheim, así como para Giordano Bruno, el universo es un ser viviente, dotado de alma; una identidad esencial reúne a todos los seres particulares, que no son más que emanaciones del Todo. Una relación de universal *simpatía* rige todas las manifestaciones de vida y explica la creencia de todos los pensadores del Renacimiento en la *magia*: ningún gesto, ningún acto aparece aislado, sus eficaces repercusiones se escuchan en la creación entera, y la operación mágica llega naturalmente hasta las cosas y los seres más lejanos. (Béguin 78)

[For Kepler, Paracelsus, Nicholas of Cusa or Agrippa of Nettelsheim, as for Giordano Bruno, the universe is a living being, endowed with a soul; an essential unity gathers together all the separate beings, which are merely emanations from the All. A relationship of universal *sympathy* governs all manifestations of life, and explains the belief in *magic* held in common by Renaissance thinkers: no gesture, no act, appears in isolation; rather, their effective repercussions are heard throughout all of creation, and the operations of magic naturally reach even the most distant things and beings.]

Cartesian and post-Cartesian philosophy, however, all but erased these strains of analogical-magical thought. What did survive went underground, forming the main current of the occult and Illuminist creeds abundant throughout the seventeenth and eighteenth centuries.[2]

The doctrine of cosmic unity, in its particular aspect of analogy or correspondence among all things, reemerges powerfully at the beginning of the nineteenth century with the German romantics, who absorbed ideas from Oriental as well as European occultism. Octavio Paz goes so far as to call analogy "the true religion of modern poetry, from Romanticism to Surrealism" (*Children* 55). From Novalis to Rimbaud to Breton, this belief centers upon a single crucial analogy: magic and poetry. The belief in *logos* as power is, of course, ancient, but within the Western literary-philosophical tradition it is not until the advent of German romanticism that the poet consciously cultivates language as a means of changing the world. Certain late-eighteenth-century German writers, such as Johann Georg Hamann, formed the vanguard of this new aesthetic, viewing poetry as an important vehicle for reestablishing a primordial attitude of man toward the universe.

The German romantics absorbed this notion, but went a step further, bestowing a new efficacy upon the poetic word. Paz states in this regard that "The conception of poetry as magic implies an aesthetic of action. Art ceases to be exclusively representation and contemplation; it becomes also an intervention in reality" (*Children* 60). If the poetic word is truly capable of intervening in and transforming reality, then the poet—seen as an occult initiate since the beginning of the nineteenth century—is the possessor of a secret and sovereign power. Again, the allusion is to the myth of the fall, and the movement is retrogressive: the poet attempts to retrieve "todo lo que en nosotros puede sobrevivir de nuestros poderes anteriores a la separación" [everything that may survive in us of the powers we held before the separation] (Béguin 106). For many preromantics and their successors, the recuperation of primordial powers had a particular linguistic application, for they believed in the existence of a primitive and universal language as the deity's first expression of being in the material world. To retrieve that language is to act in a reverent but irrational manner, one which depends on a faith in verbal magic.

In a poem addressed to Pizarnik, written after the younger poet's suicide, Orozco's speaker reminds her friend that "en el fondo de todo hay un jardín / donde se abre la flor azul del sueño de Novalis" [at the bottom of everything there is a garden / where the blue flower of Novalis opens] (*Mutaciones* 75). The allusion is to Novalis's unfinished novel *Heinrich von Ofterdingen* (1801), whose young protagonist dreams of a blue flower that comes to symbolize the spirit of poetry. Of all the German romantics, it is perhaps Novalis (Friedrich von Hardenberg, 1772–1801) who most clearly exemplifies the doctrine of cosmic unity and, by extension, the conception of the poet as seer and sorcerer. In this spirit, the novel's protagonist claims that the very origin of poetry resides in "this delight of revealing in the world what is beyond the world, of being able to do that which is really the original motive of our being here" (116). Béguin sees as fundamental in Novalis himself that same aspiration, "esa necesidad de integrarlo todo, de creer en la coexistencia de todo y en un futuro en que toda separación terminaría en un retorno a la armonía absoluta" [that need to integrate everything, to believe in the coexistence of everything and in a future in which all separation will end with a return to absolute harmony] (257). Nevertheless, Novalis struggled against a different reality: in both nature and human existence he saw not unity and harmony but dispersion and discord, imperfection and alienation. The only means of reconciliation between the ideal world and the real, for Novalis, was the magic of the poetic word. He expressed a belief in the identity between magician and poet, one being the alter ego of the other.

Novalis longed for death as a release, as a reunion with his beloved, yet what most often manifests itself in his writing is a repeated striving toward a communication *hic et nunc* with a supreme reality. The poet's perfected consciousness of the beyond from within life can effect a transcendence not only of his or her own being; it can result in what Novalis terms "the raising of mankind above itself" (qtd. in Willson 69). In his singular affinity for the night and in his striving for union with the beyond, Novalis recalls the sixteenth-century Spanish mystic poet San Juan de la Cruz. In his insistence on the power of the poetic word, he prefigures Baudelaire, Rimbaud, and Mallarmé.

Novalis and the romantics that succeeded him fashioned an aesthetic that informed much European poetry in the nineteenth and twentieth centuries. Yet their vision was rooted in notions that were centuries in the making. The true novelty and originality of this group of poets and thinkers, according to Béguin, is precisely their acute awareness of "su raigambre en las tinieblas interiores" [their rootedness in interior darkness] (198). The true romantic poet, recognizing that he is not the only "author" of his work, and having learned that poetry is above all a song springing from the abyss, "trata *deliberadamente y con toda lucidez* de provocar la subida de las voces misteriosas" [tries *deliberately and with complete lucidity* to call the mysterious voices up from the depths] (199; emphasis in original). This deliberate calling-forth of occult voices and powers will become the supreme poetic action for Baudelaire and the French symbolists.

The nineteenth-century symbolic conception of the universe is a rather direct echo of certain strains of neo-Platonic thought of the Renaissance. According to many Renaissance thinkers, it was only from the interior of each individual that the exterior world could be perceived (by means of analogy), since the visible creation held a symbolic value, and each of its manifestations were mere allusions to the One. In a purely interior sphere, it was Baudelaire who first emphasized the unity of psychic dimensions, the proximity of the highest and lowest regions of the spirit. This fascination with the darker side of the human psyche had been born with the romantics and would culminate in the fin de siècle consciousness of the so-called *poètes maudits*.

Baudelaire's particular brand of analogical thought tended to concentrate on the possibility, for the poet-adept, of communication with the occult. The visible universe, to recall Baudelaire's famous metaphor, was a "forest of symbols," a veil that only those with secret, mystical powers could rend (42). Raymond says of Baudelaire that, like Novalis, he saw a transcendental mission for poetry, which was "to open a window on this other world, which is actually our world, to enable the self to escape from its limitations and to expand to the infinite" (11). Baudelaire's doctrine of *correspondances*, derived largely from the writings of the eighteenth-century Swedish scientist and visionary Emanuel Swedenborg (1688–1772), asserted the preeminence of spontaneous or unconscious associations among multiple sensory data, or between materiality and mental-spiritual states. Given that the visible universe is an analogue of the invisible beyond, claims Baudelaire, it is the poet who, with "les vastes éclairs de son esprit lucide" [the vast flashes of light of his clear soul] must translate the true meanings of things for the noninitiated (34). With the deliberate utilization of his magical powers—an awareness inherited from the romantics—the poet renders the perceived correspondences in their literary forms of symbol, metaphor, simile, or allegory. Had Novalis not aptly prefigured this development in his fragment "Mankind: metaphor" (qtd. in Willson 72)?

In aesthetic and literary terms, Baudelaire's determination to extend the mind's grasp beyond visible appearances freed poetry from the principle of the representation of nature, to which even the romantics had been largely bound. From Baudelaire forward, poetic language was to be associative rather than logical, and the intersecting planes of sensual, mental, and spiritual apperception opened nearly infinite possibilities within the old law of universal analogy. With Baudelaire, observes Raymond, "the poet's art was becoming an 'evocative magic,' a sacred function" (20).

One line of influence leading away from Baudelaire, and drawing as well upon the theories of Edgar Allan Poe, emphasized the aesthetic function of poetry, the poet's skill in crafting the raw materials provided to him by the unconscious and the sensory world. In the nineteenth century, this line culminated in the French poet Stéphane Mallarmé. Two aspects of Mallarmé's approach are pertinent to the present study. First, Mallarmé's determination to distill poetic language, to remove the communicative function and concentrate the remaining material into a pure form—in short, his striving toward the essential word—leads to a new valuation of poetry as an instrument of power. He returns thus to the notion of poetic creation as a sacred act: in this case, the poet imitates divine powers by creating language anew. These notions, to reiterate, are not new. Mallarmé's singular contribution to the reshaping of this tradition was to carry to unforeseen limits the possibilities of poetic rhythm and musicality, of suggestiveness, of the resonance created by the unexpected juxtaposition of words and images. This was a legacy that immeasurably enriched the poetry of the twentieth century in Europe and the Americas.

Secondly, the very purifying function of poetic language—its suggestive and associative, as opposed to mimetic, powers—connects Mallarmé with another tradition that will characterize much subsequent European and American poetry: the hermetic tradition. The term *secret* often coincides with a reference to the magical powers of poetry. Adherents of the hermetic tradition maintain that if the communicative function of language belongs to all human beings, the creative function belongs only to a select few. In order for the poem to fulfill its highest potentialities, both poet and reader must be initiates. Clearly, such an approach connects poetry with both shamanistic magic and occult religion. The assumption is that there is a sort of mythical residue that subsists in words, and that a true spark between poet, poem, and reader is capable of "bringing back, for the span of a second, the day when words poured forth from the mouths of men to worship the gods or to exorcise their hatred" (Raymond 15). From a rationalist point of view, obscurity in poetry is a failure, since communication is valued above any other linguistic purpose. But within the hermetic tradition, a certain degree of obscurity is indispensable, and may even allow for a "miraculous" communication on a higher plane than the purely rational mind can fathom.

The vatic, or oracular, power of poetic language, a tradition upon which Orozco, Pizarnik, and Fijman all draw heavily, is concentrated in the last of the nineteenth-century French poets that we will consider, Arthur Rimbaud. Nearly a century before Rimbaud, Novalis had claimed that the poetic mind was closely related to the prophetic and religious mind, to all forms of seership. More than any of his contemporaries, Rimbaud follows Novalis in this prophetic vocation.

The tradition of poet as *voyant* and as *vates*, as one possessed of the supernatural power to penetrate the mysteries of the universe and interpret them, has made an appearance in virtually every culture in human history. Of particular importance to the Occidental religious and aesthetic traditions are the ancient Greek and the biblical manifestations of this conception: the synthesis of poetry and prophesy. The European revival of arcane beliefs and practices in the eighteenth and nineteenth centuries brought into the foreground once again the prophetic vocation of the poet. In Rimbaud's famous "Lettre du Voyant," written to his friend Paul Demeny in 1871, he outlines the method he has adopted for himself and which he advocates for other poets: "The Poet makes himself a *seer* by a long, gigantic and rational *derangement* of *all the senses*. All forms of love, suffering, and madness. He searches himself. He exhausts all poisons in himself and keeps only their quintessences. Unspeakable torture where he needs all his faith, all his superhuman strength, where he becomes among all men the great patient, the great criminal, the one accursed—and the supreme Scholar!—Because he reaches the *unknown!*" (307; emphasis in original). Like his predecessor Baudelaire, Rimbaud attempts a direct communication with the dark side of his own psyche, firm in the belief that his interior self, in all its illuminated and horrifying facets, is but a reflection of a larger reality, the unknown, God. But Rimbaud surpassed Baudelaire in the revolutionary form of his poetry and in its visionary and hallucinatory effects.

Both Rimbaud and the French symbolists found in the Orphic tradition a mythic framework for their own poetic attitudes and practices. The oracular quality of Rimbaud's celebrated collection of poetry *Une Saison en enfer* [A season in hell] (1873) is detectable in its multiple and often contradictory poetic speakers and its enigmatic language. Its particular connection with the Orphic myth is obvious in the central motif of the poet's descent into hell, an archetypal journey that Orozco will call "mi descenso al olvido" [my descent into oblivion] (*Obra* 95). In both this work and in Rimbaud's second major collection, *Les Illuminations* [Illuminations] (1875), the speaker-poet consciously adopts the role of oracle: "I intend to unveil all mysteries: religious mysteries or those of nature, death, birth, the future, the past, cosmogony, the void" (185). The Orphic tradition, like so many others that came to form a part of esoteric thought, is grounded in the remembrance of a Golden Age. The Orphic cosmogonies recall a totality centered in the deity Phanes, himself centered in the primordial Night. Unity is splintered and differentiation occurs over five successive reigns, ending in the birth of Dionysus (Detienne 111–14). Accordingly, Rimbaud opens *Une Saison en enfer* with an allusion to a personal-universal golden age: "Long ago, if my memory serves me, my life was a banquet where everyone's heart was generous, and where all wines flowed" (173). In *Illuminations,* the theme of the fall from paradise is a recurrent one, concentrated especially in the poem "Après le déluge" [After the flood], in which a hotel is erected "in the chaos of ice and polar night" (215).

The mythical figure of Orpheus, musician and enchanter from Thrace, was a priest in the temple of Apollo, that is, one initiated into the mysteries. Apart from his repeated allusions to himself as "magus or angel" (209), Rimbaud's lyric speaker ponders the notion of "les élus," the elect or chosen ones. In "L'Impossible," he claims that in daily existence, the only "elect" we see are the false ones; he warns the reader, however, that "They are not blessers!" (203). After his descent into hell, the mythical Orpheus becomes an initiate in an even more profound sense: he is one who has seen what ordinary mortals never see. It is his experience in hell, surely, that enables Orpheus's severed head, after his violent death, to out-prophesy even the oracle at Delphi. For the symbolists (and later the surrealists), the descent into hell was associated with a delving into the unconscious, often with the aid of hashish or absinthe. "I am really from beyond the tomb," Rimbaud's speaker declares (231). Within the Orphic cults, true initiation promised the possibility of victory over death; within circles of the decadent poets, initiation seemed to deliver one to death's threshold.

The most celebrated element of this tradition is perhaps that of the Orphic song, a primordial and pure sound, a spellbinding voice that existed before the splintering of cosmic unity, thus one that preceded human speech. In Novalis's *Heinrich von Ofterdingen,* the legend is told of poets of antiquity "who by the strange sounds of marvelous instruments awakened the secret life of the woods and the spirits hidden in trees, aroused the dead seed of plants in deserts and waste places, and called forth blossoming gardens" (32–33). The Orphic song embraces all things, celebrating differentiation; thus in Rimbaud we read: "I loved the desert, burnt orchards, musty shops, tepid drinks. I dragged myself through stinking alleys, and with my eyes closed, gave myself over to the sun, the god of fire" (197). The poet is at home in any wilderness; in fact, he possesses the power to recreate, to transform the deathly landscape: "I have created all celebrations, all triumphs, all dramas. I have tried to invent new flowers, new stars, new flesh, new tongues" (207).

Rimbaud's attempts to make of himself a seer and an angel, to attain wisdom by means of "l'hallucination des mots" [the hallucinations of words], ended in the same Promethean failure as did Mallarmé's (195). The very "sacred" quality of his experiment is called into question with bitter irony in *Une Saison en enfer*: "At the end I looked on the disorder of my mind as sacred" (195). The penultimate poem of this volume juxtaposes the poet's supreme frustration—"*I have forgotten how to speak!*"—with the height of his oracular speech: "Where shall we go beyond the shores and the mountains, to salute the birth of the new work, and the new wisdom . . . ?" (207; emphasis in original). The three poets presented in the present study represent the same uneasy coexistence of the Orphic song and its own self-silencing. In this sense, they share their lot with many twentieth-century writers, since, as Paz observes, *Une Saison en enfer* marks the turning point in the modern conceptualization of poetry. From Rimbaud forward, argues Paz, the poetic word sustains itself with the very negation of the word (*Bow* 236–37).

"Rimbaud is a Surrealist in the way he lived, and elsewhere," writes Breton in his 1924 *Manifestoes of Surrealism* (27). Indeed, most surrealists looked to Rimbaud as their literary predecessor, and with good reason. Rimbaud represents the gathering-point of several currents of esoteric thought that were subsequently revived and reworked in surrealism, a movement that first arose in France early in the decade of the 1920s. In this vein, the dadaist and surrealist poet Tristan Tzara enumerates certain treasures of the nineteenth century that he and his contemporaries found valuable in their quest for the materials of poetry: "the cult of the phantom, magic . . . the dream, insanity, passion, folklore, and real and imaginary voyage" (qtd. in Balakian, *Literary Origins* 12–13). With the coming of the new century, European and American poets took up, once again, the task of redefining their art. But this new art owed much to the old. Raymond rightly observes that "the idea that poetic activity is a way to occult knowledge of a super-nature was, in the years preceding the world war, enriched by a mysticism and a spirit of revolt originating in Rimbaud" (201). Surrealism is the literary tendency of the early twentieth century that most closely follows the traditions of esoteric thought. In retrospect, there is an obvious irony in the fact that this movement initially proclaimed itself to be in total rebellion against nearly all literary, religious, and philosophical traditions. To cite only one example, Breton both appropriates and dismisses the oracular function of poetry so central to Rimbaud and his predecessors: "The Surrealist voice that shook Cumae, Dodona, and Delphi is nothing more than the voice which dictates my less irascible speeches to me" (*Manifestoes* 45).

Paz claims that the history of modern poetry is one of oscillation between revolutionary and religious sensibilities (*Children* 37). An argument can be made that the foundations of revolutionary, atheistic surrealism were fundamentally sacred. The surrealist vision is, once again, one of a primordial and ideal unity. Creation—and with it the human condition—represents the tragic fragmentation of that unity. One can never be satisfied with life in the ordinary here and now, since, as Breton claimed, "existence is elsewhere" (*Manifestoes* 47). Thus, the poet (in the tradition of the occult adept) is charged with the act of *conciliatio oppositorum*: "Everything tends to make us believe that there exists a certain point of the mind at which life and death, the real and the imagined, past and future, the communicable and the incommunicable, high and low, cease to be perceived as contradictions. Now, search as one may one will never find any other motivating force in the activities of the Surrealists than the hope of finding and fixing this point" (123–24). Nevertheless, the means by which the surrealists proposed to bridge the gap between existence and essence diverged fundamentally from previous occult and mystic traditions. Viewed accurately, claims Balakian in *Literary Origins of Surrealism*, the shared territory of the romantics, the symbolists, and the surrealists can be reduced to a single metaphysical concern: a passion for the unknown (31). In the years since the height of the symbolist aesthetic (1885–95), Freud's experiments with the unconscious had profoundly changed the prevailing views on nature and on artistic creation, among other things. Surrealism became "the result of a long struggle to abandon the Romantic devotion of an earlier age to the exterior manifestations of nature and the habit of turning the known forms of nature into the symbols of the poet's mysticism" (Balakian, *Literary Origins* 9). What counted now, more than ever before, was the poet's own interiority: if there existed a sacred realm, it was to be found not in nature but in the human unconscious. This explains the value the surrealists placed on oneiric imagery, as well as their devotion to *l'écriture automatique,* a method of writing in which the unconscious was thought to freely dictate images and symbols whose juxtaposition, jarring to the conscious mind, would unveil the true content of the soul.

In sum, surrealism—at least in its early formulations—appears indeed to be more an exorcism of modern demons than an embracing of the sacred. The surrealists as a whole rejected any notion of orthodox monotheism, as well as any sense of religious *merveilleux*. The marvelous becomes identical with the absurd, and is more likely to be found in fairy tales than in religious doctrine. "Fear, the attraction of the unusual, chance, the taste for things extravagant," comments Breton in his circular way, "are all devices which we can always call upon without fear or deception" (*Manifestoes* 16).

Paramount to the surrealist aesthetic was an absolute freedom of the mind, that is, a freedom from the constraints of rational thought. Reason's role in creative activity, says Breton, must limit itself to "taking note of, and appreciating, the luminous phenomenon" (*Manifestoes* 37). Such a view would lead Breton and others to embrace mental illness as one of the possible paths to "total authenticity" both in everyday life and in the sphere of artistic production.[3] This was in essence a reaction to the scientific reductionism and philosophic optimism embodied in nineteenth-century positivism. In this regard the surrealists adopted a skeptical view, born of the failure of science to deliver on its early promises, and of the all-too-real experience of the First World War. Science had failed, claimed the surrealists, precisely because of its dependence on reason, its attempt to analyze and classify the unknown. Consequently, a new value was placed on disorder, on chance. Mallarmé's long poem "Un Coup de dés" [A dice throw] (1897) prefigured this approach.

One of the important outcomes of the rejection of rational thought was the dissolution of the logical categories of time and space, or for that matter any of the laws of nature. The next step, of course, was the discrediting of the rational properties of language. It is perhaps this facet of surrealism as an aesthetic that has exercised the most profound and lasting influence on later twentieth-century poetry. In fact, the surrealists' views on language encapsulate their entire vision. Paz, in his essay on Breton, summarizes this phenomenon: "Man, even man debased by the neocapitalism and pseudosocialism of our time, is a marvelous being because he sometimes *speaks*. Language is the mark, the sign, not of his fall but of his original innocence. Through the Word we may regain the lost kingdom and recover powers we possessed in the far-distant past. These powers are not ours. The man inspired, the man who really speaks, does not say anything personal: language speaks through his mouth" (*Alternating Current* 48).

The surrealist worldview is not without its contradictions. Balakian points out that, in spite of their rejection of rational thought, the surrealists adopted from science "the method of untiring objective investigation, experimentation, cooperative activity, and collective discovery" (*Literary Origins* 13). Likewise, there is irony in their rejection of religion, given their ceaseless attempts to transcend ordinary life, to dissolve the self, to escape to a nameless beyond. If religion as such was rejected, the value of the sacred was exalted. Language (born of the unconscious and merely witnessed by the conscious mind) provided the key to transcendence because of its magical properties. Paz observes that Breton "not only made no distinction between magic and poetry; he also was convinced all his life that poetry was a force, a substance, an energy truly capable of changing reality" (*Alternating Current* 50).

Raymond concludes that ultimately, the surrealists found themselves in a difficult situation, since "they are more violent in negating the appearances of reality than in affirming its spiritual, mystical existence" (319). It was left to later poets, perhaps, to effect once again a creative tension between those opposing perceptions.

The sacred character of the *logos*, or poetic word, is the fundamental esoteric principle upon which the poetics of Orozco, Pizarnik, and Fijman are based. This belief bears a correspondent risk, one fully acknowledged by the romantics. Poetry is the ultimate "dangerous game" in this view, because it promises access to forbidden knowledge. We have here an aesthetic, linguistic reworking of the ancient prohibition against "beholding the face of God," an experience that, according to the mythical accounts, no one survives. The saint, perhaps, can prepare adequately for the force of the "total knowledge" by means of spiritual purification and ascetic practices; his or her experience is thus, by definition, transcendent. But the poet is simply the invader, the transgressor. In the romantic myth of the poet, to step across the threshold into what Orozco and Pizarnik both refer to as the "forbidden garden" is to risk the ultimate punishment, madness. Orozco, while she assiduously explores the realms of occult knowledge as a poetic frame of reference, actively resists any association with madness. Pizarnik's work reveals a continual fascination with the limits of experience, with evil and unreason. Fijman, in his lyric production as well as in the author-persona he presents, bears the marks of both madness and transcendent understanding.

2

Gnostic and Hermetic Discourse in the Poetry of Olga Orozco

The general principles of the esoteric traditions outlined in Chapter 1 function as a broad context within which certain Argentine writers develop their own highly personal poetics. As we have seen, the immediate precedent, the focal point in which the main tenets of occultism converge in the early twentieth century, is surrealism. Far from being a movement of the literary past, surrealism, as a rebellious and dynamic reconfiguration of centuries-old traditions, continued to operate throughout the twentieth century as a prominent aesthetic in Buenos Aires. No single figure illustrates the vital presence of this aesthetic more than Olga Orozco. The chronological span of her work, from the 1940s to the 1990s, as well as its sober and refined treatment of the principles in question, places Orozco in a position of centrality with regard to Argentine poetry of the twentieth century. Taking Orozco's appropriation of the esoteric traditions in literature as a critical vantage point, we are able to look ahead to Pizarnik and back to Fijman and to follow Ariadne's thread out of the labyrinth of the poetic avant-garde and its *sequela*.

Olga Orozco was born in 1920 in the small town of Toay on the Argentine pampa. Her mother was a descendent of Basque and Irish immigrants who had come to Argentina in the eighteenth and nineteenth centuries; her father was Sicilian.[1] Orozco cites the significance of her maternal grandmother (who was of Irish stock) in the matter of early influences: "Es importante, sobre todo por el lado de mi abuela materna, porque ella tenía una concepción bastante mágica, bastante animista del mundo, que sin duda venía de sus antepasados celtas. De modo que todo el mundo era algo en movimiento. Los objetos siempre estaban en acecho para ayudarte o para condenarte, para protegerte o para llevarte al abismo. Todo era un peligro y un asilo" [This is important, especially considering my maternal grandmother's side of the family, because she maintained a rather magical, animistic view of the world, which undoubtedly was inherited from her Celtic ancestors. For her, the entire world was made up of things in movement. Objects were always lying in ambush, waiting to help you or to condemn you, to protect you or to take you into the abyss. Everything was a danger or a refuge] (qtd. in Sefamí 96). The supernatural or magical worldview that Orozco is describing does indeed become the basis for her poetics, as I intend to show in this and the following chapter.

The other significant factor in the formation of Orozco's worldview, according to the poet herself, is the geography of her native province of La Pampa, an extremely arid land of "fantastic" proportions, with winds so powerful that entire sand dunes would shift places from one day to the next. "Además," adds Orozco, "como hay grandes zonas desérticas, sin vegetación, cada pequeño objeto—un hueso, una piedra—toma un relieve importantísimo, desmesurado, como podría suceder dentro de un cuadro surrealista. Cualquier presencia aislada adquiere las características de una revelación, de una aparición" [Moreover, since there are wide reaches of desert, with no vegetation, each little object—a bone, a rock—takes on a striking relief, it appears huge, as it could happen in any surrealist painting. Any isolated presence takes on the characteristics of a revelation, of an apparition] (qtd. in Sefamí 97). All in all, the formation of Orozco's poetic voice is grounded in the "spectacle" of this geography: "Tiene que ver con ese espectáculo casi hasta la alucinación, como para hacerme saltar a otro mundo" ["It has to do with that spectacle that almost becomes hallucination, as if it could make me leap into another world"] (97).

At eight years of age, Orozco moved with her family to Bahía Blanca (a coastal city in the southern portion of the province of Buenos Aires), and at the age of sixteen to the capital, Buenos Aires, where she remained until her death in 1999. Frequenting the family library from an early age (she remembers having read Dostoyevsky at age eleven or twelve), and following the lead of both her parents, who read to her from the classics, Orozco developed a passion for literature. At the age of eighteen she published her first poem, the same age at which she began to frequent the informal gatherings of poets whom critics later called the Argentine "Generation of 1940." From that day forward, Orozco participated more or less visibly in the literary life of Buenos Aires, publishing literary essays, reviews, and translations (from French and Italian), in addition to her own poetry and prose. Although she traveled often and widely, she never resided outside Argentina. One trip in particular bears mention in the context of this study: in 1961, Orozco traveled on scholarship to France, Spain, Italy, and Switzerland in order to carry out research on "The Occult and the Sacred in Modern Poetry." This research undoubtedly fomented the process by which Orozco integrated into her poetic voice an interest that she had carried with her since childhood.

Orozco declared herself to be an ardent reader of Nerval, Rimbaud, and Baudelaire; furthermore, she acknowledged her affinity with the surrealist aesthetic and with the antecedents of this movement.[2] A student not only of world literature, but also of all the esoteric traditions, Orozco eventually hit upon gnosticism as the basis for a worldview that could take into account all that she saw as comprising those antecedents of surrealism. In the present chapter, I will outline briefly the literary world into which Orozco stepped when she published her first volume in 1946, as well as provide an overview of Orozco's poetic production. I will then explore certain principles of gnosticism and, to a lesser degree, hermeticism, that constitute the philosophico-religious framework of Orozco's poetry.

Orozco can be included chronologically—if by no other definitive means—within a group of poets who began publishing in Buenos Aires around the year 1940. Critics most often include in this group Enrique Molina, César Fernández Moreno, León Benarós, Ana María Chouhy Aguirre, Juan Rodolfo Wilcock, and Alberto Girri, as well as Orozco. The majority of the "Generation of 1940" demonstrates a clear aesthetic kinship with the Austrian poet Rainer Maria Rilke. This explains in part their general classification as *neoromantics,* by which critics have alluded to their preoccupation with the themes of love, death, and human anguish, and the rather constant elegiac note in their poetry. Undoubtedly, the other literary father of this generation of poets—and of similar groups of poets throughout the South American continent—was the Chilean poet Pablo Neruda. Neruda's three-volume *Residencia en la tierra* [Residence on the earth] (1933, 1935, 1947) exercised a clear and direct influence on Orozco and her contemporaries. The poetry of the first two books of *Residencia* is most often described as introspective, hermetic, and surrealistic. Reflecting the powerful impact of Breton's school and of the other avant-garde movements that had shaken Latin American poetry in the first two decades of the century, Neruda's imagery in these poems is oneiric, irrational, intentionally obscure. It is important to note, however, that this is not surrealism as Breton envisioned it. "Breton wanted to capture the voice of the subconscious," observes René de Costa; "Neruda wanted only to create the style of that voice" (44). It is precisely Neruda's surrealistic orientation or aesthetic vision, rather than the method of automatic writing or the mere recording of unconscious outflow, that was to be adopted by the young poets who held him in such high regard.

This decade in European poetry generally signaled a return to individual, existential concerns, after the primarily social orientation of the 1930s. Spanish poets such as Luis Cernuda and Vicente Aleixandre, who wrote in both metaphysical and neoromantic veins, were widely read and highly regarded by young poets throughout the Hispanic world. The poets who succeeded those of the Argentine *vanguardia* found themselves in rebellion against the self-consciously inventive approach to language; they also sought to reestablish human sentiment as the prime mover of poetry. But these younger poets also recognized the debt they owed to the avant-garde movements, which had freed poetry from the linguistic stagnation into which Spanish-American *modernismo* had fallen. They also, for the most part, continued to give primacy to the poetic image. Speaking for his own generation, Fernández Moreno observes: "La hueste de 1940 no está, pues, divorciada de la anterior: vendría más bien a ser su faz perfilada, humana" [The 1940 group is not necessarily divorced from the previous one: rather, it becomes the more polished, human side of the coin] (229). Some avant-garde movements, most notably surrealism, even managed to adapt themselves, without a change in essence, to the new concerns of the 1940s.

The Spanish Civil War also played its part in shaping Orozco's generation, bringing to Buenos Aires such influential poets as Rafael Alberti, Juan Ramón Jiménez, and Juan Larrea, as well as the writer of brief prose Ramón Gómez de la Serna. The bitter experience of these *exiliados,* as well as that of prominent Latin Americans who had traveled to Spain in these years (Neruda and Peruvian poet César Vallejo among them), intensified the note of anguish and the pessimistic tone of the young writers. To these factors must be added, of course, the outbreak of World War II. The sobering effect of these international events was exacerbated by Argentina's own political turmoil of the day. After a period of relative democratic stability and economic prosperity in the 1920s, Argentina's infrastructure had begun to crumble. A military coup in 1930 toppled the liberal government of Hipólito Yrigoyen, under whose leadership social programs had been advanced and university reform had been carried out. The rise of Juan Domingo Perón to power in 1945 saw a tightening of governmental control of the media and a marked restriction of the role that intellectuals played in the cultural life of the nation. Lyric poets in particular—and the members of the Generation of 1940 invariably defined themselves as such—found themselves in a marginalized position. The fundamental theme of Neruda's *Residencia I*—the perpetual disintegration of life and the preeminence of death—found ample historical corroboration in the decade that followed its publication. For these reasons, Fernández Moreno synthesizes the poetry of his generation as "quejosa, saturada de pesimismo: el tiempo corre hacia la perdición, y con él se van todas las dudosas apariencias de las cosas, flotando en inacabable confusión" [plaintive, saturated with pessimism: time flows toward ruination, and with it go all the questionable appearances of things, floating in endless confusion] (226).

In an homage to Orozco in 1972, Enrique Molina commented on the exemplary internal unity of her work. Years later, taking into consideration several more volumes of Orozco's poetry, Jacobo Sefamí remarked of her work that "un poema puede ser todos los poemas; un libro puede ser todos los libros" [one poem can be every poem; one book can be every book] ("Nota introductoria" 7).[3] It is this internal coherence of Orozco's poetry—formal, tonal, and thematic—that has dictated to a great degree my approach in the present study. Rather than considering her work in its chronological progression, I have chosen to examine certain elements reflective of the esoteric traditions as they appear throughout her work, although I draw heavily on her later volumes.

Los juegos peligrosos [The dangerous games], published in 1962, is the first of Orozco's books to employ an allusive system directly based on the occult traditions. What had been a partial approach in her previous volumes, a shamanistic tone or an occasional reference to magic and ritual, now becomes the organizing principle of the book.[4] We could say that, with this book, Orozco's orientation toward an esoteric worldview had finally found its center. In what sense are these games to be considered dangerous? First, it is evident that the practices involved in the occult sciences—magic, witchcraft, and divination, among others—have the potential for disastrous personal and social consequences. The mythical proscriptions against eating of the tree of knowledge, or looking upon the face of God, provide a broadly based cultural understanding of the dangers faced by the practitioner of the occult sciences. Orozco draws the material for much of her poetry from the consideration of these potentially negative consequences. Second, as Lindstrom points out, there is a purely literary danger involved in the utilization of an occult-oriented lexicon: "El riesgo es de producir un texto efectista, sensacionalista" [The risk is that of producing a showy, sensationalist text] ("La voz poética" 771). The aesthetic risk taken by Orozco is overcome by several means, most notably the metaphysical depth from which her rhetoric springs. In brief, Orozco's use of a suprarational system of tropes is solidly grounded in a worldview that gives precedence to the hidden, the unknown, the unreachable. Magic is for this poet not a facile trick or a cheap spectacle. It is, rather, one of several plausible means by which an attempt is made to cross the threshold into the desired "other side." Orozco leads the reader to conclude that poetry itself is the most dangerous game, a topic I will discuss in greater depth in my Conclusion.

Cantos a Berenice [Songs for Berenice, 1977] is a poetic cycle of seventeen poems that serve as an extended epitaph for a cat. Orozco's approach is to link Berenice with legends and myths surrounding the feline species from Babylonian times onward. This book takes the reader back into the realm of the occult, but here there is a new focus: in *Cantos a Berenice*, Orozco begins the cultivation of a distinctively feminine orientation. The speaker as witch, with the black cat as her familiar, is only one of several ways in which Orozco explores the world of the occult arts through female archetypal figures.[5]

With her next volume, *Mutaciones de la realidad* [Mutations of reality] (1979), Orozco effectively abandons the practice of organizing a book around a clearly identifiable thematic unit. The organizing metaphor here is, in true postmodern fashion, a lack of metaphor, or a metaphor in constant disintegration. Though the subject of the book is "reality," both the poetic speaker and the reader are constantly thwarted in the attempt to grasp that reality as any sort of meaningful whole. The assumption underlying *Mutaciones de la realidad*, in sum, is that reality is unknowable by rational means. In *La noche a la deriva* [Night adrift] (1983), Orozco continues to explore motifs associated with knowing, with escaping the bounds of visible reality, and with magic as a means of crossing the threshold into the realm of the absolute. Several poems of this volume build upon the well-known allegory of human existence as the dream of a superior dreamer. The dream state evoked in much surrealist imagery is an artistic or literary version of the shaman's leap into other realms of consciousness. *La noche a la deriva* can be seen as a poetic testimonial to this sort of extramundane experience.

En el revés del cielo [On the other side of the sky] (1987) takes up the same transcendental themes as the previous books, but the tone seems to darken, and the motifs of silence, abandonment, and frustration prevail.

The image contained in the book's title recalls the lost paradise that the speaker finds increasingly remote and unattainable. This book, perhaps more than any other of Orozco's oeuvre, conveys a gnostic pessimism regarding the primordial human condition and the failure of all attempts to transcend it. The book is "framed" by two poems whose subject is speech, or the *logos* of the written (poetic) word. In both poems (as in "The Cumaean Sibyl of Cumas," another of this collection), the possibility of oracular discourse as a means to knowledge is examined and ultimately rejected. In Orozco's last book of poems, *Con esta boca, en este mundo* [With this mouth, in this world] (1994), silence, loss, and the imminence of death seem to overwhelm the lyric voice. There is a deepening sense of the impossibility of contact with the realm of the invisible, and of the failure of poetry to effect that contact.

As the preceding overview has shown, Orozco's sequence of nine volumes of poetry, spanning the period from 1946 to 1994, displays a remarkable internal coherence in its principle concerns as well as in its rhetorical modes and formal presentation. The later books are characterized by a darkened tone or a more pessimistic approach to the metaphysical problems presented. With regard to its esoteric character, which will be the focus of this study, Orozco's poetry has displayed from the first volume onward a tendency toward oracular discourse and heavily rhythmic, repetitive structures that echo liturgy, ritual, or even incantation. The use of organizing tropes and a semantic field directly related to the occult arts rises to the surface in *Los juegos peligrosos* and *Cantos a Berenice*, but can be found in varying degrees in all her volumes. Each of these elements— tone, rhythm, figurative language, and diction—reflects a worldview predicated upon alienation and loss. At the heart of all Orozco's work we discover the conviction that truth or reality always resides *elsewhere,* and that the human endeavor to regain this lost paradise, or to cross the threshold into absolute being, is doomed to failure.

> Estoy hecha con la misma sustancia del abismo
> y oficio contra la nada mi caída en las inmóviles tinieblas.
>
> [I am made with the same substance as the abyss
> and I officiate against the void my fall into the unmoving darkness.]
>
> Orozco, *Mutaciones*

Orozco's poetry is structured around the dichotomy of sacred and profane. Gnosticism, one of the major lines of esoteric tradition upon which her worldview is built, carries this dichotomy to an extreme that all but obliterates it. For the gnostic, even those elements of human existence that we deem sacred are permeated with evil; our perception of this dichotomy and others, therefore, is merely part of the boundless ignorance that separates us from the absolute. In this chapter, I explore gnosticism and, to a lesser degree, hermeticism, as key elements in what one critic has aptly called "the doctrine that organizes an entire worldview" in Orozco's work (Tacconi 116). Jill Suzanne Kuhnheim claims that "It would be reductionist to read [Orozco's] poetry on this level, to use gnostic principles as keys to unlock a set of clearly defined meanings" (81). As I will argue in the pages that follow, a clearer understanding of gnostic thought and, in particular, an examination of the major tropes of gnostic literature, can in fact broaden our appreciation of Orozco's poetry. Kuhnheim's concern that "the influence of gnosticism begs historicization, contextualization" is one that I hope to address in some depth in my Conclusion.

Orozco herself has affirmed in an interview that "más que cristiana, mi poesía es gnóstica" [more than Christian, my poetry is gnostic] (qtd. in Torres Fierro 202). In order to elucidate this distinction, I begin with a brief overview of the subject.[6] Definitions of gnosticism tend to be incomplete and inexact, in large part because the gnostics' very disdain of worldly existence—and therefore of human structures—precluded the establishment of an organized church with a well-defined and well-recorded system of beliefs. Furthermore, the gnostics' increasingly conflictive relationship with the early Christian church led them to function secretly. Much of what we know of gnosticism has been gleaned from Christian texts that decried the heretical nature of gnostic writings. The extant body of treatises by gnostic writers themselves displays a wide range of views that has eluded uniform codification.

The German historian of philosophy Hans Jonas, considered "the eminent authority on gnosticism," identifies gnosticism as the outstanding unifying element within a diverse field of beliefs characteristic of the late Hellenistic period in the Greco-Roman world (Pagels xxv). After Alexander's conquest of Eastern lands (334–323 B.C.), classical Western belief systems began to shift and fragment under the influence of the conquered cultures. By the first century B.C., secular Hellenism had been largely replaced by numerous currents of thought that Jonas characterizes as religious, soteriological (that is, concerned with salvation), transcendent, and dualistic (31–32).

Recent scholarship stresses both Hellenistic and Jewish origins of gnostic thought, which began to take shape in cosmopolitan urban centers such as Alexandria and Tyre (Quispel 567). Gnosticism's rise to the status of a major religion concurred with the rise of Christianity, with the first true gnostic texts dating to the second century A.D. Early gnosticism virtually disappeared, owing to persecution by the orthodox Christian church, by the end of the fourth century A.D. In medieval times, however, sects such as the Cathars (in southern France and northern Italy) and the Bogomils (in Bosnia) developed doctrines that closely resembled those of the early gnostics. Modern gnosticism took shape in the seventeenth century with Jakob Boehme, who is generally characterized as a Protestant mystic, but whose writings reflect both gnostic and hermetic worldviews. In the late eighteenth and early nineteenth centuries, these doctrines were reexamined by Johann Wolfgang von Goethe, by the German romantics, and by the Italian and English romantic poets Giacomo Leopardi, Percy Bysshe Shelley, and William Blake.

The scholarly study of gnosticism received a strong stimulus with the 1945 discovery of a set of fifty-two well-preserved texts of gnostic and hermetic origin at Nag Hammadi, Egypt. These texts—including secret gospels, poems, mythico-philosophical accounts of the origins of the universe, magical formulas, and instructions for mystical practices—provided scholars for the first time with a substantial body of documents apparently written by and for the gnostics themselves. Elaine Pagels, in *The Gnostic Gospels* (1979), provides a fascinating account of the discovery at Nag Hammadi, the mystery that shrouded the texts for three decades, and an overview of modern scholarship on the subject of gnosticism. Pheme Perkins, in *The Gnostic Dialogue* (1980) examines the gnostic writings as a unique form of religious and literary discourse. The epilogue to this book, entitled "Gnosis and the Modern Spirit," studies the reappearance of gnostic thought in the modern novel, in Jungian depth psychology, and even in modern Western politics.

Finally, it is worth noting that the renewed scholarly interest in gnosticism has been duly reflected in contemporary literature. Harold Bloom's *The Flight to Lucifer: A Gnostic Fantasy* (1979) is a work of fiction whose characters are "reincarnations" of historical gnostic personages such as Valentinus, or of figures from gnostic mythology such as the Primal Man, Sophia, and Ialdaboth. Bloom has also incorporated gnostic thought into his theories of literary criticism, stressing the similarities between gnosticism and cabalistic thought, most notably in *Kabbalah and Criticism*

(1975). Umberto Eco's *The Name of the Rose* (1980)—like Bloom's "fantasy," a work that is complex and difficult to classify—explores the relationship of orthodox Christianity to the numerous heresies, some with gnostic underpinnings, arising in the late Middle Ages. Finally, the fiction of Orozco's compatriots Enrique Anderson Imbert and Jorge Luis Borges provides further evidence of the richness of gnostic conceptual and symbolical possibilities for contemporary literature.

The Greek word *gnosis* means *knowledge*, particularly in the Latin sense of *cognoscere*, as opposed to *sapere* (Layton, *Gnostic Scriptures* 9). The early sects that began referring to themselves as *gnostics* held as a basic doctrine that salvation was to be gained by knowledge of—that is, direct acquaintance with—God. The belief in the saving power of mystic knowledge, gained by rites of initiation and ritualistic practices that became highly and disparately developed within the different sects, was consciously opposed to the orthodox Christian doctrines of faith or grace as the primary means to salvation. To become a true gnostic was to escape the primary human condition, not of sin, but of ignorance, a condition acknowledged repeatedly in Orozco's work.

The gnostic myth of origins, which Bentley Layton calls "the literary creation of theological poets," contains important elements from both Platonic and Hebrew traditions (12). The quintessential element of this myth is dualism: God, or the first principle, is entirely separate from the created cosmos. The first principle, initially sufficient unto itself, underwent a fall, a change resulting either from an inherent error or weakness, or from the coexistence of a principle of evil that rebelled against the godhead.[7] A crucial point here is that the true god of gnosticism is not the Judeo-Christian creator god. Yahweh is, in fact, seen as an inferior god, one concerned primarily with earthly justice. Gnostic texts often identify the creator-god with the demiurge, a secondary deity (probably modeled after the Demiurge of Plato's *Timaeus*) who embodies evil as well as good. Such a belief leads directly to the doctrine of cosmic evil. The world of matter, including the entire cosmos as humans perceive it, is the result of an error, a weakness, a rebellion by evil forces. The true god is utterly alien to reality as we know it. In Orozco's work this belief is patent, borne out by reiterated claims that reality is merely "ese relámpago de lo invisible / que revela en nosotros la soledad de Dios" [that lightning bolt out of the invisible / that reveals in us the solitude of God] (*Mutaciones* 37).

Orozco's use of an image of light—"relámpago"—to characterize the human portion of godliness is entirely appropriate to gnostic symbolism. The gnostics held that human beings consist of body (matter), soul, and spirit. The soul (akin to the Greek concept of *psyche*) belongs to the cosmos; it is still conditioned by contingency. But the soul contains the true particle of deity within each human, called by gnostics the *pneuma*. Orozco reflects this emphasis on spirit as qualitatively distinct from soul in the image of "la lámpara enterrada en el borde de tu alma" [the lamp buried at the edge of your soul] (*Obra* 122). *Pneuma* means *breath* in Greek; gnostic imagery related to this term incorporates this meaning, as well as the sense of a fragment of light or a spark. Interestingly, Orozco appropriates images corresponding to *pneuma* as both breath and spark in her own cosmogony: "Fue una chispa sagrada en el infierno, / la ráfaga de un cielo sepultado en la arena" [It was a sacred spark in hell, / the gust of wind from a sky buried in the sand] (*Mutaciones* 33). All gnostic doctrines agree on the general principle that human life holds meaning only to the extent that it tries to free the *pneuma* from its earthly confines and reunite it with the spirit from which it emanated. This is precisely the function of gnosis itself, and the origin of all gnostic practices and rituals. Orozco appears to have gleaned from gnosticism the sense of avid striving for such a reunion. She also shares with many gnostic writers a profound pessimism regarding the efficacy of such efforts, despairing that "ningún fulgor del cielo hemos logrado con tantas migraciones arrancadas al alma" [we haven't achieved a single heavenly glimmer with so many migrations wrenched from the soul] (23).

The historian of religions Mircea Eliade draws a fascinating parallel between notions such as the gnostic *pneuma* and the very phenomenon of "occultism," a parallel that helps to explain the confluence of esoteric beliefs in writers like Orozco. According to him, the notion of the "occultation" of the spirit in the flesh, symbolic of the fallen condition of humanity, can be seen as analogous to the occultation of certain beliefs within a given body of orthodox religious doctrine. This phenomenon occurs when a society is in the process of radical transformation. Speaking of the "underground" movement of currents of thought throughout history, he claims: "The same thing came to pass in Europe, after the urban societies had been Christianised; the pre-Christian religious traditions were conserved, camouflaged or superficially Christianised, in the countryside; but above all they were hidden in the closed circles of the sorcerers" (*Myths* 203). Ultimately, the gnostics' absolute insistence upon the evil nature of the world and its creator, their refusal to see holiness in anything but a truly occult spark, led to their expulsion from mainstream Christianity, and therefore to a choice, for many, between secrecy and death.

The radical dualism that characterizes most gnostic thought lies at the heart of Orozco's symbolic system; it is, in fact, the primary assumption behind the term *revés*, which is one of the leitmotifs of her work. Orozco's cosmology is essentially gnostic; that is, her poems reflect the belief that the world we inhabit is not divine in itself. Instead, she views human life as being trapped in a space located "en el revés del cielo" [on the other side of the sky]. Orozco insists in her work on a division between "this side" and "the other side."[8] Such a dichotomy is the poetic expression of the gnostic worldview, which claims that true life is alien to earthly human existence. A key passage from *En el revés del cielo* reads:

> Ésta es la tierra esquiva,
> la tierra de no llegar jamás, la tierra del fantasma en la pared.
> Otro es sin duda el sitio del encuentro, del combate invisible,
> de la línea de fuego donde se cierra el foso entre la piel y el alma.

(*Revés* 41)

> [This is the elusive land,
> the land of never arriving, the land of the ghost on the wall.
> Surely the site of encounter is elsewhere, that of the invisible battle,
> of the line of fire where the pit between skin and soul closes up.]

A certain tension between the gnostic view of world as evil and the hermetic view of the world as a reflection of the divine can be detected in the following passage from "Miradas que no ven" [Looks that don't see], a poem that ponders the existential situation of the biblical figure of Lazarus:

> ¡Ah, volver a nacer es volver a morir también del otro lado!
> Andará entre los vivos lo mismo que un fantasma, como un ala extraviada,
> sin acertar siquiera si este remoto mundo es un reflejo del sospechado paraíso,
> o sólo un engañoso lugar para probar la medida del alma.

(*Boca* 80)

[Oh, to be born again is to die again, also on the other side!
She will wander among the living like a ghost, like a mislaid wing,
never knowing exactly if this remote world is a reflection of a suspected paradise
or merely an illusory space for testing the measure of the soul.]

It is the latter view, that of the world as a deceptive place in which our spiritual mettle is constantly tested, that clearly prevails in Orozco's poetry.

In addition to the primary duality of good and evil, the secondary dualities characteristic of gnostic literature are also common in Orozco's poetry. Light and darkness are fundamental gnostic symbols for the "first principle" and the created cosmos, respectively. The created cosmos, it should be noted, becomes essentially identical with the evil from which it sprang. The mixing of pure light with impure darkness resulted in the material world; hence, Orozco's speaker echoes a gnostic lament: "Ah, si pudiera separar otra vez la luz y las tinieblas" [Oh, if I could only separate once again the darkness from the light] (*Noche* 14). The rare moment of transcendence is recounted in her poetry with similar images: "Se abre por un instante la trama entretejida por el humo y el brillo del abismo" [For a brief instant it opens: the weft interwoven by the smoke and the gleam of the abyss] (13). Gnostic symbolism is particularly clear in this passage, since "Abyss" was one of the names given to the alien first principle (Jonas 180).[9] In Orozco's work, darkness is often indicated by the more modulated term *sombra*. The poet's success in utilizing such broad or abstract symbols as darkness, light, and shadow while still maintaining an intensity of tone may result from the subjective, concrete, and highly visual contexts in which she places them. The poem ironically titled "Lugar seguro" [Safe haven], for instance, ends with a visually powerful image alluding to a purely metaphysical state: "Yo con la sombra hasta el cuello" [I, with shadow up to my neck] (*Noche* 12).

The utter separation from the godhead is a gap that is bridged, in some gnostic literature, by a sign or a voice, a "call from without." "At the gate of the worlds stands Kushta (Truth) and speaks [sic] a question into the world," reads one gnostic text, and another states: "He called with a heavenly voice into the turmoil of the worlds" (qtd. in Jonas 74). The otherworldly call of gnostic literature is related to a motif common to the Hebrew scriptures, in which the essentially inscrutable Yahweh gives a sign indicative of his will. Orozco's work is permeated with the motif of the enigmatic sign or call, which represents the possibility of communication between worlds that is a source of both faith and frustration.

The sign in Orozco's poetry virtually never functions as evidence of efficacious communication from one world to another. It tends to represent, rather, "un pálido signo que perdió su sentido" [a pale sign that has lost its meaning] or a series of "oscuros jeroglíficos" [dark hieroglyphs] employed by the speaker to underscore the improbability of such communication (*Obra* 182). I would argue that the purpose behind these fragmented attempts at transmundane communication is fundamentally gnostic. Separated from the absolute by the very condition of birth, the speaker spends her days in a futile search for "un indicio como de un talismán que me revierta la división y la caída" [a sign like a talisman that would revert for me the separation and the fall] (*Mutaciones* 91).

The poem "Pequeños visitantes" [Little visitors] is constructed as a sort of dramatization of the act of perceiving and deciphering signs. It demonstrates, perhaps better than any other poem, the centrality of the sign motif to Orozco's poetics:

Sé que hay algún avaro lugar donde se guardan pedazos del pasaje,
escenas incompletas como cualquier escena de este mundo,
poblaciones y gentes aferradas a un solo atardecer,
a una sola tormenta.
Se dirían imágenes arrebatadas al pasar por un golpe de viento,
retazos del pasado recogidos como por un rastrillo para el último
    día,
quizás como testigos, quizás como una prueba destinada a la
    hoguera final.

(*Boca* 43)

[I know there is some miserly place where fragments of landscape
    are kept,
scenes incomplete as any scene from this world,
whole populations clinging to a single dusk,
to a single storm.
They could be images snatched up by a passing windgust,
scraps of the past gathered up, as if by a rake, for the final day,
perhaps as witnesses, perhaps as a proof destined for the final
    blaze.]

In this poem, the signs of another reality are personified as "pequeños visitantes" or characterized negatively as "mezquinos tesoros" [petty treasures]. They have escaped, through some mysterious crevice, from a "sitio imantado" [magnetized place] in which fragments of this world are preserved. But the speaker insists that these visitors, or "testigos" [witnesses], are not simply pieces of a personal or cultural past: "¡Ah, porque no se trata de momentos guardados para la gran memoria!" [Oh, but it's not a question of moments saved for the great memory!]. Their purpose is somehow more sinister: they represent a "ciega ronda de ratones" [blind round of mice] who pursue and ambush the speaker. In the process of pondering the meaning of these visitors, their ontological status, the speaker comes up against the most intriguing possibility: that they are signs not from the past but from the future, hints of an unknown *elsewhere* that represents her "verdadera vida" [true life]. This last phrase recalls almost verbatim Breton's famous statement "Existence is elsewhere," and underscores the gnostic sense of division between a false or deceptive worldly existence and the true, real absolute (*Manifestoes* 47). The "pequeños visitantes" as signs from a transcendental beyond ultimately underscore, for Orozco, the negative condition of life on earth. Finally, it is worth noting that a gnostic sense of ignorance is represented structurally in "Pequeños visitantes." The confident affirmation of knowledge that opens the poem ("Sé que hay algún lugar") crumbles, by the end, into a series of unanswerable questions. The final question reads, "¿Y si fueran, opacos, andrajosos, con su gris aterido, / los fieles anticipos de mi verdadera vida, más allá?" [And what if they were, opaque, ragged, with their freezing gray, / the faithful foretastes of my true life, there beyond?] (*Boca* 44). The subjunctive "what if" of this question, coupled with the negative images conjured by the speaker, textually demonstrate a condition of terrifying ignorance.

The radical dualism of gnostic thought leads inexorably to the conviction that the world itself is a "reign of shadows," the embodiment of error and evil (*Noche* 13). Consequently, in Orozco's poems gnostic allusions to the material world often occur in images similar to those Jonas categorizes as "fall," "sinking," or "capture" (Jonas 62–64). The term *caída* [fall], broadly applicable to Judeo-Christian mythology, functions as a leitmotif throughout Orozco's work. Her insistence on the purely fatalistic aspects of the fall, together with the conviction that "la caída es una ley más fuerte que cualquier ascensión" [the fall is a law that is stronger than any ascension] echoes the pessimism conveyed by many gnostic writers (*Obra* 122).

A characteristically gnostic interplay between the fall, earthly matter, and darkness is apparent in the poem "Atavíos y ceremonial" [Finery and ceremonial]: "Estoy hecha con la misma sustancia del abismo / y oficio contra la nada mi caída en las inmóviles tinieblas" [I am made with the very substance of the abyss / and I officiate against nothingness my fall into the unmoving darkness] (*Mutaciones* 87).

According to Jonas, gnostic writers often employed terms such as *cast out* or *thrown down* to describe the human condition in its separation from God. The metaphysical sense of these very physical verbs is apparent in Orozco's images. In one passage the speaker laments: "Me arrojaron al mundo en mi ataúd de hielo" [They cast me into the world in my icy casket] (*Obra* 98); in another she remarks that "Siempre hay sendas que vuelan y me arrojan en un despeñadero" [There are always paths that take flight, casting me over the precipice" (*Revés* 18). The object of the verb *arrojar* [to cast or throw] is typically the speaker herself, who describes the resultant situation as one of captivity. "Outcast" and "captive" are, of course, familiar Platonic metaphors for both world and body, but in gnostic literature they take on an unusual intensity. One gnostic writer asks of God: "Why did ye carry me away from my abode into captivity and cast me into the stinking body?" (qtd. in Jonas 63). In the poem "Operación nocturna" [Nocturnal operation] Orozco puts into play all of the semantic elements thus far identified as pertaining to the gnostic worldview:

> ¿No había para mí nada más que esta cárcel,
> estos muros aviesos, fatales hacia abajo,
> esta tensa tiniebla que me arroja de subsuelo en subsuelo?

(*Mutaciones* 19)

> [Was there nothing for me but this prison,
> these twisted walls, fatal in their depths,
> this tense darkness that tosses me from subsoil to subsoil?]

The final phrase of this passage is particularly germane to the present discussion, since gnostic mythologies divided the world into multiple levels. Hellenistic gnosticism accounted for seven or twelve "aeons," or worlds, and some later systems claimed the existence of as many as 365. In any case, life or the human soul is seen as being cast away from the godhead and falling through these numerous lower spheres, or *subsuelos,* as Orozco aptly designates them.

In gnostic literature the primordial ignorance that characterizes the human psyche, reinforcing its separation from God, is conveyed through metaphors of numbness, sleep, and intoxication (Jonas 68–73). This state of oblivion is profoundly related to the innate evil of the world, and redemption through gnosis means—to maintain the primary analogy—awakening. To read in Orozco of "la desmedida inercia frente al rito vampiro de la fatalidad" [boundless inertia facing the vampire rite of fatality] (*Noche* 34), or of "ojos estancados donde se ahoga el sueño" [stagnant eyes where dreams drown] (39), is certainly to be reminded of the gnostic sense of oblivion. Curiously, however, in the depiction of human consciousness, Orozco seems more often to deviate from the gnostic figures. Far more common than sleep metaphors are the terms *insomnia, velar,* and *testigo.* If anything, the speaker here is hyperconscious. Nights as well as days are lived "con los ojos abiertos bajo el insorportable parpadeo del sol" [with eyes open under the unbearable blinking of the sun] (*Mutaciones* 91). Far from being lulled into psychic sleep, she appears plagued by incessant mental activity: "¡Qué taller inaudito mi cabeza!" [What a monstrous workshop, this head of mine!] (85).

Does Orozco represent here the state of spiritual awakening toward which the gnostics strove? Does the speaker depict, by way of this hyperconsciousness, the achievement of some degree of true gnosis? To answer these questions it is necessary to recall, first, that the "call from without" of gnostic literature appears in Orozco as a frustrated communication, a sign with no clear meaning. Secondly, upon examination, the images related to wakefulness fail to reveal any real acquaintance with the absolute. The speaker of "Atavíos y ceremonial" recalls the garments she has donned in her attempts to reach the beyond: "El traje de humaredas y telarañas rotas que permite cruzar alguna vez /—aunque jamás indemne—/ esas grietas que entreabren en los muros" [The suit of smoke clouds and broken webs that sometimes allows one to pass /—although never unharmed—/ through the chinks that open in the walls] (*Mutaciones* 85). Significantly, among these articles is "el sombrero de ortigas insomnes para forzar los sueños hasta la pesadilla" [the hat made of sleepless nettles for forcing dreams into nightmare] (85). Forcing the dream leads not to an enlightened wakefulness but to a nightmare. Moreover, there is among the garments a "capa de ráfaga emplumada" [cape of feathered windgusts] that allows her to be sucked into "[el] vacío donde se pierde el yo" [the emptiness where the self is lost] (85), suggesting that the leap into transcendental consciousness may lead to the loss of the self. At the end of her enumeration of magic vestments, liturgies, and ceremonies, the speaker rediscovers that there is only the body itself—the flesh despised by the gnostics: "Solamente el precario, desnudo tegumento sin costuras que me ciñe a los huesos, / que me vuelve de pronto del revés y me arrastra hacia adentro" [Just the precarious, naked, seamless integument that binds me to my bones, / that turns me suddenly inside out and drags me inwards] (86).

In some gnostic texts, most notably a fascinating parable known as "The Hymn of the Pearl," the garment symbolizes salvation, the "robe of glory" which humans once wore and which will be attained again upon the soul's ascent after death (Jonas 112–29). The central figure of this parable, akin to the biblical prodigal son, returns triumphantly to his parents' house after a long period of exile, and is given the robe he wore as a child. "And I cast the royal mantle about my entire self," he says; "Clothed therein, I ascended to the gate of salutation and adoration" (qtd. in Jonas 115). How utterly different, then, is Orozco's "traje de humaredas y telarañas rotas," the miserable garment that may allow her a momentary crossing to the other side, but that finally throws her back into the density of matter and reminds her of the absurdity of her desires: "Qué frágiles envolturas para el juego perverso de la tentación y el desafío!" [What fragile wrappings for the perverse game of temptation and duel!] (*Mutaciones* 85).

The symbolism of the garment in "The Hymn of the Pearl" is far more complex than it might appear in the passages just cited. In Egypt, the exiled son is visited by messengers from his father, who deliver to him the robe he wore as a child: "As I now beheld the robe, it seemed to me suddenly to become a mirror-image of myself: myself entire I saw in it, and it entire I saw in myself, that we were two in separateness, and yet again one in the sameness of our forms" (qtd. in Jonas 115). In this text, the garment becomes fully personified; it speaks to the son and even hastens of its own will from the messenger's hands to the son's. Its verbal message allows us to identify it as a duplication of the son himself, one who stayed behind in the father's house, and whose moral stature there grew in accordance with the son's trials in exile. Jonas explains that the robe thus symbolizes "the heavenly or eternal self of the person, his original idea, a kind of double or alter ego preserved in the upper world while he labors down below" (122). In fact, texts postulating this sort of duplication abound in gnostic literature, and lead to the doctrine of the "transcendental self" or "heavenly twin." The concept is Platonic in origin: in the realm of the absolute there exists the perfect idea or image of each soul. The soul, in its descent to earth, becomes temporarily obscured; in the moment of salvation, earthly and celestial selves recognize one another and are fused.

Historically, the notion of the spiritual twin was revived by the eighteenth-century German Illuminists. In nineteenth-century France, it forms the basis of Nerval's semiautobiographical novel *Aurélia,* and of Rimbaud's well-known poem "Génie." Orozco seems to have drawn as well from this tradition in several of her poems. The mythicized cat of *Cantos a Berenice,* itself a double of the speaker, is said to have "una constelación por cabellera en tu doble del cielo" [a constellation for hair in your heavenly double] (*Obra* 169). In several passages, the awareness of the *other* comes from the speaker's sense of being watched from afar: "A veces surgen grietas por las que me contempla mi testigo invisible" [Sometimes fissures appear through which my invisible witness watches me] (*Noche* 12). The celestial double is clearly depicted in the poem "Catecismo animal" [Animal catechism], whose initial vision closely parallels the gnostic view of the human condition, created "por obra de error" [by means of error] (*Revés* 13). Here the speaker expresses a desire to recover the spiritual "lost half":

> Ah descubrir la imagen oculta e impensable del reflejo,
> la palabra secreta, el bien perdido,
> la otra mitad que siempre fue una nube inalcanzable desde la
>   soledad
> y es toda la belleza que nos ciñe en su trama y nos rehace.
>
> (*Revés* 13)

> [Oh, to discover the hidden and unthinkable image of the reflection,
> the secret word, the lost good,
> the other half that was always a cloud, unreachable from this solitude
> and that is all the beauty that wraps us in its weft and remakes us.]

The celestial double is not personified in this poem as it is in gnostic mythology; nevertheless, it possesses the same qualities of beauty, eternal perfection, and devotion to its earthly twin. Although this other half has the potential of remaking the human self in its divine image, it remains remote, *inalcanzable.* Once again, Orozco's poetry oscillates between possibility—union with the spiritual double—and failure: "Nunca con este cuerpo donde siempre tropieza el universo" [Never with this body where the universe always stumbles] (*Revés* 14).

The final feature of gnosticism I will examine in relation to Orozco's work is the doctrine of plurality. To reiterate, gnostic mythologies view the fall as a fracturing of the original unity into multiplicity, what Orozco calls "una lluvia de piedras desprendida del cielo" [a rain of stones unloosed from the sky] (*Obra* 125). The very multifaceted nature of the cosmos, its illusive quality, and its capacity for perpetual change thus become associated with error and evil. The symbolism of many key gnostic texts portrays plurality as a dispersal of the original light, or a mixing of light with darkness. This is the origin of the association of the *pneuma* with the spark as the fragment of divinity enclosed within the human body. Orozco's imagery, in similar fashion, often recalls the notion of the universe as a broken and dispersed version of an original unity. In one poem, the speaker sees the present as nothing but "restos esparcidos bajo el grito del sol" [remains scattered under the cry of the sun]; the future is also described as "despedazado" [shattered] (*Revés* 26). Correspondingly, in these lines a fragmented present is contrasted with a vision of paradise lost: "Aún no hace mucho tiempo, / cuando el mundo era un vidrio del color de la dicha, no un puñado de arena" [Not very long ago, / when the world was a window the color of happiness, not a mere handful of sand] (*Revés* 33). The translucent, perfect whole of the past is left shattered when someone or something "rompió el reflejo ... enturbió el azogue ... deshizo el embrujo de la transparencia" [broke the reflection ... clouded the quicksilver ... undid the spell of transparency] (33).

When Orozco's speaker does allude to the possibility of personal salvation, she does so in the gnostic terms of reunion of dispersed fragments. Telma Luzzani Bystrowicz has analyzed this metaphysical position as it manifests itself on a purely textual level. Noting the internal coherence, the "organic" nature of Orozco's work, she observes that while this poetry speaks overtly of duality and contradiction, "en su nivel profundo produce una síntesis, una fusión que debe leerse también como la búsqueda de una originaria unidad perdida" [on the deepest level it produces a synthesis, a fusion that should also be read as the search for an original, lost unity] (227). The concept of plurality manifests itself in specific rhetorical devices often associated with a baroque style, such as antithesis, oxymoron, and syntactic inversions. Luzzani Bystrowicz emphasizes what she calls the "specular structure" of Orozco's poetry, noting a whole semantic field related to the term *espejo* [mirror] (228). This structural device, she argues, contributes markedly to an effect of equilibrium, a balancing or gathering-in of otherwise contradictory or dispersed elements. Stylistically, the tension inherent in dialectical opposition is resolved by means of two devices: first, by the very constancy of such elements, which converts them into a textual norm; and second, by the use of modifiers to accompany contradictory elements that, "lejos de resaltar su oposición, los fusionan" [far from stressing their opposition, actually fuses them] (228).

In addition to these devices, Luzzani Bystrowicz cites Orozco's use of reiterated semantic (and, I might add, symbolical) elements and the sense of circularity given to many poems by the similarity of opening and closing lines. These structural and rhetorical devices, as Bystrowicz observes, serve to integrate the written text into the pluralistic gnostic worldview upon which it is based (229). The poem "Rara sustancia" ends with a question that underscores the plurality of existence: "¿Cuál podrá ser mi reino en esta mezcla . . . ?" [What could be my kingdom in all this mixture?]. This question is followed by an answer that tentatively affirms a gnostic sense of salvation: "Tal vez el reino de la unidad perdida entre unas sombras, / el reino que me absorbe desde la nostalgia primera y el último suspiro" [Perhaps the kingdom of lost unity among shadows, / the kingdom that absorbs me from the first nostalgia and the last sigh] (*Noche* 29).

The textual evidence presented here affirms that Orozco's attitude toward what may be broadly termed *salvation* is pessimistic at best. An overwhelming majority of images depicts the sentiment encapsulated in the title "No hay acceso" [No access]: there is simply no way into the desired space of transcendence or reintegration. Occasionally, however, the sense of possibility triumphs. Such is the case in "Desdoblamiento de Dios en máscara de todos" [God's unfolding in everyone's mask], a relatively early poem that affirms a sense of shared essence among disparate human appearances: "Desde adentro de todos no hay más que una morada bajo un friso de máscaras" [Within all of us there is only a dwelling beneath a frieze of masks] (*Obra* 124). The *morada*, or spiritual dwelling, a term used by mystics such as Santa Teresa de Jesús to connote union with God, is viewed as the sole integral element at the base of multiple falsities. The final strophe of this poem opens with an allusion to what may be the transcendental self, or, in Borgesian fashion, to a creator-dreamer whose dream is the universe: "Despierto en cada sueño con el sueño con que Alguien sueña el mundo" [I awaken in each dream with the dream in which Someone dreams the world] (125). The strophe concludes, significantly, with a vision of spiritual reintegration that is characteristically gnostic: "Es víspera de Dios. / Está uniendo en nosotros sus pedazos" [It is the eve of God. He is unifying his fragments in us] (125).

The preceding examination of the abundant gnostic imagery in this poetry leads me to conclude that gnosticism, more than any other belief system, provides an apt philosophico-religious framework for Orozco's major concerns: namely, the alien place of the human spirit within its surroundings, and the seeming impossibility of attaining a state of union with the divine, which the speaker, nevertheless, desperately desires. Jonas's conclusions regarding gnostic thought may offer a further clue to its appeal for Orozco: "The beginning and end of the paradox that is gnostic religion is the unknown God himself who, unknowable on principle . . . is yet the object of a knowledge and even asks to be known. He as much invites as he thwarts the quest for knowing him; in the failure of reason and speech he becomes revealed; and the very account of the failure yields the language for naming him" (288). What better way to characterize Orozco's poetry than as "the very account of the failure"? For Orozco, the quest for the unknown begins and ends with poetry itself. Her sense of defeat at this task is underscored in a final image of gnostic dispersal: "Un puñado de polvo, mis vocablos!" [A fistful of dust, my words!] (*Mutaciones* 92).

The philosophical and spiritual tendencies of the late classical and early Christian era in the Greco-Roman world produced another set of texts related to many gnostic writings, yet with a distinctive flavor. These writings are the basis of a tradition that became known as hermeticism, a tradition upon which the German romantics and their literary successors drew heavily. Although the hermetic worldview does not inform Orozco's work as closely as does the gnostic, it is the source of several important symbols and images that characterize her worldview, and as such bears brief examination here. Taken together, gnosticism and hermeticism provide a complete framework within which Orozco's esoteric belief system can be analyzed.

Unlike classic gnosticism, hermeticism never solidified into a set of doctrines forming the basis of a religion. The primary body of hermetic texts was written in Alexandria between the first century B.C. and the second century A.D., but was based on much older works (Mahé 289). These texts display a unity of literary genre (consisting mainly of "sentences" passed from father to son in Egyptian scribal tradition, comments on these sentences, and prayers) and remain as "outstanding testimonials to the spiritual concerns of late paganism" (292). Hermetic writings, like their gnostic counterparts, are eclectic in origin, showing influence from late Hellenistic thought, from Judaism, and from ancient Egyptian traditions. Of uncertain and apparently varied authorship, these treatises were attributed to Hermes Trismegistos ("Thrice-great Hermes"), a semihistorical, semimythological figure traditionally associated with Thoth, the Egyptian god of wisdom and inventor of writing. Written in Greek, the texts purport to be the teachings of Thoth and his disciples, which were translated from the Coptic (288).

The importance of hermetic writings for modern scholarship and literature dates to 1463, when the *Corpus Hermeticum*, until then relatively unknown in Europe, was translated by Marsilio Ficino and introduced into Florence as "a precious newly found revelation which might just possibly antedate Moses himself" (Tuveson 8). Renowned Renaissance scholar Frances Yates argues in her pivotal book *Giordano Bruno and the Hermetic Tradition* (1964) that hermetic thought was at the very core of Renaissance humanism. Although more recent research has shown her claims too far-reaching, Yates is credited with reorienting modern scholarship with regard to the historical significance of hermetic thought. In *The Avatars of Thrice Great Hermes* (1982), Ernest Tuveson traces the philosophical and literary development of hermeticism from Ficino's translation of the *Corpus* through the English romantic poets, to modern poets such as Walt Whitman. Claims Tuveson: "One might say that the idea *of* the universe underwent a most drastic upheaval, in the seventeenth and eighteenth centuries; but, in the hermetist tradition, ideas *about* the universe remained constant. Finally, they led to what we know as romanticism" (12).

As a whole, the body of hermetic writings shares with gnosticism the cardinal myth of the fall and its corollary, the doctrine of salvation through reintegration. Moreover, hermeticism is often linked with gnosticism precisely because both profess the importance of gnosis for salvation, a belief which led to a secret transmission of knowledge from master to adept. Some gnostics even invoked Hermes Trismegistos and appropriated portions of the hermetic scholarly tradition for their own purposes (Mahé 291–92). The two currents of thought diverge, however, in their radically opposed conception of divinity, and, therefore, of humanity. I have discussed the dualism that pervaded gnostic thought, which located the true god at an unreachable distance from the inhabited universe. For hermeticism, in contrast, the universe is a direct and visible unfolding of God. All that makes up the world is therefore a manifestation of divinity, a symbolic representation of the divine mind. This was the crucial premise upon which the doctrine of *correspondances*, so fundamental to the work of Baudelaire and the symbolists, was based.

Orozco clearly positions herself more along gnostic than hermetic lines. However, certain aspects of hermetic thought, or of the philosophical and artistic traditions they engendered, do contribute to the wealth of sources upon which Orozco has drawn. The first derives from the stress placed in the Hermetica on the positive, symbolic value of the created universe. The *Tabula Smaragdina*, attributed to Hermes Trismegistos and widely circulated in late medieval and Renaissance periods, sets forth hermeticism's fundamental premise: "That which is above is like to that which is below, and that which is below is like to that which is above" (qtd. in Holmyard 97). The reflection of macrocosm in microcosm is explicit in certain passages of Orozco's work. "Si observas al trasluz," claims the speaker, "verás pasar el mundo rodando en una lágrima" [If you look against the light, you'll see the world roll by in a tear] (*Revés* 65). Here the hermetic sense of the world reflected in a drop of water is tempered by gnostic pessimism: the drop is in fact a tear.

The analogous relationship of the terrestrial to the divine produces a symbol common to almost all esoteric thought, that of "the world as mirror of the divine and object of contemplation" (Faivre, "Hermetism" 294). I have already mentioned one critic's observation of the specular structure of Orozco's work and the frequent occurrence of terms related to *mirror* (Luzzani Bystrowicz 228). Although Orozco's work typically reveals a gnostic conception of the universe as a corrupted deviation from the absolute, occasionally a positive view emerges through the image of divine reflection. In one poem, for instance, spiritual reintegration is associated with divine love, which is symbolized as "el espejo donde alguien recupera el paraíso" [the mirror where someone recovers paradise] (*Revés* 61). But genuine hermetic optimism—a sense of utter confidence in divine providence—is nowhere so pointedly expressed as in the speaker's reminder that "el alma que te habita es también la mirada del cielo que te incluye" [the soul that inhabits you is also the gaze of the sky that includes you] (*Noche* 39).

The hermetic notion that the human intellect is reflective of the divine *Nous*, or Mind, leads to the conception of the world as a text to be deciphered, an idea adopted by later esoteric currents of thought. Orozco employs the metaphor of the text in several passages. In the allegorical poem

"Al pie de la letra" [Word for word], the speaker tells of writing her existence as a "confesión" that she herself is then unable to decipher (*Noche* 38). The poem is fraught with images of judgment and martyrdom (more reminiscent of Judaic or Christian than of Hermetic thought). The text in question, being written with the speaker's own blood, is cast as "la escritura fatal" [fatal writing] (38). And though she asks herself what might be the "whole sense" of this written testimony, no answer presents itself: "Delación o alegato, no alcanzo a interpretar las intenciones del esquivo mensaje" [Denunciation or plea, I'm unable to interpret the intention of the elusive message] (38). In another poem, the speaker reinforces the notion that the symbolic text remains elusive, as she pleads for "Algo con que alumbrar las sílabas dispersas de un código perdido" [Something with which to illuminate the disperse syllables of a lost code] (*Mutaciones* 91). These allusions to meaning as written text bear resemblance to the references to the "call from without" discussed with regard to gnostic mythology. In both cases, the message fails to be deciphered or to offer the "total sense" that the speaker desires.

A final, somewhat curious connection between hermetic mythology and Orozco's work may be found in the motif of the human statue. As Silvia Pellarolo notes, the statue of salt is one of Orozco's most fundamental symbols.[10] On a primary level, the image clearly alludes to the biblical account of Lot's wife, who was turned into a pillar of salt as punishment for her disobedience in looking back at the destruction of Sodom and Gomorrah. Orozco's poetic speaker is identified with Lot's wife in her perpetual desire to look back, that is, to express nostalgia for the lost primordial unity. From the purely mineral pillar of the Genesis account, this image gradually takes on life in Orozco's poetry, until the statue becomes an image of the speaker herself, posterior to a spiritual death: "Me embalsaman en estatua de sal a las puertas del tiempo. / Soy la momia traslúcida de ayer convertida en oráculo" [They embalm me in a statue of salt at the doors of time. / I am yesterday's translucent mummy that has become an oracle] (*Mutaciones* 16).

In the *Asclepius,* one of the most influential books of the *Corpus Hermeticum,* Hermes discusses the ancient Egyptian belief that mortals have the power to create gods. This may occur when the soul of a god is induced to enter a statue, whereby the statue becomes an oracle capable of prophesying and of inflicting or curing disease (Mahé 290). For Orozco, the inanimate statue signifies matter in the gnostic sense of dense, spiritless substance—the pillar of salt, after all, means death for Lot's wife. But the statue inhabited by a spirit is a miracle of human making, an apt symbol for the poet and her voice. In the poem "La caída" [The fall], this symbol is integrated with the motif of the celestial twin, the "estatua de azul" [blue statue] who addresses her earthly counterpart in the voice of a personal oracle: "Bella estatua de sal: tú no puedes llegar" [Beautiful statue of salt: you cannot arrive] (*Obra* 105). In Orozco's account, the hermetic oracular statue speaks from a gnostic perspective, insisting on the impassable threshold separating the sacred from the profane.

Hermetic mythology details the fall of man, largely due to his vulnerability to Eros. But the theme of the fall is countered with a positive emphasis on rebirth, regeneration, or reintegration by means of the soul's ascent. Reascent can be accomplished by means of the intellect (which effects a connection with intermediary spiritual intelligences) or by theurgical means (Faivre, "Hermetism" 294). This explains the traditional association of hermeticism (particularly in its development from the Renaissance forward) with initiatory rites, magic, astrology, and alchemy. The following chapter will examine Orozco's own poetic exploration of these occult paths to knowledge and reintegration.

3

The Occult as Revelation and Power of Passage in Orozco's Poetry

> Yo elegí los delirios, las magias y el amor.
> [I chose delirium, the magic arts, and love.]
> —O. Orozco, "Feria del hombre" [The fair of man]

Gnosticism and hermeticism, as we have seen, are intricate tapestries in which mythological, religious, philosophical, and literary threads intertwine. Both exalt the idea of gnosis, building their speculative systems upon the conviction that certain human beings are capable of attaining a special knowledge that will allow them access to a hidden realm. Of the two, gnosticism maintains a more pessimistic stance, seeing the material world as fundamentally evil and as a hindrance to human attempts to commune with the godhead. Hermeticism, though more varied in its approaches, tends toward an optimistic stance that posits the material world as a reflection of the divine, and therefore as worthy of sustained contemplation.

Both of these belief systems may be seen as partial constructions within a more comprehensive framework of human thought. According to the sociologist Edward Tiryakian, Western and non-Western societies, modern and premodern alike, have been characterized by "a general perspective that the world of appearance is an outward manifestation of a background reality, that the relationships and interrelationships among observed phenomena derive from their linkage to covert factors or forces 'behind' the world of appearance" (4). Knowledge of these hidden truths is a source of power. Thus, although gnosticism and hermeticism are highly structured and codified elaborations of the concept of gnosis, they are by no means isolated systems of thought. They are, in fact, two particular manifestations of a broader set of cultural patterns commonly referred to as the esoteric, or the occult.

The previous chapter examined certain correlates between the gnostic worldview and the system of tropes utilized by Orozco; we have also seen how Orozco has adapted some of hermeticism's primary symbols (the statue with prophetic powers, the mirror, the world as text) to her own poetic purposes. The present chapter moves beyond the paradigms of gnosticism and hermeticism to an examination of "dangerous games" themselves: alchemy, divination, and magic. In a prose commentary, Orozco herself makes explicit the ties between the occult arts and the gnostic sense of existential exile: "Y bien, sólo desde este territorio del destierro, de la nostalgia y la esperanza, puedo hablar de 'Los Juegos Peligrosos,' precisamente porque son peligrosos todos los juegos que intentamos para salir de él, para cambiarlo o para anexarle otros cielos y otras tierras con sus flores y sus faunas" [And so it is only from this territory of exile, of nostalgia, and of hope, that I can speak of "The Dangerous Games," precisely because all games are dangerous if we play them in order to leave it, to change it, or to attach it to other heavens and other earths with their flora and their fauna] (*Páginas* 100). These occult arts—or sciences, as they have been variously called throughout their long traditions—do not belong to a particular religious or philosophical body of thought. Rather, they have always been molded to fit some broader context. Although the occult arts embody widely divergent creeds and methods, I intend to focus on certain portions of their shared territory: first, the conviction that there exists a hidden realm beyond the grasp of the senses, and even beyond the reach of rational knowledge; and second, that a praxis may be established for reaching into that realm. My intention is to demonstrate that such convictions underlie Orozco's poetry and that the occult arts provide Orozco with a figurative paradigm that determines to a significant degree the praxis of her poetry.

> Just as universal substance (*materia prima*) can only be grasped by means of knowledge of Pure Being, whose shadow it is, so also the true ground of the soul can only be known in its response to the pure Spirit.
>
> —Titus Burckhardt, *Alchemy*

Alchemy provides a bridge between the religious and philosophical worldviews of late Hellenistic and early Christian times, and the practice of the occult arts, which spans the centuries leading into our own. Throughout its development in Western cultures, alchemy has manifested a strong correlation with all major esoteric and mystical traditions (Eliade, "Alchemy" 183). In fact, alchemy, the attempt to produce an elixir of immortality or to create gold from common metals, has traditionally been considered the quintessential hermetic art. Hermes, or Thoth, was known as the founder of alchemy, and writers of alchemical texts frequently attributed their works to Hermes Trismegistos. Occult literature from late Hellenistic Egypt, dating from the second to fourth century A.D., establishes clear links between alchemy, gnosticism, and hermeticism. From this fact, historians argue that "alchemy, beyond being a craft devoted to changing matter, has a place also within the history of religions," and moreover, that "in the alchemist's religious beliefs the general gnostic tenets blended with his specific alchemical approach to the world" (Kahane and Kahane 193). In his book *Yeats and Alchemy*, William Gorski observes that "The alchemical implication of [the gnostic] myth is that spirit penetrates all matter, and therefore the entire cosmos retains its potential divinity" (9). The so-called *Tabula Smaragdina*, or Emerald Tablet, from the ninth century but based on hermetic sources and traditionally included within the *Corpus Hermeticum* (c. 1460), was regarded by late medieval and Renaissance alchemists as a divine revelation of secret teachings in the art. The role of alchemy within Islam was particularly strong; thus, in the Middle Ages, the art was reintroduced into Christianized Europe through Arab-dominated Spain. In fact, many Medieval and Renaissance texts on alchemy were first translated into Arabic from Greek, then from Arabic into Latin and the vernaculars. The term *al-kimiya'* in Arabic probably derives from the Greek *chumeia* (or *chemeia*), denoting the "art of transmutation" (Rahim 196).

The goal of the practical alchemist was to perfect the transmutation of base metals into silver and gold, by means of complex methods involving first the "blackening," then the bleaching, and finally the "reddening" of a mysterious materia prima. The practical means by which these methods were carried out varied widely, and can seem incomprehensible or arbitrary from a modern rationalistic perspective. Although Renaissance alchemists agreed upon the black-white-red color sequence, there was little agreement on the particular substances to be used or the processes by which these changes were to be effected. To begin with, the materia prima was nowhere clearly defined, and many alchemists spent years of experimentation in discovering what they considered to be the true primal substance. The entire process was directed toward the production of the so-called philosopher's stone, which was then to be applied in the actual work of transmutation. In addition to the myriad procedural choices facing the alchemists, numerous practical difficulties arose, such as the regulation of the fire without accurate thermometers. In spite of all this, alchemy did produce, over the centuries, a limited body of knowledge that has been regarded as protochemistry. In some cases, the alchemists believed that they had indeed produced gold, although modern chemistry has demonstrated the misconceptions that led to these false conclusions (Holmyard 138). But for most alchemists, the practical experiments were an acknowledged failure.

With the triumph of rationalism and the discoveries of empirical science beginning in the seventeenth century, the very notion of the transmutation of substances was discredited, and alchemy as a practical enterprise or protoscience virtually disappeared. But modern scholars are quick to point out that it is not the methods or material goals of these early chemists that accounts for the power of the alchemical legacy (Eliade, "Alchemy" 183). The notion of transmutation itself held not only a physical meaning, but a symbolic, redemptive meaning as well. Symbolically, the alchemical opus becomes "the art of the transmutations of the soul" (Burckhardt 23), or, in more secular terms, "a series of specific experiences aimed at the radical transformation of the human condition" (Eliade, "Alchemy" 184). The *opus alchimicum* in each of its phases, in fact, can be interpreted as an allegory for the ascent of the fallen or divided human soul (as materia prima) into pure spirit. Or, conversely, it allegorizes the descent of spirit into human form, whereby the form is consecrated. "Spiritually understood," concludes Burckhardt, "the transmutation of lead into gold is nothing other than the regaining of the original nobility of human nature" (26). In sum, long after the natural death of alchemy as a science or craft, the tradition survived in its symbolic aspect. Having lost its "exoteric" component to chemistry, "alchemy was reduced to its 'esoteric' questions about man's relation to the cosmos" (Kahane and Kahane 196). Goethe's *Faust*, to cite one well-known example, is a drama filled with alchemical allusions. Nor was the symbolic value of alchemy lost on such nineteenth-century poets as Rimbaud, who alluded to the poetic transmutation of experience into metaphor in his poem "Alchimie du verbe" [Alchemy of the word] (192). William Butler Yeats, likewise, "valued alchemy as a metaphor for transformation, applicable to both the creative act and to spiritual work" (Gorski 24). In the twentieth century, the psychologist C. G. Jung maintained that the mystical side of alchemy, as distinct from its historical aspect, was essentially a psychological problem (*Studies* 105). The work of the alchemist, with its goal of freeing the spirit from its material bonds, was a concretization, in projected and symbolic form, of the universal quest for Self, a process he termed *individuation* (105).

Throughout her nine volumes of poetry published to date, Orozco has utilized a symbolic language deriving from alchemy. In its general application, the term *alquimia* for Orozco connotes change (that is, transmutation), often related to secret knowledge. The blood of her own body, for instance, suggests to the speaker "[la] alquimia de animal iniciado en todos los arcanos" [the alchemy of an animal initiated into all mysteries] (*Obra* 161). In another passage, alchemy is a metaphor for a conscious change resulting in the ability to forget: "¡Ah tu alquimia secreta para lograr el filtro del olvido!" [Ah, your secret alchemy for achieving a potion for forgetting] (*Boca* 26). But for Orozco, alchemy represents far more than a generalized metaphor for change. In the pages that follow, I will outline Orozco's appropriation of particular figures in the alchemical allegory, in particular her focus on the failure of the operation in its spiritual or psychological sense.

The basic hermetic principle of universal sympathy, or the interrelated nature of all phenomena, underlies the alchemical principle of the transmutation of matter. This principle is implied when the speaker of "Animal que respira" [Animal that breathes] classifies the act of breathing as "esta mutua transfusión con todo el universo" [this mutual transfusion with the entire universe] (*Obra* 154). Self and universe are likened in this prose poem to "dos organismos esponjosos fijados a la pared de lo visible" [two spongy organisms stuck to the wall of the visible], locked into a perpetual double fluctuation whose meaning is unknown to them (154). Eliade has pointed out the analogies between respiratory processes and alchemical operations in Chinese alchemy (*Forge* 124–25). In Orozco's poem, the process of breathing, and with it the olfactory sense (related primarily to memory), are summarized in terms that allude directly to the methods of alchemy: "Una alquimia volátil se hacina poco a poco en los resquicios, evapora las duras condensaciones de los años, y me excava y me sofoca y me respira en grandes transparencias que son la forma exangüe de mi última armazón" [A volatile alchemy gathers slowly in the chinks, evaporates the hard condensations of the years; it excavates me and suffocates me and breathes me in great transparencies that are the bloodless form of my final framework] (*Obra* 155). "Armazón" in this context refers to the barrier that effectively separates the self from the universe (in psychological terms, the ego). The "resquicios," as cracks in that structure, are metaphorically those places where self and universe can fuse. But as the imagery of this poem suggests, such fusion is an unstable, momentary reaction. The only permanence here is the repetitive process of respiration itself.

In the poem just cited, the speaker refers to the materia prima of the alchemical process in entirely subjective terms: it is some part of herself that is dug out, suffocated, and aspirated. This reading suggests an interesting parallel to Jung's association of the primal material with the unconscious, particularly given Orozco's choice of verbs, which reinforce Jung's claim that "the divine process of change manifests itself . . . as punishment, torment, death and transfiguration" (*Studies* 105). The *Tabula Smaragdina* declares that "As all things were by the contemplation of one, so all things arose from this one thing by a single act of adaptation" (qtd. in Holmyard 97). Orozco's speaker ponders this same possibility when she considers that "tal vez quién, cuándo y dónde sean las variaciones de una sola sustancia" [who, when, and where may be variations on a single substance] (*Noche* 41). In Christian alchemy, this original "one thing" was equated with the clay from which Adam was formed, the "barro luminoso" [luminous clay] of Orozco's poem "Génesis" (*Obra* 130).

Until the scientific discoveries of the seventeenth century, it was generally held (following Aristotle) that all matter was constituted of four basic elements. For the alchemist, these elements arose, in their turn, from the materia prima, which, though a tangible substance, was but a manifestation of divinity. The speaker of "Rare Substance" draws upon these notions in her attempt to classify her own being: "Mi especie no es del agua ni del fuego, ni del aire o la tierra, / solamente" [My kind does not come from water nor fire, nor from air or earth / alone] (*Noche* 28). In moments of acute perceptual clarity, she ventures, "verán que pertenezco a esa extraña familia de las metamorfosis transparentes, / a ese orden inconcluso que se fija a un color como a la sal del mundo" [they will see that I belong to that strange family of transparent metamorphoses, / to that unfinished order that affixes itself to a color as if to the salt of the world] (28). Such transparent or qualitative changes (perceptible by a change in color) were exactly what the alchemists were after. The reference to salt in this passage is particularly apt, since, in alchemical operations, "Salt is the ash that remains over and serves to fix the 'volatile' spirit" (Burckhardt 147).

The alchemist's work, if successful, would transform the undifferentiated primal substance into gold, the "noblest" of the metals. The alchemical symbol for gold was a circle with a dot at its center, representing the sun; thus, both gold and the sun came to symbolize the transcendent consciousness (gnosis) to which humans could aspire. In the attempt at transmutation, comments Eliade, the alchemist is only assisting nature in the fulfillment of an ideal, "which is the perfection of its progeny—be it mineral, animal or human—to its supreme ripening, which is absolute immortality and liberty (gold being the symbol of sovereignty and autonomy)" (*Forge* 52). The notion of the sacredness of gold is recalled in several passages of Orozco's work, sometimes coupled directly with sun images. The poem "En la rueda solar" [In the solar wheel], which builds upon an extended metaphor for the human eye, alludes to "la alquimia del oro en aguas estancadas" [the alchemy of gold in stagnant waters] (*Obra* 144). The symbol may be associated with knowledge and power—"el oro de la revelación al sol del mediodía" [the gold of the sun's revelation at midday] (120)—or with immortality, as in the case of the lovers who "transmutaban en oro de eternidad / el resplandor de un día" [transmuted the brightness of a day / into the gold of eternity] (98). The sacred character of gold, its quality of absolute plenitude, is integrated into a vision of a lost paradise in which "se llenaban los huecos con una lluvia de oro" [the hollows were filled with a rain of gold] (*Revés* 33).

One of Orozco's most original applications of the metaphor of transmuted substances occurs in several images of "reverse alchemy," in which gold is stripped of its sacred character. A prose poem from *Museo salvaje* reads: "Has hurgado en la lumbre de la fiebre y el ocio para extraer esa tinaja de oro que irremediablemente se convierte en carbón" [You have stirred up the fire of fever and idleness in order to extract that jar of gold that irremediably turns into coal] (*Obra* 162). The very same figure is recalled in the poem "La mala suerte" [Bad luck], in which the speaker enumerates the signs of her adverse fortune: "¿No vuelan en bandadas azules mis amigos y se trueca en carbón el oro que yo toco?" [Do my friends not fly away in blue flocks, does the gold I touch not turn to coal?] (*Boca* 35). This transmutation of precious metal into common substance, of gold into carbon, recalls perhaps the tension between the gnostic images of divine spark and dense, corporeal matter. In another poem, a similar alchemical reversal is used to symbolize a marriage which love has failed to redeem: "—¡tanta alquimia al revés!—/ y caer como cae una llovizna de oro trasmutada en cenizas y en adiós" [so much alchemy in reverse! / and to fall like a drizzle of gold transmuted into ashes, into good-byes] (*Mutaciones* 64). Taken together, these images of reverse alchemy reiterate the speaker's insistence on the unfulfilled potential of occult powers.

Alchemical operations upon the primal matter were performed within a vessel—the crucible—often a glass sphere that had been hermetically sealed. As Jung has shown, the vessel symbolized the soul in some al chemical writings (*Studies* 86). Orozco utilizes this image to describe the very nature of reality as "Cautiva, como yo, con las constelaciones y la hormiga, / quizás en una esfera de cristal" [Captive, like me, with the constellations and the ant, / perhaps in a crystal sphere] (*Mutaciones* 10). This passage also serves to underscore the mirroring of macrocosm and microcosm that permeated hermetic thought. Continuing her characterization of mutable reality, the speaker claims that "la he visto reducirse hasta tomar la forma del ínfimo Jonás dentro de la ballena" [I have seen her reduce herself until she took on the shape of minuscule Jonas inside the whale] (10). Aptly, Jonah's emergence from the belly of the whale was used in alchemical texts as a symbol for the spiritualization of matter (von Franz 148, plate 42).

The alchemist worked with many substances, but chief among them were sulfur, quicksilver (mercury), and salt. These substances symbolized, respectively, spirit, soul, and body. References to the latter two can be found in several passages of Orozco's work. Of quicksilver, or *argentum vivum*, Jung states that "philosophically it means the *spiritus vitae*, or even the world-soul, so that Mercurius also takes on the significance of Hermes, god of revelation" (*Portable Jung* 384–85). Changeable and fluid, mercury, as the "bearer of all forms," was the *primum agens* of alchemical operations (Burckhardt 89). Thus, when Orozco's speaker demands of her interlocutor, "Gira . . . con tu fauna de azogue disuelta en una lágrima" [Spin . . . with your quicksilver fauna dissolved in a tear], she is alluding to both dynamism and creativity as positive qualities of mercury (*Obra* 121). Quicksilver may even possess magical and redemptive properties. Described as "un pequeño amuleto" [a little amulet], the essence found in the depth of the speaker's heart is "una gota de azogue que libra a quien se mira de la expiación y de la muerte" [a drop of quicksilver that frees the one who looks from atonement and death] (*Noche* 39).

Salt often symbolizes for Orozco, as it did for the alchemists, corporeal matter. Its metaphysical implications in this context are conveyed clearly by the phrase "la sal del destierro" [the salt of exile] (*Obra* 123). *Destierro* in this context, as elsewhere in Orozco's poetry, does not refer to a geographical exile, but rather to the condition of alienation from the absolute. Salt serves to symbolize material existence, diametrically opposed to transcendent spirituality. Salt also plays a part in the pseudoalchemical ritual described in the poem "Para un balance" [Toward a balance], whose subject is the speaker's own head, alchemically identified with the primal matter: "La volví del revés la puse a evaporar al sol de la inclemencia / hasta que se fundió en la menuda sal de la memoria que es apenas la borra del olvido" [I turned it inside out, I laid it out to evaporate under the inclement sun / until it melted into the minute salt of memory, which is scarcely the dregs of forgetting] (*Noche* 39). But when the speaker later describes her existence as "apenas un reguero de sal bajo la lluvia" [barely a trickle of salt in the rain], she alludes not to the solidity of salt, but to its solubility, symbolizing the ephemeral quality of a single human life (40).

When transmutation is effected by the alchemical opus, matter becomes spiritualized. This goal, elusive for the practical alchemist, yielded the central symbol of alchemy: the *coniunctionis*, or marriage of opposites. An elaborate pattern of associations arose: sun-king-sulfur-red was joined to moon-queen-mercury-white, producing the so-called "Hermetic androgyne." In an unmistakable allusion to this symbolism, Orozco's speaker affirms that "Entre las ceremonias del amor / ninguna es comparable al matrimonio del sol y de la luna" [Among all the ceremonies of love / none is comparable to the marriage of the sun and the moon] (*Obra* 94). Significantly, this passage is taken from "Para ser otra" [To be another], a poem rich in occult terminology. The motif of the tension between opposites, of which "sol/luna" is the prototype, recurs throughout this poem: "el éxtasis y el pavor" [ecstasy and terror], "la distancia que llamamos nunca" [the distance we call never], "este solo recuerdo del porvenir desde el comienzo de los siglos" [this single memory of the future from the beginning of the centuries] (94–96). Since these opposites retain their polarity, this poem suggests that the marriage of sun and moon will remain for the speaker, as it did for the practical alchemists, an unrealizable potential. The particular significance of the marriage symbolism in this context derives from the poem's concern with the fracturing of personal identity. The speaker's declaration, near the end of the poem, that "Ya soy ajena a mí" [I am alien to myself] (96) implies that within the self, opposites sometimes cannot reconcile.[1] In Jungian terms, individuation is not achieved in "To be another," since the separate facets of the psyche are unable to fuse into a meaningful whole.

The symbol was undoubtedly the device upon which alchemical writers relied most heavily in the expression of their arcane knowledge. A second device, the antonym, deserves mention for its prevalence in alchemical literature and in Orozco's work. In addition to the sun/moon pairing discussed above, the alchemists stressed dichotomies such as spirit/matter, male/female, hot/cold, moist/dry, fire/water, and so forth. Scholars have noted the connection between these sets of contraries and the radical dualism (good versus evil) of the gnostic worldview (Kahane and Kahane 194). An incomplete but representative list of antithetical terms appearing with some frequency in Orozco's work would include: día/noche [day/night], luz/tinieblas [light/darkness], fuego/hielo [fire/ice], mañana/ayer [tomorrow/yesterday], palabra/silencio [word/silence], partir/volver [leave/return], memoria/olvido [memory/forgetting], unidad/multiplicidad [unity/multiplicity], and subida/caída [ascent/fall]. By way of analogy, if the purpose of the alchemist's work was to resolve antonym into synonym, that is, to fuse impure, opposing substances into pure, singular gold, a poet may attempt to resolve existential tensions by means of poetry. In a prose commentary on her work, Orozco speaks of the power of the poetic word to "reduce" each perceptual plane to a spiritual plane. Having accomplished this, she says, poetry has "transmuted" the world into images and symbols (*Páginas* 102). In this regard, she is the descendant of the literary alchemists whose master was Rimbaud. Orozco's commentary, significantly, ends on a note of failure: the poetic word "se declara vencida" [declares its defeat] (102). She spoke for the alchemists as well, for whom pure gold, or the elixir of immortality, remained merely a tantalizing potentiality.

Western alchemy is closely linked with astrology. Each planet was said to correspond to a certain metal: Mars to iron, Saturn to lead, and so forth. Similarly, the steps of the alchemical process corresponded to the signs of the zodiac.[2] Alchemists often consulted the stars for guidance in their art, and it was held that particular operations could be performed successfully only under certain favorable astral conditions. The assumption underlying this thinking was, of course, the hermetic doctrine of universal sympathy. All things above affect all things below, and genuine gnosis consists of comprehending as fully as possible the patterns of those effects, especially when those patterns are hidden from the senses.

The attempt to gain knowledge by supranatural means may be termed *divination*, and it plays a fundamental role in all branches of the occult arts. As its etymology suggests, divination is linked with a religious view of the world, in most cases predicated upon the belief that otherworldly beings or forces can communicate with humans regarding worldly events.

(We have already seen instances in Orozco's poetry of the related situation of interpretation of signs or "calls from without.") The anthropologist Evan Zuesse, observing that divination implies more than simply predicting outcomes, defines it as "the art or practice of discovering the personal, human significance of future or, more commonly, present or past events" (375). Divination stems from the human need to know more than natural phenomena or personal experience can reveal in a given moment. Psychologically speaking, it is rooted in some form of anxiety, and, when successful, provides the diviner or the client with relief from that anxiety. Considering these factors, it should come as no surprise that divination is a pervasive presence in the poetry of Orozco. The anxiety conveyed by the speaker throughout this body of work springs from her need to glimpse, or to comprehend on some level, the *otro lado*. Divination, in a variety of forms, provides the poet with a fitting metaphor for the endeavor to achieve gnosis, to know that which cannot be known.

Zuesse has devised a typology of divination that is applicable to a study of Orozco's poetry (376). The first type, intuitive divination, includes hunches and presentiments, and involves a spontaneous comprehension on the part of the diviner. Orozco highlights this type in the poem "Presentiments in ritual dress," in which forebodings are personified as "ladrones en la noche" [thieves in the night] (*Mutaciones* 15). These presences, poking "con frías uñas en el costado abierto por la misma condena" [with cold fingernails in the side laid open by the same condemnation] are perceived as entirely evil (15). Evidently, the omens are a form of future knowledge ("una bocanada que asciende a borbotones desde el fondo de todo el porvenir" [a gust that gushes up from the bottom of all the future]), but that knowledge presents itself to the speaker as either spurious or dangerous (15). This follows a pattern common to all strains of esoteric thought, in which the desired knowledge is forbidden precisely because the possessor becomes vulnerable to forces beyond human control. Transgression of the taboo against superhuman knowledge constitutes one of the primary dangerous games.

The somewhat more complex possession divination, as the term suggests, involves communication by spiritual beings through an intermediary. Possession may be linked to inanimate agents or to spiritual forces (animate or abstract). Orozco's poem "El presagio" [The omen] is constructed upon auguries of the first sort: "Estaba escrito en sombras. / Fue trazado con humo ... / lo propagó la hierba" [It was written in shadows. / It was drawn with smoke ... / the grass spread it] (*Noche* 49). The veracity and the power of these omens for the speaker is conveyed with great emotional tension in the conclusion of this short poem:

> Un gran pájaro negro cayó sobre tu plato.
> ....
> Llega desde las más remotas plantaciones de tu presentimiento y de
>   tu miedo,
> llega incesantemente exhalando el misterio.
> Está sobre tu plato y no hay distancia alguna que te aparte
> ni escondite posible.
>
> (*Noche* 49)
>
> [A great black bird fell on your plate.
> ....
> It comes from the most remote plantations of your presentiment
>   and your fear,
> it comes incessantly exhaling mystery.
> It lies on your plate and there is no distance that will take you
>   away,
> no possible place to hide.]

In *Cantos a Berenice*, a book-length poem in which the speaker addresses the spirit of a cat, Orozco provides a small catalogue of the possibilities of divination through inanimate objects. In poem VIII, the cat is seen

> interrogando en vano a un hueso ambiguo,
> a una indescifrable cabeza de pescado,
> a un hermético claustro de semillas,
> por si en ellos estaban el aguijón y la respuesta,
> por si acaso sabían.
>
> (*Obra* 172)
>
> [vainly questioning an ambiguous bone,
> an undecipherable fish-head,
> a hermetic cloister of seeds,
> to see if perhaps in them were the spur and the answer,
> to see if perhaps they knew.]

The motif of divination in this poem is given an extra twist of complexity by the fact that the speaker is attempting to read the cat's enigmatic character, while the cat is in turn attempting to read the signs of her own origin and destiny. In both cases, the omens fail to communicate meaning: the qualifiers "en vano," "hermético," and "indecifrable" underscore the inefficacy of divination.

In the second subtype of possession divination, according to the scheme suggested by Zuesse, a human agent receives knowledge from some spiritual source (376). In the long tradition of divination, this subtype has included such important categories as divination by dreams (oneiromancy), divination by glossalalia (speaking in tongues), and divination by full mediumism or oracular trance. The human body itself may serve as augurial object, traditionally through the interpretation of twitches and pains. Orozco's speaker places the human body in a divinatory role when she instructs her interlocutor to "interrogar el desvarío de tu sangre convertida en oráculo" [question the raving of your blood that has become an oracle] (*Obra* 122). In addition to the numerous nonhuman omens in "The omen" there appear certain "oscuros personajes girando siempre a tientas" [dark figures always groping as they spin] (*Noche* 49). However, like the presentiments discussed above, these mysterious figures seem to be personifications of psychic states, rather than actual human beings.

Possession divination through partial mediumism, in which the medium is possessed by a spirit but maintains awareness of self and surroundings, is apparent in several passages of Orozco's poetry alluding to prophecy and oracle. In the long and complex poem "La cartomancia" [Cartomancy] the tarot reader acts as a partial medium, announcing a fearful destiny to her client. This poem, which opens the volume *Los juegos peligrosos*, is a virtual compendium of references to divination in its varied forms, from prophecy and astrology to lithomancy (divination by stones) and numerology. Strictly speaking, the use of a tarot deck for conjecture, particularly the archetypal figures constituting the cards of the Major Arcana, falls within the third and final class of divination in Zuesse's typology, wisdom divination. This practice involves the decoding of impersonal patterns of reality. It is a kind of organized divination that does not rest upon a belief in invisible spiritual beings, but rather affirms a mysterious congruence of cosmic forces. In the Western tradition, chief among the forms of wisdom divination is astrology, which arose in ancient Babylonia and was codified in the Hellenistic world. Astrology, claims Zuesse, "came to function as nothing less than a universal and syncretistic religious perspective that underlay or influenced all the religions of late antiquity" (378). This explains, perhaps, the importance of astrology in the hermetic worldview and its persistent ties to alchemy and other occult arts.

In an essay titled "Anotaciones para una autobiografía" [Notes for an autobiography] Orozco states: "Con sol en Piscis y ascendente en Acuario, y un horóscopo de estratega en derrota y enamorada trágica, nací en Toay (La Pampa), y salí sollozando al encuentro de temibles cuadraturas y ansiadas conjunciones que aún ignoraba" [With the sun in Pisces and ascendant in Aquarius, and the horoscope of a ruined strategist and a tragic lover, I was born in Toay (La Pampa), and I went forth sobbing to face the fearful quadratures and the longed-for conjunctions of which I still knew nothing] (*Páginas* 217). The metaphorical, rather than literal, sense of this autobiographical narrative is evident. Orozco follows astrological tradition in ascribing to an individual human destiny the particular confluence of heavenly bodies at the moment of birth. Implicit is the notion that personal character and life circumstance were somehow predetermined by the stars. However, Orozco's deviation from modern popular astrology, which tends toward emotionally neutral or positive statements that reassure the reader, is apparent in "Anotaciones." Destiny here is couched in entirely baleful terms. In this brief passage, failure, tragedy, grief, fear, and anxiety are all explicit. Ironically, the final word is "ignoraba" [did not know], implying that impersonal forces of the cosmos predetermine a person's destiny, part of which is her own ignorance regarding that destiny. It will be recalled that, for the gnostics, ignorance was the condition that determined, more than any other, the misery of life on Earth. Thus, the astrological metaphor serves here to reinforce a genuinely gnostic—that is, fatalistic—sense of human existence.

An implicit question underlies the "scene of divination" represented by "La cartomancia": is astrology an authentic source of knowledge? Yes, answers the tarot reader: "Las Estrellas alumbran el cielo del enigma" [The stars illuminate the sky of the enigma]. But a caveat follows immediately: "Mas lo que quieres ver no puede ser mirado cara a cara / porque su luz es de otro reino" [But what you want to see cannot be looked at face to face / because its light belongs to another kingdom]. In the astrological trope of this poem, the stars symbolize the cosmic forces that fix a human destiny; for one suffering the implacability of that destiny, the temptation to uncover the stars' fullest meaning is strong. But can a person withstand the force of such knowledge? This passage reiterates a warning about the outcome of human striving for gnosis, particularly by way of the sophisticated methods of wisdom divination. Like Yahweh of the Hebrew scriptures, the object of desire ("lo que quieres ver") is otherworldly and may destroy the one whose gaze falls upon it.

> Hay un juego peligroso, hay un gran salto que no conseguiré realizar jamás.
> [There is one dangerous game, one great leap that I will never execute.]
> —O. Orozco, "La poesía como juego peligroso" [Poetry as a dangerous game]

Of all the occult arts, magic is perhaps the one that most deserves the epithet of "dangerous game." In divination, the practitioner asks for knowledge that may prove perilous. But the practitioner of magic takes a greater risk by attempting to affect the outcome of events, to alter the natural patterns of cause and effect. For Orozco, as for Novalis and other German romantics, the practice of magic is analogous in certain respects to the writing of poetry, with danger inherent in both: "Me entrego a juegos peligrosos en los que creo adquirir poderes casi mágicos. Intento explorar en las zonas prohibidas, en los deseos inexpresados, en las inmensas canteras del sueño.... Trato de cambiar las perspectivas, de presenciar la soledad, de reducir las potencias que terminan por reducirme al silencio" [I surrender myself to dangerous games in which I believe I acquire nearly magical powers. I attempt to explore dangerous zones, unexpressed desires, the immense quarries of dream.... I try to change perspectives, to witness solitude, to reduce the powers that end by reducing me to silence] ("La poesía como juego peligroso" 102). As this passage implies, the poet and the magician both enter a forbidden zone, both tamper with "potencias" that they do not fully understand and cannot fully control.

The belief in and practice of magic, essentially out of place in classical Greek rationalism, found a home in the religious and philosophical syncretism of the Hellenistic period. While the Skeptics, the Epicureans, and the Cynics had rejected magic outright, the Neoplatonic philosophers and the writers of hermetic treatises made magic an integral part of their systems of thought. Central to this thought was the doctrine of cosmic unity and its corollary, the interrelationship by analogy of all things. The term *sympathetic magic* thus points to the possibility of cause-and-effect relationships that may be illogical and invisible. Orozco associates this type of belief with the craft of writing when she comments that "Magia y poesía están profundamente unidas en sus raíces: ambas intentan una conversión analógica del universo, un encadenamiento que no es el de causa a efecto reglamentarios" [Magic and poetry are profoundly joined at their roots:

both attempt an analogical conversion of the universe, a linking that is not that of normal cause and effect] (*Páginas* 279). To the ancient belief in the powers of magic, Orozco adds the more modern belief in the irrational power of the unconscious (repressed desire and the "immense quarries" of dreams) in the formulation of her analogical approach to poetry.

The Venezuelan critic Juan Liscano ties figurative magic to religion in his observation that "La poesía de Olga Orozco es acto de magia religiosa" [Olga Orozco's poetry is an act of religious magic] (Qtd. in *Páginas* 80). Theories of magic formulated in the nineteenth and early twentieth centuries (arising mainly out of anthropology) tended to see magic and religion as distinct realms of human endeavor, often placing magic in a prelogical, "primitive" level of human evolution (Middleton 83–84). In his influential book *The Idea of the Holy* (1928), theologian Rudolf Otto acknowledged that magic was an aspect of the numinous, yet placed it (along with fairy tale, myth, fetishism, and shamanism) in "the vestibule of religion" (117). Since midcentury, scholars of magic have tended to view it in broader cultural contexts that admit a coexistence of magic and religion (Betz 88). Gnosticism, as demonstrated by the text *Pistis Sophia* (dating from the third century A.D. and discovered in 1772), as well as many of the Nag Hammadi writings, incorporated the use of talismans and amulets, and also certain magical incantations (Pavitt and Pavitt 76–79). Within the Jewish tradition, magic was generally considered to be outside the law and foreign to the true religion. But certain practices of what may be considered verbal magic, such as the use of blessings and curses, survived even within orthodox Judaism. The mysterious name of God, invoked but not pronounced, was believed to wield a great power that was inexplicable, and therefore *magical* in the broad sense of the term. In fact, it was not until the Christian Middle Ages—when magic lost its positive connotations and came to be equated with demonolatry—that an effective split between magic and religion occurred.

The reduction of magic to "black magic," which led to the identification of magic with heresy, cut off any acceptable transmission of its traditions within an increasingly Christianized European society. It should be noted that this is one aspect in which magic differs from other branches of the esoteric tradition. Alchemy, for instance, remained "remarkably free from the taint of black magic, invocations of demons, necromancy, and other evil practices contemporaneous with it for practically the whole period during which it flourished" (Holmyard 158). Although alchemy certainly situated itself on the periphery of Christianity, its symbolic concern with the transmutation of the soul allowed it some degree of religious legitimacy. Divination, likewise, could be associated with the attempt to discover the will of a *deus absconditus*. But magic, lacking these moral underpinnings, became a "taint" at best, and at worst, a scourge.

For Orozco, magic is "la creencia en la eficacia inmediata del deseo y del sentimiento; es una tentativa esperanzada de posesión" [the belief in the immediate efficacy of desire and feeling; it is a hopeful attempt at possession] (*Páginas* 286). This definition carries echoes of the anthropologist Bronislaw Malinowski's well-known claim that magic "ritualizes man's optimism" (90). As a poetic trope, then, magical ritual symbolizes the speaker's desire to transcend the limitations placed on her by time and space, by the physical body and the rational mind.

The human heart, as the traditional seat of emotion, can be said to represent both body and spirit. For Orozco's speaker, the heart is at once a "residencia hechizada" [haunted residence] and a magical being "distribuyendo un filtro que absorbe la distancia y acrecienta la sed de todo lo imposible" [distributing a potion that absorbs distance and increases the thirst for everything impossible] (*Obra* 137). Here, the magic implied in the term *hechizada* seems to be reversed. Instead of alleviating the thirst of desire, the heart's potion—that is, the blood—augments it. The nature of this thirst, abstract and unquenchable, is like the gnostic's zeal to know the unknowable. The image of the heart as a closed magical sphere that represents both enchanter and enchanted calls to mind Jung's claim that "Magical practices are nothing but projections of psychic events, which then exert a counter-influence on the psyche and put a kind of spell on the personality" (*Studies* 24–25). Thus, the heart becomes ironically a "talismán de catástrofes" [talisman of catastrophes], reversing its function as a charm against evil, and even drawing disaster to itself (*Obra* 137).

Charm magic, in the tradition that extends back through Greco-Roman antiquity to ancient Egypt, commonly made use of amulets and talismans. These were objects thought to concentrate magical power (usually for the purpose of warding off evil), and were typically worn around the neck or placed on doors or thresholds. They were often made of semiprecious or precious gems and were engraved with magical symbols, images of deities, or inscriptions. Amulets were sometimes placed in capsules that were known as *bullae*. Orozco presents a variation of the encapsulated amulet as a metaphor for the human soul, "un raro amuleto soterrado en la espesura inmensa" [a strange amulet buried in an immense thicket] (*Revés* 57). In another passage, a small amulet—a drop of quicksilver—is discovered in the depths of the heart (*Noche* 39). It is interesting to consider these images in relation to the gnostic and cabalistic symbol of the *pneuma* as a divine spark buried within the dense materiality of the physical body.

Talismans appear frequently in Orozco's poems as symbols of psychic self-protection or integration. Significantly, these potentially magical objects are typically characterized as being ineffective or entirely absent. The tarot reader, for example, admonishes her client: "No trates de encontrar tu talismán de huesos de pescado, / porque es mucha la noche y muchos tus verdugos" [Do not try to find your fish-bone talisman, / because the night is great, and many are your executioners] (*Obra* 86). One key poem in *Los juegos peligrosos*, "Para hacer tu talismán" [To make your talisman], describes a ritual for converting the heart into a powerful charm:

> Se necesita sólo tu corazón
> hecho a la viva imagen de tu demonio o de tu dios.
> Un corazón apenas, como un crisol de brasas para la idolotría.
> Nada más que un indefenso corazón enamorado.
> Déjalo a la intemperie,
> donde la hierba aúlle sus endechas de nodriza loca
> y no pueda dormir,
> donde el viento y la lluvia dejen caer su látigo en un golpe de azul escalofrío
> sin convertirlo en mármol y sin partirlo en dos,
> donde la oscuridad abra sus madrigueras a todas las jaurías
> y no logre olvidar.
> . . . .
> Si sobrevive aún,
> si ha llegado hasta aquí hecho a la viva imagen de tu demonio o de tu dios;
> he ahí un talismán más inflexible que la ley,
> más fuerte que las armas y el mal del enemigo.
> Guárdalo en la vigilia de tu pecho igual que a un centinela.
> Pero vela con él.
> Puede crecer en ti como la mordedura de la lepra;
> puede ser tu verdugo.
> ¡El inocente monstruo, el insaciable comensal de tu muerte!
>
> (*Obra* 100–101)

[Only your heart is needed,
made in the living image of your daemon or your god.
Merely a heart, like a crucible full of live coals for idolatry.
Simply a helpless, enamored heart.
Leave it in the wild,
where grass will howl its dirges like the mad wetnurse
and it cannot sleep,
where the whip of rain and wind cracks like a blue chill
without splitting it nor turning it to marble,
where darkness opens its dens to every pack
and it cannot forget.
. . . .
If it still survives,
if it has come this far as the living image of your daemon or your
   god,
behold a talisman more inflexible than the law,
stronger than the enemy's weapons or his evil.
Guard it in the vigil of your chest like a sentinel.
But keep watch with it.
It can grow within you like the bite of leprosy,
it can be your executioner.
The innocent monster, insatiable guest at the table of your death!]

The talisman in this poem is an object created by means of ritual acts associated with violence, bestial aggression, pain of every sort, fury, and even madness. The speaker acknowledges the transgressive nature of this act, which creates an object that reflects the living image of either god or devil; in fact, it represents a space of idolatry. The magic represented by the heart-talisman is potent (even stronger than the enemy's evil) but dangerously reversible. Far from offering an assurance of protection—its presumed function—this object requires extreme vigilance, because it bears the power to destroy its maker. All in all, the amulet or talisman functions as a trope in Orozco's work for human (or superhuman) forces that offer themselves as allies, but whose efficacy ultimately fails or turns against the human subject.

Historically, magic has maintained a special kinship to poetry. Magic is believed to grant a supernatural energy to certain objects or images, but it also, like poetry, springs from a faith in the power of the spoken or written word. (Interestingly, the word *talisman* derives from the Greek *telesma*, which means "incantation.") To speak of the *logos* of magic is to consider the incantation not only as means to an end, but as a force in and of itself. Malinowski placed particular stress on incantation in his studies of magic, arguing that "the ritual centers around the utterance of the spell" (73). If the shaman wields his magic through the word, the poet, likewise, effects changes in the listener/reader by nonrational means. It was Novalis in Germany and, later, Mallarmé and other French symbolists who brought the synthesis of poetry and magic into the modern aesthetic consciousness. Orozco, speaking along the same lines, has suggested that "El poeta tiene una toma de conciencia mucho más mágica que lógica ... y el poema mismo obra mucho más por encantamiento que por persuasión" [The poet acquires an awareness that is much more magical than logical ... and the poem itself works more by enchantment than by persuasion] (*Páginas* 279).[3] The key word in this statement is *encantamiento*. While the object-talisman is represented as either absent or present-but-useless, the "enchanted" poetic word may serve a more positive and efficacious function.

Orozco's interest in occult powers—alchemy, divination, or magic—returns insistently to a fascination with the power of language itself. Certain poems, in fact, directly represent poetic language in the ipso facto function of magical incantation. For the subsequent analysis, I rely principally on Northrop Frye's essay "Charms and Riddles," published in the collection *Spiritus Mundi: Essays on Literature, Myth, and Society* (1976). The age-old association of magic and poetry is apparent in the Latin word *carmen*, which encompassed the meanings of charm, poetry, and song. The verb *to enchant*, likewise, is rooted in the Latin *in + cantare*, "to sing into." In the Classical world, all of these notions were bound up in the myth of Orpheus, whose primordial and otherworldly song held animals and humans alike under a powerful spell. Thus Orpheus with his lyre takes his place in the pantheon as the god of poetry and song, and stands as the symbol par excellence of voice as power.

One key poem from *Los juegos peligrosos* employs techniques that I will call, after Frye, "the rhetoric of enchantment." That is, it relies much more heavily than do other poems of Orozco's corpus on repetition, rhyme, hypnotic rhythms, and alliteration. Moreover, portions of the poem imitate to some degree an actual rite of sorcery. "The more closely the magical aspect of charm is adhered to in poetry," observes Frye, "the more likely the poem is to present some kind of specific ritual" (136). I have already examined briefly the text as imitation of an act of magic in reference to "Para hacer tu talismán." In a similar but much more extensive way, "Para destruir a la enemiga [To destroy the enemy] represents textually certain of the conventions of verbal incantation. The object of the ritual black magic (marked as feminine in the Spanish *enemiga*) is a sort of cryptic doppelgänger, perhaps a sorceress, perhaps even an allegorical representation of death itself. The speaker's obsession with her may be related to what Frye identifies as magic that begins at the human level and searches for powers greater than itself. Rather than invoking higher deities, such magic "is more likely to turn to the mysterious beings in the lower world, who in the Christian centuries were nearly all demonic, and had been sinister and dangerous long before that" (131). Despite the focus on a manifestly evil being, an elegiac tone is not absent from "Para destruir a la enemiga," with its long, plaintive lines and its allusions to death, grief, and memory. I cite here the opening stanzas of the poem:

> Mira a la que avanza desde el fondo del agua borrando el día con
>   sus manos,
> vaciando en piedra gris lo que tú destinabas a memoria de fuego,
> cubriendo de cenizas las más bellas estampas prometidas por las dos
>   caras de los sueños.
> Lleva sobre su rostro la señal:
> ese color de invierno deslumbrante que nace donde mueres,
> esas sombras como de grandes alas que barren desde siempre todos
>   los juramentos del amor.
>
> Cada noche, a lo lejos, en esa lejanía donde el amante duerme con
>   los ojos abiertos a otro mundo adonde nunca llegas,
> ella cambia tu nombre por el ruido más triste de la arena;
> tu voz, por un sollozo sepultado en el fondo de la canción que nadie
>   ya recuerda;
> tu amor, por una estéril ceremonia donde se inmola el crimen y el
>   perdón.
> Cada noche, en el deshabitado lugar adonde vuelves,
> ella pone a secar la cifra de tu edad al bajar la marea,
> o cose con el hilo de tus días la noche del adiós,
> o prepara con el sabor del tiempo más hermoso ese turbio brebaje
>   que paladeas en la soledad,
> ese ardiente veneno que otros llaman nostalgia
> y que tan lentamente transforma el corazón en un puñado de
>   semillas amargas.

No la dejes pasar.
Apaga su camino con la hoguera del árbol partido por el rayo.
Arroja su reflejo donde corran las aguas para que nunca vuelva.
Sepulta la medida de su sombra debajo de tu casa para que por su boca la tierra la reclame.
Nómbrala con el nombre de lo deshabitado.

(*Obra* 108–109)

[See the one who comes forth from the depths of the water, erasing the day with her hands,
emptying onto gray stone what you had allotted to the memory of fire,
covering with ash the loveliest images offered by the two faces of dreams.
On her skin she wears the mark:
that color of dazzling winter, born where you die,
shadows as of great wings eternally sweeping away the oaths of love.

Each night, far away, in that remote place where the lover sleeps with eyes open to another world where you never arrive,
she exchanges your name for the saddest whisper of sand;
your voice, for a sob buried at the bottom of a song no one remembers;
your love, for a sterile ceremony immolating crime and reprieve.
Each night, in the vacant place to which you return,
she sets the cipher of your age out to dry at low tide,
or sews the night of goodbye with the thread of your days,
or prepares, with the flavor of the most resplendent hour, that turbid potion you savor in solitude,
that fiery poison others call nostalgia
and that turns the heart by slow degrees to a fistful of bitter seeds.

Don't let her pass.
Extinguish her path with a bonfire from the tree that lightning split.
Throw her reflection into the current so it never returns.
Bury the length of her shadow beneath your house so that earth's mouth will reclaim her.
Name her with the name of the uninhabited.]

The lyric, elegiac tone conveyed by phrases such as "Cada noche, a lo lejos" and "la canción que nadie ya recuerda" belongs to one rhetorical mode of this poem, that in which the speaker laments the loss of an edenic state probably associated with romantic love. But the nostalgic mood is overshadowed by images of violence, vengeance, and evil. The speaker engages in a one-sided dialogue with an invisible and silent interlocutor, to whom she gives instructions regarding the destruction of the female enemy (perhaps the despised third in a lovers' triangle) by means of black magic. To this end, the verbal strength of speaker's discourse is discharged most powerfully in a series of imperatives that lend the poem its imprecatory character: "No la dejes pasar. / Apaga su camino . . . / Sepulta la medida de su sombra debajo de tu casa para que por su boca la tierra la reclame."

In order to comprehend the technique of this and other passages, I cite Frye's definition of the rhetoric of charm: "The rhetoric of charm is dissociative and incantatory: it sets up a pattern of sound so complex and repetitive that the ordinary processes of response are short-circuited. . . . Such repetitive formulas break down and confuse the conscious will, hypnotize and compel to certain courses of action" (126). It follows from this definition that a poem such as "Para destruir a la enemiga" operates on two levels. On the first, the speaker is literally trying to compel action on the part of her interlocutor. Taken out of its poetic context, the repetitive imperatives could literally constitute the words of a magical spell. Yet this text is not the transcription of a spell, but rather a poem that adopts the spell's hypnotic technique. On this second level, it is the reader who is somehow compelled—if not to action, then to a particular frame of mind— by the rhythms set up by the speaker's commands.

One imperative in particular is crucial: "Nómbrala" [Name her]. Occult traditions, particularly that of magic, are permeated with the power of naming. Frye states pointedly that "You may compel the evil by possessing a name" (125). Once again there arises the connection between gnosis and power: to possess the knowledge of a name, particularly a secret name, is to hold sway over the object named. The repetitive force of the passage that follows those previously cited is indeed spellbinding:

Nómbrala con el nombre de lo deshabitado.
Nómbrala.
Nómbrala con el frío y el ardor,
   con la cera fundida como una nieve sucia donde cae la forma de su
      vida,

con las tijeras y el puñal,
con el rastro de la alimaña herida sobre la piedra negra,
con el humo del ascua,
con la fosa del imposible amor abierta al rojo vivo en su costado,
con la palabra de poder
nómbrala y mátala.

(*Obra* 109)

[Name her with the name of the uninhabited.
Name her.
Name her with chill and with burning,
with wax melted like a tainted snow where the shape of her life
    falls,
with scissors and with dagger,
with the track of the wounded beast across the black rock,
with the smoking ember,
with the hollow pit of impossible love open to the vivid red in her
    side,
with the word of power
name her and kill her.]

Structurally, it is worth noting that the preposition *con* [with], heading the enumeration of the implements of sorcery, is repeated seven times. The number seven, like the number three, has long been held in esoteric circles (as well as in Judeo-Christian tradition and in Western folkways) to hold magical and mystical powers. According to Cirlot's *Dictionary of Symbols*, the number seven symbolizes perfect order, a complete period or cycle; notably, it is also the symbol of pain (233). In a twist of rhetorical complexity, the seven implements of naming are themselves named. Only after this incantatory naming can the final imperative be pronounced, in which naming wields the power of killing.

The speaker commands her interlocutor, finally, to bury a coin face down: "Y no olvides sepultar la moneda. / Hacia arriba la noche bajo el pesado párpado del invierno más largo. / Hacia abajo la efigie y la inscripción" [And do not forget to bury the coin. / Face up, the night beneath the weighty eyelid of the longest winter. / Face down, the effigy and the inscription] (*Obra* 109). In the history of magic, the act of burying a stone or metal object inscribed with a curse was not uncommon. These objects were believed to be particularly powerful, since the efficacy of the curse would last as long as the object remained hidden (Hole 108). The coin's inscription in Orozco's poem reads:

"Reina de las espadas,
Dama de las desdichas,
Señora de las lágrimas:
en el sitio en que estés con dos ojos te miro,
con tres nudos te ato,
la sangre te bebo
y el corazón te parto."

(*Obra* 109)

["Queen of swords,
Mistress of griefs,
Lady of tears:
wherever you may be, with two eyes I see you,
with three knots I tie you,
your blood I drink,
your heart I cleave."]

This passage is a tour de force of poetry as curse. The inscription is broken into seven verses. The enemy is addressed by three epithets, each syntactically parallel, each ending in a three-syllable noun with a feminine plural ending. The fourth line, significantly longer than all the others, establishes a structural border between the first three lines, which constitute the invocation, and the last three, which constitute the curse itself. The magical three appears again as the number of knots tied. The fifth, sixth, and seventh lines end in a verb of the first-person singular, present tense, echoing the ending of the fourth line. These verbs, with the pronominal *te*, follow the "as this, so that" pattern that reflects the analogical thinking fundamental to magical spells (Frye 130). Simply put, the enunciation of an action ("la sangre te bebo") is considered by the charmer as equivalent to the action itself, and, by extension, to its effect. Given the overwhelming power granted to the spoken word in such formulas, it is not difficult to comprehend the identity some poets claim between their art and the art of magic.

Frye comments in the conclusion to his essay: "Wherever we turn in charm poetry, we seem to be led back to some kind of mythological universe, a world of interlocking names of mysterious powers and potencies which are above, but not wholly beyond reach of, the world of time and space" (136). Not charm poetry alone, but the occult arts as a whole, establish themselves in a universe in which desire—whether for the blood sacrifice of an enemy or for the discovery of the primordial word—finds efficacious allies. Orozco's poetic speaker continually presents herself as a transgressive subject, willing to play even the most dangerous games in order to tap into those potencies. Nevertheless, careful examination of textual evidence reveals that many poems also represent a failure on the part of the allies and a breakdown of magical powers. The force of the curse in "Para destruir a la enemiga," for example, is largely undermined in the poem's concluding lines by the speaker's realization that her identity has fused completely with that of the enemy: "Porque ella te fue anunciada en el séptimo día, /—en el día primero de tu culpa—, / y asumiste su nombre con el tuyo" [Because she was announced to you on the seventh day—/ on the first day of your guilt—, and you assumed her name along with her own] (*Obra* 109).

In the final analysis, Orozco's poetic world does resemble the world of invisible yet accessible powers described by Frye. But it is also, and perhaps more importantly for the speaker,

el mundo que huye,
el mundo que se va como por una grieta,
y aunque vuelve y me tienta una vez más no consigo ceñir los
   nudos
no encuentro la manera.

(*Revés* 94)

[the world that flees,
the world that slips away, as if through a fissure,
and though it returns and touches me once again, I cannot bind the
   knots
I cannot find the way.]

Orozco's lyric voice explores the occult—alchemy, divination, and magic—as means of revelation and power of passage. On one level, the failure is patent. Alchemical operations go awry, turning gold into carbon. Signs from "the other side" remain unclear; secret alphabets are indecipherable. Black magic directed against the despised other turns back upon the self. Yet on another level, these explorations yield a richness of figurative language and rhetorical technique that powerfully shapes the contours of Orozco's discourse. As "Para destruir a la enemiga" so forcefully demonstrates, the failure of the curse is the success of the incantatory poem.

4

Alejandra Pizarnik and the Literature of Evil

> Mi oficio ... es conjurar y exorcizar.
> [My work ... is to conspire and to exorcise.]
>
> —A. Pizarnik, "Extracción de la piedra de locura" [Extraction of the Stone of Folly]

In the annals of Argentine literature, the story of Alejandra Pizarnik almost always begins with her death by suicide. This fact can be attributed in part to the inherently sensational nature of suicide, and to its association, since romanticism, with the figure of the socially alienated poet. Yet suicide, in Pizarnik's story, is not only biographical but also literary. As virtually every critic has pointed out, death figures significantly in Pizarnik's work from its inception, not as an abstract, metaphorical theme, but as a presence, a companion, the supreme object of desire. To a writer interested in threshold experiences (*la experiencia límite*), suicide represented the ultimate experience. Pizarnik herself prefigures the critical connection between poetry and suicide in two diary entries from 1961. In the entry dated January 14, she writes:

> Soñé con Rimbaud.
> *Par litterature,*
> *j'ai perdu ma vie.*
>
> (*Semblanza* 246)

> [I dreamed of Rimbaud.
> *For literature*
> *I lost my life.*]

On April 15, she glosses Rimbaud's lines with the following observation: "La vida perdida para la literatura por culpa de la literatura. Por hacer de mí un personaje literario en la vida real fracaso en mi intento de hacer literatura con mi vida real pues ésta no existe: es literatura" [Life lost for literature, because of literature. Because in real life I make of myself a literary character, I fail in my intent to make literature with my real life, since real life doesn't exist: it is literature] (*Semblanza* 253).

In 1978, six years after Pizarnik's death, Olga Orozco published the poem "Pavana para una infanta difunta" [Pavane for a deceased child], dedicating it to the younger poet:

> Pequeña centinela,
> caes una vez más por la ranura de la noche
> sin más armas que los ojos abiertos y el terror
> contra los invasores insolubles en el papel en blanco.
> Ellos eran legión.
> Legión encarnizada era su nombre
> y se multiplicaban a medida que tú te destejías hasta el último
>   hilván,
> arrinconándote contra las telarañas voraces de la nada.
> El que cierra los ojos se convierte en morada de todo el universo.
> El que los abre traza la frontera y permanece a la intemperie.
> El que pisa la raya no encuentra su lugar.
> . . . .
> Sólo había un jardín: en el fondo de todo hay un jardín
> donde se abre la flor azul del sueño de Novalis.
> . . . .
> Pero otra vez te digo,
> ahora que el silencio te envuelve por dos veces en sus alas como un
>   manto:
> en el fondo de todo hay un jardín.
> Ahí está tu jardín,
> Talita cumi.[1]
>
> (*Mutaciones* 75–77)

> [Little sentinel,
> once again you fall through the groove of the night,
> unarmed except for your open eyes and your terror
> against the insoluble invaders of the blank paper.
> They were legion,
> pitiless legion was their name,
> and they multiplied as fast as you could unweave yourself, down to
>   the last stitch,

cornering you against the voracious webs of emptiness.
He that closes his eyes becomes the dwelling-place of the whole
  universe.
He that opens them draws the boundary and is left out in the open.
He that steps on the line cannot find his place.
. . . .
There was only a garden: at the bottom of everything there is a
  garden
where the blue flower of Novalis's dream still opens.
. . . .
But I'm telling you again,
now that silence has wrapped you twice in its wings as in a blanket:
at the bottom of everything there is a garden.
There is your garden,
Talita cumi.]

Orozco, one of Pizarnik's closest friends and in many ways her poetic mentor, alludes to suicide in this poem ("esa perversa tentación") not in order to participate in the sensationalism surrounding Pizarnik's death, but in order to situate it within her very literary life. Jill S. Kuhnheim observes that in her poetry Orozco "does not embrace silence or death but struggle and transformation" (81). Thus, the "Pavana" reflects Orozco's understanding that the end of Pizarnik's life came when poetry as a process could no longer sustain or protect her. The poetic speaker characterizing much of the work of both Pizarnik and Orozco, as Kuhnheim has convincingly argued, often loses her agency and is reduced to a position of stasis, an inability to speak or act (78). This is why, in the "Pavana," the blank paper became the site of the terrifying "invasores insolubles" that multiplied in number even as Pizarnik herself disintegrated. When the speaker of Orozco's poem asks "¿Quién habló de conjuros para contrarrestar la herida del propio nacimiento?" [Who spoke of a spell to counteract the wound of one's own birth?], the reader may well answer that it was Orozco herself who spoke of such things (*Mutaciones* 75). As I demonstrated in the previous chapter, Orozco presents the praxis of poetry as the most sustainable means of "seeing" into the invisible world, of gaining a fleeting access to the absolute; her work is a continual affirmation of the belief that poetry can act as an incantation to counteract the "wound" that life represents. But Orozco herself offers a constant caveat in this regard. The poetic process, like the alchemical operation or the use of talismans, is doomed to repeated failure. Thus, in the poem for Pizarnik, the blue flower of

Novalis's dream—a metaphor for poetic language—is treacherous and represents an extreme danger: "jamás se alcanza sin dejar la cabeza o el resto de la sangre en el umbral" [it can never be reached without leaving the head or the rest of one's blood on the threshold] (76). Pizarnik, who for her own reasons could not heed the warning, retreated increasingly into language, and at some point stepped too far. From this perspective, the key line in Orozco's poem is "El que pisa la raya no encuentra su lugar" [He who steps on the line will not find his place]. Pizarnik's death-by-poetry was a matter of transgression.

> No quiero ir más allá que hasta el fondo.
> [I do not want to go farther than to the bottom.]
> —A. Pizarnik, notation found among her papers at the time of her death

Flora Alejandra Pizarnik was born in 1936 in Avellaneda, a suburb of the Argentine capital. Her parents, fleeing Jewish persecution, had immigrated to Argentina from Russia scarcely two years earlier. According to Alejandra's older sister, Myriam, the girls' childhood was overshadowed by the parents' melancholy, a reaction to their awareness of Nazi horrors and in particular of news of several family members killed in Rovne (Piña, *Alejandra Pizarnik* 32). Alejandra's mother never worked outside the home, and never mastered Spanish entirely; Russian and Yiddish were the languages most often spoken within the home. The father earned a living as a salesman and accountant, and the family, solidly established within the urban Argentine middle class, prospered. Alejandra attended both public schools and a progressive Jewish school.

Alejandra was, by all accounts, a "chica rara," an awkward and insecure adolescent (Piña, *Alejandra Pizarnik* 33). She suffered from asthma, saw herself as overweight, and had a slight stutter. In her late teens she developed a dependency on amphetamines and barbiturates, a habit that she would never lose, and that would eventually lead to her suicide by overdose in 1972 (42).

After high school, Alejandra began university studies in Buenos Aires, attending courses in both journalism and the humanities (filosofía y letras). These studies were soon curtailed (in spite of her intelligence, she seemed unable to complete a single course), but her contact with university life brought her friendships and literary associations that would prove invaluable in her development as a writer (see Piña, *Alejandra Pizarnik* 50, 65, 73–89). These writers and scholars included Juan Jacobo Bajarlía (a professor and poet who introduced her to the writings of Marcel Proust, André Gide, Paul Claudel, James Joyce, and the French surrealists), Silvia Molloy, Roberto Yahni, and Susana Thénon. With Bajarlía's help, Pizarnik began translating French poetry. Her affinity with the surrealist aesthetic dates from these early university contacts. Cristina Piña underscores the significance of this association: "[Q]uienes más profundamente la marcaron fueron los poetas surrealistas, cuya influencia . . . resulta verdaderamente configuradora de su vida y su poesía a partir de la incorporación del aspecto más esencial y revolucionario del programa surrealista: la concepción de que lo poético va más allá de la escritura concreta del poema y afecta la vida misma" [Those who marked her most profoundly were the surrealist poets, whose influence . . . unquestionably shapes her life and her poetry, beginning with the incorporation of the most essential and revolutionary aspect of the surrealist program: the notion that the poetic extends beyond the concrete writing of the poem; it affects life itself] (Piña, *Alejandra Pizarnik* 53). Pizarnik carried the fusion of art and life to its most extreme interpretation, but this is a principle that also profoundly affected the orientations of Orozco, and, as I will later demonstrate, Jacobo Fijman.

Pizarnik's friendships with prominent writers in Buenos Aires grew in number and depth during the years of 1954–1955, just prior to the publication of her first book of poetry. Already close to Olga Orozco, Pizarnik met the well-known avant-garde poets Aldo Pellegrini, Oliverio Girondo, and Enrique Molina, as well as the fiction writer Norah Lange. At age nineteen, she published her first volume of poetry, *La tierra más ajena* [The most alien land] (1955), a book she would later reject as immature. Although uneven as a collection, many of these early poems display the mastery of the surrealist image and the sharp-edged diction that would come to characterize her mature work. It was in this period of her life that Pizarnik began frequenting the gatherings of the group associated with the literary magazine *Poesía Buenos Aires,* a prominent publication during the decade of the sixties. Instrumental to the group's productivity was the somewhat older poet Raúl Gustavo Aguirre, who was to become one of Pizarnik's most avid supporters. It was through Aguirre that Pizarnik came to deepen her appreciation of the French surrealists and to read widely among European avant-garde poets.

Although Pizarnik's next two books of poetry, *La última inocencia* [The last innocence] and *Las aventuras perdidas* [The lost adventures] were published in 1956 and 1958, respectively, she is generally considered by critics to form part of the Argentine Generation of 1960. During this decade Pizarnik would publish her most important collections of poetry: *Árbol de Diana* [Tree of Diana] (1962), *Los trabajos y las noches* [Works and nights] (1965), and *Extracción de la piedra de locura* [Extraction of the stone of folly] (1969). The last volume published in her lifetime, *El infierno musical* [The musical inferno], saw the light shortly after the close of the decade, in 1971.[2] In spite of her chronological affiliation with the Generation of 1960, Pizarnik stands at odds with almost everything these writers came to stand for: rejection of the highly subjective and universalizing neoromantic lyrical mode, appropriation of language and imagery characterizing popular culture (especially film and the tango), and greater engagement with social and political realities, both domestic and international. Pizarnik's literary affinities clearly show greater ties with poets who began writing in the 1940s, like Orozco and Enrique Molina, or with certain poets of the Generation of 1950, especially those centered around the magazine *Poesía = Poesía*, who emphasized a more purely literary function of poetic discourse. In her introduction to the recent anthology *Poesía argentina de fin de siglo* (1996), Piña situates Pizarnik's aesthetic against the prevailing aesthetic of the 1960s, and alongside that of the acclaimed poet Roberto Juarroz, in a metaphysical line emphasizing the "transcendentalization of the poetic act": "En tal sentido, para Alejandra—como para la línea de poetas con la que se identifica: Rimbaud, Mallarmé, Lautréamont, Artaud—la poesía no aparece como una mera práctica sino como un destino, una ética y una ontología" [In this sense, for Alejandra—as for the line of poets with whom she identifies: Rimbaud, Mallarmé, Lautréamont, Artaud—poetry does not manifest itself as a mere exercise, but as a destiny, an ethic, and an ontology] ("Estudio preliminar" 33–34).

Orozco, as we have seen, chose not to incorporate the "real world" in any recognizable form into her poetic expression. For Pizarnik, the acceptance of poetry as destiny, ethic, and ontology would have as its corollary in what Piña calls "una especie de inadecuación radical ante la realidad" [a kind of radical inadequacy before reality] (*Alejandra Pizarnik* 81). The political and social realities of her day, including the increasing presence of repressive military forces and a dangerously unstable economy, went virtually unnoticed by this young writer who strove, above all else, to follow the models of the decadent poets. Even the larger events of the decade of the 1960s made no notable impression on her. As Piña wryly observes: "'¿Y cómo sabes que el dólar cuesta eso?,' podría haber preguntado con los ojos como platos, e ignorar, sobre todo, que había hambre en África, revoluciones militares en el país, un grupo de hombres que darían vuelta la conciencia de América Latina imponiéndose gloriosamente en Cuba" ["And how do you know that's what the dollar is worth?" she might have asked, wide-eyed, not knowing that there was hunger in Africa, that there were military revolts in her country, that a group of men who would turn America's consciousness around were gloriously taking power in Cuba] (81). Pizarnik was not unaware of the dangers of living her life as poetry. In a diary entry dated July 25, 1965, she writes: "En el fondo yo odio la poesía. Es, para mí, una condena a la abstracción. Y además me recuerda esa condena. Y además me recuerda que no puedo 'hincar el diente' en lo concreto" [Fundamentally, I hate poetry. I feel that it sentences me to abstraction. What's more, it reminds me of that sentence. And what's more, it reminds me that I can't "sink my teeth" into materiality] (*Semblanza* 271).

Pizarnik's bohemian dreams would lead to at least one reality that would profoundly mark her consciousness as a writer: in 1960, she traveled to Paris, where, for the next four years, she would experience both debilitating periods of depression and periods of rich literary stimulus and output. Her friendships there extended beyond the Argentine expatriates—most notably Julio Cortázar—to an intellectual group of influential writers such as Italo Calvino and Octavio Paz. Pizarnik's crucial connection with the French writer Georges Bataille will be sketched in more detail in the following pages.

As a system of literary tropes, the esoteric tradition does not rise to the surface in Pizarnik's poetry as it does in Orozco's. In broad terms, Pizarnik's highly subjective poetry does not have the metaphysical character of Orozco's; nor is it possible to determine any philosophico-religious framework such as gnosticism or hermeticism that might help the reader to discover its central tensions. Nevertheless, I would claim that certain fundamental tenets of esoterism—those that were filtered through surrealism—underlie Pizarnik's poetry. A number of these tenets are discernible in the prose poem "Cantora nocturna" [Night singer], the initial poem of *Extracción de la piedra de locura*, which Pizarnik dedicated to Orozco:

> La que murió de su vestido azul está cantando. Canta imbuida de muerte al sol de su ebriedad. Adentro de su canción hay un vestido azul, hay un caballo blanco, hay un corazón verde tatuado con los ecos de los latidos de su corazón muerto. Expuesta a todas las perdiciones,

ella canta junto a una niña extraviada que es ella: su amuleto de la
buena suerte. Y a pesar de la niebla verde en los labios y del frío gris
en los ojos, su voz corroe la distancia que se abre entre la sed y la mano
que busca el vaso. Ella canta. (*Obras* 117)

[The one who died of her blue dress is singing. She sings imbued with
death in the sun of her drunkenness. Inside her song there is a blue
dress, there is a white horse, there is a green heart tattooed with the
echoes of her dead heart's beating. Exposed to every undoing, she
sings by the side of a lost child that is she herself: her good-luck
amulet. And in spite of the green fog on her lips and the cold gray in
her eyes, her voice corrodes the distance that opens between thirst
and the hand that gropes for the glass. She sings.]

This piece, like Orozco's "Pavana," works at the crossroads of the two
writer's poetics. The surrealist technique of using violently juxtaposed
images to jar the reader's sensibility appears in such phrases as "hay un
vestido azul, hay un caballo blanco, hay un corazón verde." Death as the
idée fixe of Pizarnik's poetry, the final transgression, characterizes the
piece as a whole. The phrase "Expuesta a todas las perdiciones" echoes poems by Orozco such as "Para hacer un talismán," which create tropes for
the situation of the poet's exposure to social or psychic danger. The
myth—and the reality—of the decadent poets is manifest in this phrase, as
it is in the sentence "Canta imbuida de muerte al sol de su ebriedad." The
breakdown of the integral subject, a concern common to both writers (with
a particularly gnostic flavor in Orozco), is envisioned here as a splitting of
the adult from the child who is her psychic *other*. Paralleling Orozco's
motif of orphanhood, Pizarnik presents the child-figure as lost, missing,
gone astray (a characterization applicable to the first-person subject of
many of her poems), and yet acting as a source of magical power for the
adult she will become.[3] This is in fact a complex treatment of the surrealist
notion of a lost paradise (often located in childhood), which is in itself an
adaptation of the esoteric principle of a primordial golden age. The corollary dialectic of *este lado* versus *el otro lado*, so prominent in Orozco's
poetry, appears toward the end of this poem as "la distancia que se abre
entre la sed y la mano que busca el vaso." The pithy final phrase "Ella
canta" recalls the trope of poetry-as-song introduced in the title (where it
is romantically associated with the night) and reiterated in several places
throughout the poem. In spite of the exposure to numerous dangers—the
poem seems to say—in spite of the hovering presence of death and of the

abyss between the object of desire and the ability to reach it, the poet sings. Kuhnheim remarks that "[Pizarnik's] poetry that speaks continually of death is in fact meant to be a life-sustaining process, a means of survival but not transcendence of the situation" (78). It is an affirmation of the power of the *logos* that would become, by means of distinct modes, a pivotal issue for both Orozco and Pizarnik.

One of the trademarks of decadence for the decadent poets was the literary elaboration of the principle of evil. Two writers in particular embraced the realm of evil in their work, Baudelaire in the very title of his collected poems, *Fleurs du mal* [Flowers of evil], and Lautréamont in *Les Chants de Maldoror* [Songs of Maldoror], whose narrator-protagonist is the very incarnation of evil. While Baaudelaire explored the negative depths of the human spirit, professing to "extract *beauty* from *evil*,"[4] Lautréamont portrayed the limits of evil in human interaction, from violent pederasty to murder. Pizarnik expressed admiration for both of these nineteenth-century writers, and their work undoubtedly exercised a distant influence over her own. However, I will argue in this chapter that Pizarnik's particular approximation to the value of evil in literature was most clearly articulated by a contemporary French writer, Georges Bataille.

> Ésta es ahora mi vida: mesurarme, temblar ante cada voz, templar las palabras apelando a todo lo que de nefasto y maldito he oído y leído en materia de formas de seducción.
>
> [This is my life now: restraining myself, trembling before every voice, tempering my words by appealing to all that I have heard and read regarding forms of seduction that is ill-fated and damned.]
>
> —A. Pizarnik, "Palabras" [Words]

> Mais il s'agit de faire l'âme monstrueuse.
>
> [But the soul must be made monstrous.]
>
> —Rimbaud, letter to Paul Demeny

"Literature is not innocent," claims Bataille in his book *Literature and Evil*. "It is guilty and should admit itself so" (x). He explains the premise of his study as follows: "Literature is either the essential or nothing. I believe that the Evil—an acute form of evil—which it expresses, has a sovereign value for us. But this concept does not exclude morality: on the contrary, it demands a 'hypermorality'" (viii). Bataille's book is a series of essays on the work of Emily Brontë, Charles Baudelaire, William Blake, the Marquis de Sade, and Jean Genet, among others. To this company I would add Alejandra Pizarnik. Pizarnik's work is unrelentingly dark, death-focused, violent, and, in some cases, obscene. Rhetorically, Pizarnik seems always to be pushing toward precipitous edges, desperately seeking that *mot juste* capable of rendering extreme states of subjectivity. In fact, it is this concern with what, from a psychological point of view, might be termed "abnormal" or "perverse" states of consciousness—and with the language that strives to correspond to such states—that places Pizarnik alongside Bataille's group of nineteenth- and early-twentieth-century writers. Her poetry is "guilty" to the degree that it challenges norms of conventional morality and pushes irremediably across borders into "forbidden" and dangerous zones. And this, Bataille would argue, is exactly what literature should do.

How, then, does Pizarnik's work merit association with the term *literary evil*, in the sense that Bataille gives the term, and how would the acceptance of such an epithet modify the way in which we read her? These are the questions I propose to address in the following pages. After first examining Bataille's rather complex notion of evil in literature, I will consider fragments from Pizarnik's work—both lyric poems and prose pieces—in order to determine how she might fit into the strange company of Bataille's subjects.

Certain critics have noted Pizarnik's propensity toward transgressive writing, particularly with regard to *La condesa sangrienta* [The bloody countess] (1971) and many of the prose pieces she produced in the two years prior to her death. D. W. Foster speaks of the "evil lesbian erotic" that characterizes the narrative stance of *La condesa sangrienta* (*Gay and Lesbian Themes* 101). Suzanne Chávez Silverman explores the relationship of transgression to the critical question of the "lesbian text" in her essay "The Look That Kills: The 'Unacceptable Beauty' of Alejandra Pizarnik's *La condesa sangrienta*". For the most part, however, critical assessment of Pizarnik's poetry has failed to recognize the extent to which Pizarnik explored notions of evil in her work. A vast majority of essays published to date emphasize, understandably, Pizarnik's preoccupation with language (that is, the power and the limits of the poetic word) and with death and its corollary, silence.[5] Indeed, these are the concerns to which she returns with nothing less than obsessive regularity. In both cases, Pizarnik is interested in the *experiencia límite*, the point beyond which all meaning disappears. When Pizarnik's speaker declares that "la rebelión consiste en mirar una rosa / hasta pulverizarse los ojos" [rebellion lies in looking at a rose / until the eyes are pulverized] (80), she mocks the classical aesthetic appreciation of the rose by carrying it to an extreme of self-disintegration, and in doing so points to Bataille's own call to revolution, in which the bourgeois sense of beauty and morality is overturned. In brief, I do not wish to dispute the approach most critics have taken to Pizarnik's work, but rather to suggest that by considering her body of poetry and poetic prose under the rubric of "the literature of evil," we might find an approach that will take account of all the prominent concerns of her writing: not only language and death/silence, but also childhood, sexuality, obscenity, violence, and suicide.

Pizarnik's work stands on its own as sufficient testimony, I believe, to the parallels between her thinking and Bataille's with regard to questions of transgression as a value in literature. However, anecdotal evidence of a personal relationship between the two writers seems appropriate to present here, if for no other reason than to underscore the vital intellectual presence that Bataille represented for the young poet from Buenos Aires. As I indicated earlier, Pizarnik resided in Paris from 1960 to 1964, a period of intense literary activity for her, both in terms of her own production and of her circle of acquaintances. She crossed paths with Bataille on several occasions, most often in the renowned Café Flore, and conversed with him on the passions they both shared—most notably literature and art. Although there appears to be no written record of her impression of Bataille as a person, we do know that she became an avid reader of Bataille's writings while in Paris. In an undated letter to Yvonne Bordelois, Pizarnik speaks of her enthusiasm for the work of Isak Dinesen (Karen Blixen), then adds: "Pero mi lectura de fondo sigue siendo Georges Bataille" [But my most fundamental reading continues to be Georges Bataille].[6]

Years later, when Pizarnik returned to Paris in what turned out to be an abortive attempt to relive the transformative experience of her first journey there, she reported to friends the desperate sense of disillusion and loss she felt. Paris, in those brief five years between 1964 and 1969, had been spoiled for her: it had become Americanized and commercialized, and most of her literary and artistic companions had gone elsewhere or were dead. Piña sums up Pizarnik's reaction to this second experience of Paris with these words: "Porque tanto como Elías Pizarnik, el padre real, había muerto en la patria adoptiva, Georges Bataille—cuyos ojos azules duplicaban, en la patria literaria, los ojos del padre íntimamente amado y rechazado, permitiéndole a Alejandra designarlo su padre en el reino de la creación—había muerto en París" [Just as Elías Pizarnik, her real father, had died in his adoptive homeland, Georges Bataille—whose blue eyes duplicated, in her literary homeland, the eyes of the father who had been deeply loved and rejected, allowing Alejandra to designate him her father in the territory of creation—had died in Paris] (*Alejandra Pizarnik* 210).

Who was this man that became, at the end of his life, a "living fetish" for Pizarnik?[7] Georges Bataille (1897–1962) was, by the decade of the fifties, a prominent figure of the French intellectual avant-garde.[8] Biographical information is scarce, but according to his own statements, he was raised by a blind, syphilitic father who subjected him to various forms of cruelty. He and his mother abandoned his birthplace of Reims in 1915, on the eve of the German invasion. A high school dropout, Bataille eventually studied at the prestigious École des Chartes and completed his preparation as a medievalist librarian, whereupon he spent twenty years at the Bibliothèque Nationale (1922–42).

But Bataille was far more colorful than these black-and-white facts would indicate. He was active until shortly before his death as a writer and political-intellectual organizer. Allan Stoekl, editor of Bataille's *Visions of Excess: Selected Writings, 1927–1939*, comments wryly that Bataille "was far from being a calm and orderly librarian" (x). Early in his career he wrote a book called "W.C." but burned the manuscript before it could be published, claiming that it was a book "violently opposed to all dignity" (qtd. in Stoekl x). He was instrumental in the founding of avant-garde journals such as *Documents* (an art review) and *La Critique Sociale* (an anti-Stalinist Marxist review), where many of his essays first appeared in print. Bataille also helped to found, in 1935, a group called Contre-Attaque, which was dedicated to political change through agitation and even violence. On the eve of the Second World War, Bataille became involved in two other groups, Acéphale and the Collège de Sociologie, the first clearly subversive and the second more politically moderate. Stoekl, noting Bataille's long-standing interest in historically marginal groups such as gnostics, madmen, and heterodox Christian mystics, observes that "The Acéphale group was . . . outside the mainstream of political life: subversive yet not intended to lead an organized mass movement, the activities of the group would help stimulate a rebirth of the kind of social values Bataille had espoused in the *Critique Sociale* essays: expenditure, risk, loss, sexuality, death" (xix).

In the years between the Second World War and his death, Bataille, often suffering from ill health, participated minimally in organized political activities but continued to write. It is in this period that *La Littérature et le mal* [Literature and evil] (1957) was first published, as well as *L'erotisme* (1957, translated as *Death and Sensuality*). By 1960, the year of Pizarnik's arrival in Paris, Bataille had gained a following as an important member of the intellectual underground, although his writings (still largely untranslated at that point) had not begun to receive the international attention they now command.[9] We can only surmise to what degree Pizarnik ascribed personally to the notions of revolution, violence, transgressive sexuality, and evil put forth in Bataille's texts. The evidence we can glean from her own poetic texts, as I intend to show here, suggests certain strong affinities.

Evil is a slippery term, and nowhere does Bataille provide us with a concise and workable definition. The various permutations of the concept emerge with fair consistency, however, as one examines his work. Clearly, Bataille means to take the term beyond its common denotations of moral depravity and wickedness; in fact, his intention in examining the works of Sade, Blake, and others is to raise these texts, and the spirit behind them, to a plane of "hypermorality." How did he arrive at these unconventional conclusions about literature and evil? Bataille was committed, first and foremost, to revolution. His revolt was a socialist one: he wished to participate in bringing down what he saw as the "crippled existence" of modern bourgeois life (*Visions* 225). This degraded existence suffered everywhere from what Bataille termed *homogeneity:* the sterile, repetitive production of forms of knowledge or social structures that suffocated creative life. All that Bataille came to stand for might be condensed into the concept of homogeneity's dialectical opposite. *Heterogeneity,* as a category of knowledge and experience, included dreams and myth—the contents of the unconscious—as well as the realms of religion and magic. All of this could be subsumed under the notion of "the sacred," which Bataille saw as having social or communal, but not necessarily transcendental, value. Bataille's originality stems from his insistence on the significance, for all of human life, of those forms of the sacred that are traditionally considered "impure": "Included are the waste products of the human body and certain analogous matter (trash, vermin, etc.); the parts of the body; persons, words, or acts having a suggestive erotic value; the various unconscious processes such as dreams or neuroses; the numerous elements or social forms that *homogenous* society is powerless to assimilate: mobs, the warrior, aristocratic and impoverished classes, different types of violent individuals or at least those who refuse the rule (madmen, leaders, poets, etc.)"

(*Visions* 142; emphasis in original). It would be difficult to find a passage in all of Bataille's writings that would better synthesize his utterly heterodox approach to social and political systems, to psychology, and to literature. Taken from an essay first published in 1933, this passage contains the ideological seeds that would flourish, more than twenty years later, in *Literature and Evil*. The fact that he includes poets among the rarefied group of individuals who "refuse the rule" hints at the fascination Pizarnik appears to have felt in the presence of Bataille and his ideas. Pizarnik also placed emphasis on the subversive element of poetry, its utter liberty in the face of societal conventions. This conviction reflects Pizarnik's allegiance to a long line of writers—Baudelaire, Lautréamont, Rimbaud, and the surrealists among them—for whom Bataille became a sort of vindicator.[10]

Evil, then—obscenity of language and image, perverse sexuality, violence perpetrated against others, self-mutilation, suicide, blasphemy, fascination with death and material decomposition in its most morbid and putrefying aspects—can be taken as a valuable element of human experience and expression insofar as it serves to excavate "the fetid ditch of bourgeois culture" (*Visions* 43). In an allusion to the image of a cut-open eye in Luis Buñuel's film *Le Chien Andalou*, Bataille remarks that such images compel us to understand "to what extent horror becomes fascinating, and how it alone is brutal enough to break everything else that stifles" (19). In sum, I would claim that *the breaking of whatever stifles* is Bataille's touchstone for aesthetic judgment. That which produces in us aversion or, in the extreme, horror, is of "sovereign value" in writing and in art. As a literary theorist, Bataille does not advocate that the writer become a perpetrator of evil in the world, but rather that he or she textually represent that evil in order to produce a certain response in the reader. This means pushing written language beyond all limits of bourgeois acceptability, as well as creating images that produce shock and horror, leading to a Nietzschean reevaluation of the very notions of "good" and "evil."

Pizarnik's poetry, although it rarely reaches the degree of horror to which Bataille alludes, is suffused with an atmosphere of suffering, fear, and malevolence. Although apparent in her early work, these elements come increasingly to dominate the lyric quality of many of the poems of *El infierno musical* (1971) and of her posthumous poetry. The text which most clearly embodies Bataille's notions of literary evil, however, is *La condesa sangrienta*, a long prose piece—part novel, part essay, part poem—that I will consider in more detail later, as the culmination of

Pizarnik's preoccupation with evil in its erotic incarnation. Initially, however, I would like to discuss Bataille's notions of evil in relation to childhood and to death as they correspond to much of Pizarnik's lyric output.

Bataille develops his notions of evil in its relation to childhood in the initial essay of *Literature and Evil*, on Emily Brontë's *Wuthering Heights* (15–31). He comments that the two young protagonists, Heathcliff and Catherine, "led their wild life, outside the world, in the most elementary conditions, and it is these conditions which Emily Brontë made tangible—the basic conditions of poetry, of a spontaneous poetry before which both children refused to stop" (*Literature* 18). It may strike us immediately that the speaker of Pizarnik's poems does not find herself "outside the world," in a wild physical environment such as that of the English moors. The speaker of an early poem makes this point explicitly:

Con todas mis muertes
yo me entrego a mi muerte,
con puñados de infancia,
con deseos ebrios
que no anduvieron bajo el sol.

(*Obras* 42)

[With all my deaths
I surrender myself to my death,
with fistfuls of childhood,
with drunken desires
that did not walk in the sun.]

Pizarnik's child-subject appears, rather, to be hermetically enclosed "inside the world." But in either case the child is painfully—we could say fatally—at odds with the surrounding human community; she is a "minúscula salvaje" [tiny savage] (*Obras* 218). This state is marked by wildness, by an elementary violence not yet subject to adult social constraints. In the long prose poem "Extracción de la piedra de locura" [Extraction of the stone of folly], Pizarnik's speaker ponders the genesis of her own madness. Looking back, she alludes favorably to "mi roja violencia elemental" [my elemental red violence], and laments losing that violence as a result of "El haberme prosternado ante el sufrimiento de los demás, el haberme acallado en honor de los demás" [Having prostrated myself before the suffering of others, having silenced myself in honor of others] (139). She pleads for a sacred space of silence for this child who has lost something vital, who is herself lost: "¿A qué hora empezó la desgracia? No quiero saber. No quiero más que un silencio para mí y las que fui, un silencio como la pequeña choza que encuentran en el bosque los niños perdidos" [When did this misfortune begin? I don't want to know. I don't want anything but a silence for myself and for those I used to be, a silence like the little hut that lost children find in the forest] (135). The connection Bataille draws between the elementary conditions of the world inhabited by Catherine and Heathcliff and the "basic conditions of poetry" is reflected in Pizarnik's own defense of the primitive quality of the poetic voice. "Hablo como en mí se habla" [I speak the way one speaks in me], says the speaker of "Extracción"; "No mi voz obstinada en parecer una voz humana sino la otra que atestigua que no he cesado de morar en el bosque" [Not with a voice determined to sound like a human voice, but with the other one that testifies that I have not stopped dwelling in the forest] (134).

There appears to be a conscious rejection here of what is human, that is, of the kind of constrained voice appropriate to human (adult) society. This rejection goes to the heart of Bataille's characterization of childhood as "evil": "But society contrasts the free play of innocence with reason, reason based on the calculations of interest. Society is governed by its will to survive. It could not survive if these childish instincts . . . were allowed to triumph" (*Literature* 18). The world of Wuthering Heights, the "spontaneous poetry before which both children refused to stop," led inexorably to physical death for Catherine and Heathcliff. Pizarnik's speaker, having survived childhood only by submitting herself to the metaphorical extraction of the stone of madness, suffers another kind of death. She ponders the loss in terms of "Haberse muerto en quien se era y en quien se amaba" [Having died in who one was and whom one loved] (135). The spontaneous child with her primitive voice has at some point been profoundly compromised: "Perdida por tu propio designio, has renunciado a tu reino por las cenizas" [Lost by your own design, you have renounced your kingdom for ashes] (135). Pizarnik seems to affirm, as does Bataille, that the kingdom of childhood, with its violence and madness, represents a more authentic existence than the one to which adult society eventually forces children to submit.

The value placed on childhood as a state of savage innocence is, in both Bataille and Pizarnik, a complex one. Thorpe Running observes that in Pizarnik's work, "That fascination with childhood, of course, becomes enmeshed with the contradictory aspects of life-death, presence-absence, which she sees in the child" ("Pizarnik" 53). One of her early lyric poems, "El despertar," illustrates these contradictions:

> Recuerdo mi niñez
> cuando yo era una anciana
> Las flores morían en mis manos
> porque la danza salvaje de la alegría
> les destruía el corazón.

(*Obras* 54)

> [I remember my childhood
> when I was an old woman
> Flowers would die in my hands
> because the wild dance of happiness
> destroyed their hearts.]

Human time does not follow its rational linear dimension here: the child is simultaneously an old woman. But the more striking contradiction occurs in the next three lines. The child's unconstrained dance of joy does not, as we would expect, reflect or add to the bounty of the natural world. In fact, it withers the life of flowers. I suspect that part of the explanation for this odd dynamic lies in the personification suggested by the image of the flowers' hearts. The traditional association of flowers with spring, with innocence, with life in its unspoiled early stages, leads us back to the child herself. In the same way that the girl is already an old woman, the flowers are already moribund; metaphorically, it is the child's own heart that is being destroyed. Bataille speaks in Nietzschean terms of "an instinctive tendency towards divine intoxication which the rational world of calculation cannot bear. This tendency is the opposite of Good" (*Literature* 22). Pizarnik's "danza salvaje de la alegría" is surely a manifestation of divine intoxication, and the destruction toward which it points in this poem reaffirms Bataille's contention that this sacred state, instinctive for the child, cannot survive the pressures of adulthood. He concludes from this that "Death and the instant of divine intoxication merge when they both oppose those intentions of Good which are based on rational calculation" (24).

It is important to underscore the fact that Bataille's portrayal of childhood has nothing to do with an idealized scenario of purity and passivity. If Heathcliff and Catherine run in the paths of evil, it is because they oppose (knowingly or unknowingly) the set of values upon which the adult world is founded. This opposition cannot last: Bataille reiterates in several passages of his essay that the destruction of the children's way of life and of their savage love for each other is inevitable. The principle he draws from this literary example is that "The road to the kingdom of childhood, governed by ingenuousness and innocence, is thus regained *in the horror of atonement*" (24, emphasis in original).

Pizarnik's poetic evocation of childhood, to which critics often allude without taking note of its complexity, is likewise permeated with a sense of suffering. To Kuhnheim's observation that "At the opposite end of Pizarnik's idealization of death is her idealization of and nostalgia for childhood" (79), I would respond that if there is a positive or nostalgic view of childhood, it is double-edged. The semantic disjointedness of the following passage reveals this ambivalence: "La hermosura de la infancia sombría, la tristeza imperdonable entre muñecas, estatuas, cosas mudas, favorables al doble monólogo entre yo y mi antro lujurioso" [The beauty of a somber childhood, the unforgivable sadness among dolls, statues, mute things, propitious for the double monologue between me and my lecherous den] (*Obras* 158). Paradoxically, a sense of the beauty of childhood arises from what is somber and sad. The child in this passage is not, I am tempted to say, well adjusted. She does not commune with the outside world, but rather with her own "antro lujurioso," an allusion to the role that sexuality has already begun to play in this dark scene. The mention of "tristeza imperdonable" here is indicative of another feature of Pizarnik's complex allusions to childhood: a bewildered acknowledgment of wrongdoing and of the need for atonement. The speaker of the passage just cited goes on to say: "Hemos intentado hacernos perdonar lo que no hicimos, las ofensas fantásticas, las culpas fantasmas. Por bruma, por nadie, por sombras, hemos expiado" [We have tried to ask forgiveness for what we didn't do, for imaginary offenses, for phantasmal sins. We have atoned for mist, for no one, for shadows] (158). This is Bataille's "horror of atonement" in its purest expression. The implication seems to be that childhood, as it is portrayed by Brontë and Pizarnik, is a state of being so completely at odds with the rigid morality of adult existence that the child is forced to pay, sometimes with life itself, for "culpas" that he or she may not even comprehend.

The notion of death arises at every point in the Bataille's discussion of childhood in particular, and of evil in general. Death is also, as many critics have noted, a thematic center of gravity for Pizarnik's work. It is not my intention in this essay to provide any comprehensive analysis of the thematics of death for either writer; rather, I wish to focus on one aspect that I consider indispensable for an understanding of both, that is, the notion of death—often in its most horrific aspect—as transcendence of the individual existence. In his seminal book *Death and Sensuality: A Study of Eroticism and the Taboo* (1957), Bataille expands upon the commonplace notion that without death there would be no renewal of life, arguing that "for us, discontinuous beings that we are, death means continuity of being" (13). In this regard, death represents a primary value for art and literature, which strive to represent continuity. Bataille's essay on *Wuthering Heights* closes with an examination of the value of death as the basis for what he calls "true literary emotion": "Death alone ... introduces that break without which nothing reaches the state of ecstasy. And what we thereby regain is always both innocence and the intoxication of existence. The isolated being *loses himself* in something other than himself. What the 'other thing' represents is of no importance. It is still a reality that transcends the common limitations" (*Literature* 26; emphasis in original). Death, then, can play a role in literature almost parallel to that of childhood: an evocation of either state can call up both primal innocence and Dionysian intoxication, each of which points to the dissolution of the individual ego and a return to a state of continuity. This concept, I might note, echoes the esoteric (and particularly the gnostic) sense of fragmented existence striving toward the unity of origins.

Not surprisingly, death in Pizarnik's work is often identified with the child, who becomes the "pequeña muerta" [little dead girl] (*Obras* 79) or, conversely, the "pequeña asesina" [little murderer] (136). In the prose piece "El sueño de la muerte o el lugar de los cuerpos poéticos" [The dream of death, or the place of poetic bodies], the lyric speaker refers to herself as the "pequeña difunta en un jardín de ruinas y de lilas" [little deceased girl in a garden of ruins and lilacs] (140). The image of the child in a garden, romantic innocence redoubled, is here given a morbid twist, since both child and garden are dead. Furthermore, the poem seems to echo Bataille's notion that death is the basis of authentic literary emotion when it alludes to "[el] lugar en que se hacen los cuerpos poéticos" [the place where poetic bodies are made] as "una cesta llena de cadáveres de niñas" [a basket filled with girls' cadavers] (140). This rather hideous image reminds the reader of Bataille's insistence on the value of representing morbid and putrefying elements in art or literature, a value which he attributes to their very capacity to horrify us, to "break that which stifles."

The rhetoric of death in Pizarnik never strays far from the horrifying. If I speak of a "sacred" evocation of death in her work, it is only within the parameters laid out by Bataille. The individual seeks to maintain his or her own circumscribed existence, but at the same time seeks to transcend that limitation. Ecstatic experiences of many kinds, including the mystic and the erotic, can provide a momentary sense of transcendence. But only death can assure it. This is why, in his essay on William Blake, Bataille claims that "What [Blake's words] describe is ultimately man's compliance with his own laceration, his compliance with death and the instinct which propels him toward it" (*Literature* 90). Few readers of Pizarnik's poetry would deny that there is a strong sense of compliance with her own laceration, so to speak. In certain moments, there is also a hint of Bataille's notion of transcendence or continuity. I take as example a passage from "Extracción de la piedra de locura," from which several textual examples have already been drawn: "Tú sabes que nunca sabrás defenderte, que sólo deseas presentarles el trofeo, quiero decir tu cadáver, y que se lo coman y se lo beban" [You know that you'll never know how to defend yourself, that you only want to present them with the trophy, I mean your cadaver, and to have them devour it and drink it up] (*Obras* 136). We do not know whom the speaker addresses here; it is likely that the interlocutor is another aspect of the speaker herself, as is common in Pizarnik's poetry. Neither do we know against what force this person must defend herself. What is clear, however, is that the interlocutor desires first her own death, then the cannibalization of her body. Bataille, discussing the ritual value of cannibalism, points out that human flesh eaten in the communion feast following sacrifice is held as sacred (*Death* 71). Transgression of the taboo against eating human flesh carries a religious significance because it points toward a reintegration of the corpse (and the individual, discontinuous life it represents) into the community. Death is consumed by life, as a means of extending life.

In another passage from the same poem, Pizarnik's speaker comes even closer to a direct espousal of the notion of death as transcendence: "Hundirme en la tierra y que la tierra se cierre sobre mí. Éxtasis innoble" [To sink into the earth and to have the earth close over me. Ignoble ecstasy] (*Obras* 136). The structure of the phrase, in particular the use of the personalized infinitive "hundirme," marks the statement as a death-wish. But here the image is not simply that of a cadaver, but rather that of a body descending into the earth, ready to be reabsorbed into the natural world. This would be, claims the speaker, an experience of *ecstasy*, a "standing outside oneself" in the purest sense. But finally, as if to remind herself that this vision carries its share of negativity, the speaker calls the ecstasy "ignoble." In its desire to protect itself, the ego can only respond to the death-wish by debasing it. This passage illustrates keenly the internal conflict of the individual who simultaneously wills both survival and self-destruction.

A less complex approach to the ecstatic or unitive aspect of death can be seen in a passage from a later prose poem: "La noche, de nuevo la noche, la magistral sapiencia de lo oscuro, el cálido roce de la muerte, un instante de éxtasis para mí, heredera de todo jardín prohibido" [The night, once again the night, the magisterial knowledge of darkness, death's warm graze, a moment of ecstasy for me, inheritor of every forbidden garden] (*Obras* 156). This passage conflates several of the semantic elements fundamental to Pizarnik's work, all rooted in the romantic tradition: night, darkness (with its promise of knowledge), death, the garden, and forbidden zones. Pizarnik, like Baudelaire, Rimbaud, Lautréamont, and Artaud, chose to locate herself within the "forbidden garden" in a literary as well as an experiential sense. The knowledge to be gained in this forbidden garden is a knowledge of absolutes. Poetry, in its most vital sense, sustained Pizarnik until her death because she attributed to it the liberating power of which Bataille speaks: "Poetry alone, which denies and destroys the limitations of things, can return us to this absence of limitations" (*Literature* 84). However, when the promise of crossing the threshold into the absolute by means of the poetic word seemed to have failed Pizarnik definitively, death appeared as the only alternative. It was a lesson well learned from those she considered her literary forefathers. It is death, in Bataille's sense of a restoration of continuity, a merging with the absolute, that constitutes the "instante de éxtasis" of which Pizarnik wrote. Her suicide, and all the rhetorical markers in her poetry that pointed toward it, may have been a desperate response to depression, but it may also have been a conscious desire to achieve "that break without which nothing reaches the state of ecstasy" (26). Bataille states the relationship between violence, life, and death in unequivocal terms: "In so far as violence casts its shadow on the being and he sees death 'face to face,' life is purely beneficial. Nothing can destroy it. Death is the condition of its renewal" (29). Pizarnik's work, though laden with a sense of horror over death's finality for the individual self, also reveals a poet's grappling with this broader and less subjective truth.

In Bataille's writings, death is inextricably linked to eroticism. This link is the principle underlying his anthropological study *Death and Sensuality*; it also provides the philosophical groundwork for many of the essays of *Literature and Evil*. He states his argument as follows: "I believe eroticism to be the approval of life, up until death. Sexuality implies death, not only in the sense in which the new prolongs and replaces that which has disappeared, but also in that the life of the being who reproduces himself is at stake.... The basis of sexual effusion is the negation of the isolation of the ego, which only experiences ecstasy by exceeding itself, by surpassing itself in the embrace in which the being loses its solitude" (*Literature* 16). Bataille goes on to say that in the realm of the erotic, intensity can reach such a degree that the destruction of the individual becomes apparent. "What we call vice," he concludes, "is based on this profound implication of death" (17). We have already seen how Pizarnik's work touches at times upon an ecstatic sense of death, but the convergence with Bataille's thought becomes even more apparent as we consider her treatment of the erotic. It is within this context that Pizarnik most fully explores transgressive values in poetry, where she plays her most dangerous games.

As we have already seen, Bataille considered obscenity to be one approach to heterogeneity in literature and art, that is, one way to confer the positive value of evil upon a work. Piña has already examined Pizarnik's use of obscenity in her extensive and well-argued essay "La palabra obscena" [The obscene word], in which she defines "lo obsceno" as "lo siniestro, lo fatal, lo *fuera de escena*" [what is sinister, what is fatal, what is *outside the scene*] (21; emphasis in original).[11] Piña reiterates the Freudian association between obscenity and death as she extends her definition:

> Tradicionalmente, la obscenidad está asociada a lo sexual, . . . al *goce* en sentido lacaniano, como lo que está más allá del placer, aquello inarticulable, ilegible, irrepresentable, pues se hunde en el tabú, en la falta primera, en la imposible "completud," que por imposible y por más allá del placer coincide con el instinto de muerte, ese Thánatos indisolublemente unido con el Eros pues va más allá de él.
>
> [Traditionally, obscenity is associated with the sexual, . . . with *jouissance* in the Lacanian sense, as that which is beyond pleasure,

that which cannot be articulated, or read, or represented, since it sinks into taboo, into original sin, into the impossible "completeness," which, due to its very impossibility and its being beyond pleasure, coincides with the death-instinct, that Thanatos indissolubly linked with Eros since it extends beyond him.] ("Obscena" 21)

Although there are evident parallels between *lo obsceno* and the representation of erotic evil, as Bataille broadly defines it, my intention here is to go beyond Piña's analysis by considering the erotic (which includes the obscene) in the larger context of its relationship with violence and death. To this end, I will examine a text by Pizarnik that has, perhaps more than any other single piece, fascinated and perplexed readers and critics.[12] I refer to *La condesa sangrienta*,[13] a collection of eleven prose vignettes that serve as meditations on a novel called *Erzébet Báthory, la Comtesse Sanglante* (1963), published in France by the surrealist writer Valerie Penrose. Báthory was a sixteenth-century Hungarian countess condemned for the sexual torture and murder of more than six hundred young women, mostly peasants from the surrounding countryside. Not surprisingly, Bataille refers to the countess and her deeds in the book that he was preparing at the time of his death, *The Tears of Eros* (139–40). Pizarnik's text thus joins the corpus that D. W. Foster calls "a literature of the horrible" and can be explicated by means of Bataille's notions of evil, particularly as they are developed in his essay on the Marquis de Sade (*Literature* 103–29).[14]

I have already discussed Bataille's arguments linking sensuality and death, in particular his claim that sexual effusion leads to the negation of the individual ego and that, when carried to extremes, this negation implies the death of the self. Such extremes are more likely to be reached in forms of sexuality that correlate the expression of desire with violence. Echoing Freud in this matter, Gilles Deleuze comments that "Both sadism and masochism imply that a particular quantity of libidinal energy be neutralized, desexualized, displaced and put at the service of Thanatos" (110). Bataille, explicating Sade's obsessive desire to exceed the limitations of the individual human psyche, claims that the only means of escape from the limitations imposed by that individuality is "the destruction of a being similar to ourselves." Ironically, by destroying another being we are able to overcome that being's limitations; extreme violence against other human beings paradoxically "returns them to immensity" (*Literature* 122).

This line of reasoning brings us once again to the notion of death as transcendence, but what is new here is the death of the other—that is, the inclusion of murder as a means for crossing ultimate boundaries. Within the realm of literature, the implication is that distinctions between subject and object are collapsed: writer, character, and reader share equally in the crime. As Foster aptly observes, in *La condesa sangrienta* "a challenge is made to the gaze of the reader, who (through the eyes of the narrator, who is the mediating voyeur) watches the countess watch herself embracing the victim through the agency of the iron maiden" ("Of Power and Virgins" 110). Pizarnik touches upon this collapse of boundaries in a diary entry in which she reflects upon her rereading of Dostoyevsky's *Crime and Punishment:* "Me duelen los brazos como si hubieran bajado el hacha homicida. Y sufro de un sufrimiento ajeno pero misteriosamente mío" [My arms hurt as if they had let the homicidal ax fall. And I suffer from a suffering that is not mine, but is mysteriously mine] (*Semblanza* 260). This ability to imagine herself, as a reader, implicated in the horrors of violent crime may explain some of Pizarnik's fascination with Penrose's text on Báthory.[15] The subject-object fusion, on whatever level it may occur, imparts a certain power to scenes, written texts, or works of art that would otherwise merely nauseate the reader/viewer/witness. Sade had the misfortune, says Bataille, to live the dream "whose obsession is the soul of philosophy, the unity of subject and object" (*Literature* 125). Echoing earlier statements, Bataille affirms that the achieved unity or identity of subject and object represents the transcendence of each individual being's limitations. Although Pizarnik may have lived a dream entirely different from Sade's, the same obsession surfaces in much of her work.

Reiterative murder, the outcome of extreme sexual and physical torture, is the only real story line of *La condesa sangrienta*. The narrator informs us of the number of victims—650—in the first line of the introduction and reminds us of it in the last lines of the final vignette.[16] The sheer numbers are reinforced by the cumulative effect of the descriptions of methods and instruments of torture: "La virgen de hierro" [The iron maiden], "Muerte por agua" [Death by water], "La jaula mortal" [The mortal cage], "Torturas clásicas" [Classic tortures]. Pizarnik's style, which often relies on an accumulation of nouns, adjectives, and condensed verbal phrases, emphasizes the repetitive, even monotonous, nature of the crimes: "Sus viejas y horribles sirvientas son figuras silenciosas que traen fuego, cuchillos, agujas, atizadores; que torturan muchachas, que luego las entierran" [Her old and horrible servants are silent figures who bring fire, knives, needles, pokers; who torture girls and then bury them] (*Obras* 373). In some passages, a parallel or anaphoristic structure imbues the descriptions with the quality of litany: "les aplicaban los atizadores enrojecidos al fuego; les cortaban los dedos con tijeras o cizallas; les punzaban las llagas; les practicaban incisiones con navajas" [they would poke them with red-hot pokers; they would cut off their fingers with scissors or shears; they would prick their wounds; they would cut them with razors] (378). The echoes of Sade here are unmistakable. Bataille claims that in his long life, the marquis was absorbed by only one occupation: "that of enumerating to the point of exhaustion the possibilities of destroying human beings, of destroying them and of enjoying the thought of their death and suffering" (*Literature* 115–16). I do not mean to imply any close analogy between Pizarnik and Sade as writers, mainly because Pizarnik is twice removed from the crimes being narrated. That is, Pizarnik did not imagine (or recall) sadistic scenes and write them down; rather, she is commenting on a text that comments on historical events. Nevertheless, the literature she chose to produce—in the case of *La condesa sangrienta*, at least—does reflect a fascination with the act of writing the sexual crime. (This fascination, as Chávez Silverman points out, may have been rooted in Pizarnik's desire to overcome the silence, imposed both from within and without, regarding her own lesbianism.)[17] Furthermore, she adopts rhetorical methods that highlight and lyricize the most horrible aspects of the crime. It is in these terms that I see her work as "guilty"—in Bataille's positive sense of pushing acceptable limits—and therefore as meriting the designation of "literature of evil."

Utilizing the same stylistic device of condensation and repetition, Pizarnik's narrator clarifies for the reader the expressly sadistic nature of the countess and her environs: "Resumo: el castillo medieval; la sala de torturas; la hermosa alucinada riendo desde su maldito éxtasis provocado por el sufrimiento ajeno" [In sum: the medieval castle, the torture chamber, the beautiful, captivated one laughing from wicked ecstasy provoked in her by the suffering of others] (379). The term *éxtasis*, as I indicated above, is one that Pizarnik reiterates in her lyric poetry, specifically in conjunction with the speaker's own imagined death. In apparent contrast to this, ecstasy for the countess is achieved by witnessing the suffering of others. Pizarnik insists, throughout this text, on the visual aspect of this enjoyment of "sufrimiento ajeno." The countess is primarily a voyeur: "Si el acto sexual implica una suerte de muerte, Erzébet Báthory necesitaba de la muerte visible, elemental, grosera, para poder, a su vez, morir de esa muerte figurada que viene a ser el orgasmo" [If the sexual act implies a kind of death, Erzébet Báthory had need of visible, elemental, crude death in order to be able to die, in turn, that figurative death which is orgasm] (380). In this regard, the sadistic act requires a separation of the object (victim) from the subject (torturer/voyeur). The moment of ecstasy—or, as Bataille would say, the temporary dissolution of the discontinuity represented by the ego—occurs at a physical distance from the being who experiences death.

There are several passages in this text, however, that signal a more physical and literal fusion of desiring subject and desired object. "La jaula mortal" contains a description of a reiterated scene in which the countess's servant would enclose the victim in a small, suspended cage into which sharp points protruded. The servant would then poke the girl with a red-hot iron, causing her to impale herself on the steel points. The countess, seated impassively below, would be covered with the victim's blood—a kind of perverse baptism. The narrator finalizes the scene with these words: "Han habido dos metamorfosis: su vestido blanco ahora es rojo y donde hubo una muchacha hay un cadáver" [There have been two metamorphoses: her white dress is now red, and where there was a girl there is a corpse] (377). The clear implication is that the girl's very life is transferred to the countess; in Bataille's terms, the countess's destruction of a being similar to herself "returns [that being] to immensity." Perhaps even more significantly in this regard, three allusions to cannibalism occur in *La condesa sangrienta*. In one, we are told that when the countess was taken ill, she would have girls brought to her bed and would tear their flesh with her teeth (379). The collapsing of subject/object boundaries is to be taken quite literally here, I believe. The countess incorporates the victims' flesh into her own; in this way, the healing of one being is predicated upon the mortal suffering of another.

We seem to have strayed a long way from any sense of the sacred with regard to either Eros or Thanatos. Yet I would maintain that Pizarnik's rendering of the Báthory story goes far beyond a mere morbid fascination with sensuality, death, or their point of intersection. If she is in any way to be considered a disciple of Bataille, it is because she sensed in him a willingness to grapple with certain "forbidden" questions in profound and unorthodox ways. Bataille says of Sade: "He did not think that he could, or should, cut out of his life these dangerous states to which his insurmountable desires led him"; rather, he dared to scrutinize these states, and by doing so, to pose "that unfathomable question which they raise for all men" (*Literature* 119). From what we know of her life, Pizarnik was not obsessed by insurmountable sexual desires, but rather by the desire to commit suicide. In either case, the work of both writers, and that of Bataille as well, is a testimony to their willingness to examine the "dangerous states" to which their desires led them.

The story of the Hungarian countess, says Pizarnik's narrator in the coda to this text, should not evoke pity or admiration; the appropriate response is "Sólo un quedar en suspenso en el exceso de horror, una fascinación por un vestido blanco que se vuelve rojo, por la idea de un absoluto desgarramiento" [Only a sense of being suspended within an excessive horror, a fascination with a white dress that turns red, with the idea of an absolute rending] (*Obras* 391). The idea of an absolute rending—laceration, rape, death, but also, perhaps, the tearing of the veil of illusion—is mirrored by the idea of absolute liberty with which Pizarnik concludes her account of *La condesa sangrienta:* "Como Sade en sus escritos, como Gilles de Rais en sus crímenes, la condesa Báthory alcanzó, más allá de todo límite, el último fondo del desenfreno. Ella es una prueba más de que la libertad absoluta de la criatura humana es horrible" [Like Sade in his writings, like Gilles de Rais in his crimes, Countess Báthory reached, beyond all limits, the ultimate depth of debauchery. She is yet another proof that the absolute freedom of the human creature is horrible] (391). Unless we take this statement to be "devastatingly ironic," as Foster suggests (*Gay and Lesbian Themes* 99), we must conclude that the narrator here chooses to unilaterally condemn the absolute freedom of which the countess is an emblem: "es horrible." Bataille's consideration of the question appears more complex and unsettling. Throughout his writings, the value of liberty is equated with the value of evil. He attributes positive worth to those actions or states of mind that free us from our limitations and that stand in opposition to the forces of good, whose only end is conservation, homogeneity, and survival. Like Heathcliff of *Wuthering Heights,* the Countess of Báthory acted in ways that ran counter to all conventional morality. She pushed the bounds of human liberty almost beyond imaginable limits. As a result, she was finally apprehended, immured within her own castle, and condemned to death. Bataille's essay on William Blake articulates the paradox that the countess's story leaves unanswered: "By affirming Evil, Blake was affirming liberty, but the liberty of Evil is also the negation of liberty" (*Literature* 93–94).

Absolute liberty, absolute evil, cannot exist in the world, since unchecked evil carries within it its own negation. It can exist, however, in literature. In Paris in 1962 Pizarnik wrote these words:

La poesía es el lugar donde todo sucede. A semejanza del amor, del humor, del suicidio y de todo acto profundamente subversivo, la poesía se desentiende de lo que no es su libertad o su verdad. Decir *libertad* o *verdad* y referir estas palabras al mundo en que vivimos o no vivimos es decir una mentira. No lo es cuando se las atribuye a la poesía: lugar donde todo es posible. (*Obras* 367)[18]

[Poetry is the place where everything happens. Like love, humor, suicide, or any truly subversive act, poetry refuses anything that does not represent its freedom or its truth. To say *freedom* or *truth*, and to refer these words to the world in which we do or do not live, is to tell a lie. It is not a lie when we attribute them to poetry, the place where everything is possible.]

The attribution of absolute liberty to poetry is a notion that arose with the romantics and was later appropriated by the surrealists. Like Lautréamont, Baudelaire, Rimbaud, or Breton, Pizarnik appears to be concerned with the transgressive power of the poetic word, its ability to reach backward into primitive states or downward into baseness, perversion, or malevolence. Like Bataille, she associates poetry with the impure elements of life: "El sabor de las palabras, ese sabor a semen viejo, a vientre viejo, a hueso que despista, a animal mojado por un agua negra. . . . Yo no sufro, yo no digo sino mi asco por el lenguaje de la ternura, esos hilos morados, esa sangre aguada" [The taste of words, that taste of old semen, of old bellies, of a bone that confuses the scent, of an animal wet by black water. . . . I don't suffer, I simply speak my disgust for the language of tenderness, those purple threads, that watery blood] (*Obras* 184). This passage, from a poem called "En contra" [Against], not only identifies poetry with decomposition and ugliness, it also charges poetry with the rebellious act of speaking passion in its harshest and least diluted forms. Such an act is not without its consequences. As the trajectory of her work shows, poetry represents for Pizarnik both a liberation and a kind of hell from which she could not extricate herself. "El infierno musical" [The musical inferno], the title poem of the last volume published in her lifetime, stands as a testimony to this contradiction:

Golpean con soles
Nada se acopla con nada aquí
Y de tanto animal muerto en el cementerio de huesos filosos de mi memoria

Y de tantas monjas como cuervos que se precipitan a hurgar entre
  mis piernas
La cantidad de fragmentos me desgarra
Impuro diálogo
Un proyectarse desesperado de la materia verbal
Liberada a sí misma
Naufragando en sí misma.

(*Obras* 155)

[They pummel with suns
Nothing couples with nothing here
And from so many dead animals in the cemetery of sharp bones
  that is my memory
And from so many nuns like crows who rush to poke between my
  legs
The number of fragments rips me apart
Impure dialogue
A desperate projection of verbal matter
Freed from itself
Sinking into itself]

Discontinuity, death and decomposition, obscenity and erotic violence, impure language, liberty that negates itself: this poem stands as an emblem of what Bataille claimed as the territory of evil in literature. It was a territory that Pizarnik was compelled to explore. The line that forms the poem's axis—"La cantidad de fragmentos me desgarra"—attests to one of the possible consequences of accepting poetry on these terms.

5

Poetry and Madness in Jacobo Fijman

Michel Foucault, in the preface to *Madness and Civilization* (1961) observes the following: "In the Middle Ages and until the Renaissance, man's dispute with madness was a dramatic debate in which he confronted the secret powers of the world; the experience of madness was clouded by images of the Fall and the Will of God, of the Beast and the Metamorphosis, and of all the marvelous secrets of Knowledge. In our era, the experience of madness remains silent in the composure of a knowledge which, knowing too much about madness, forgets it" (xii). Foucault's account of the premodern culture of madness bears a striking resemblance to what I have identified throughout this book as the esoteric tradition. Several shared elements are immediately recognizable: the notions of secret knowledge (aptly termed *marvelous* in this passage) and the secret power believed to accompany it; the mythic belief in an original, primal unity, broken by the fall; and the evocation of the Beast, incarnation of evil born of that fall, existing both without and within what has been called "human nature." That these elements characterizing a traditional view of madness should inhabit a territory common to elements of esoteric currents of thought is not surprising; in fact, the link between madness and occult knowledge is a commonplace of Western thought. Or *was*, as Foucault points out. With the shift toward a psychological view of madness that occurred in the nineteenth century, what was once linked to sacred knowledge and prophetic voice has become, in our day, a consummately profane disease: madness has become mental illness. "Since the end of the eighteenth century," says Foucault, "the life of unreason no longer manifests itself except in the lightning-flash works such as those of Hölderlin, of Nerval, of Nietzsche, or of Artaud—forever irreducible to those alienations that can be cured" (278). This observation is crucial: Foucault refers here to the one realm of human endeavor—the artistic, and in particular, the poetic—in which the extremes of irrationality may still maintain their ties to what has been considered sacred or otherworldly knowledge and expression.

Within Occidental thought, the view of poetry as linked to madness, both being of sacred origin, was already traditional in Plato's day. In *Phaedrus* 244, Socrates provides a defense of madness, associating it directly with the prophetic voice that is seen as a benefit to society:

> If it were true without qualification that madness is an evil, that would be all very well, but in fact madness, provided it comes as the gift of heaven, is the channel by which we receive the greatest blessings. Take the prophetess at Delphi and the priestesses at Dodona, for example, and consider all the benefits which individuals and states in Greece have received from them when they were in a state of frenzy, though their usefulness in their sober senses amounts to little or nothing.... So, according to the evidence provided by our ancestors, madness is a nobler thing than sober sense, in proportion as the name of the mantic art and the act it signifies are more perfect and held in higher esteem than the name and act of augury; madness comes from God, whereas sober sense is merely human. (46–47)

In the following section, Plato voices, through Socrates, the idea that poetic creation actually depends on a certain degree of irrationality:

> The third type of possession and madness is possession by the Muses. When this seizes upon a gentle and virgin soul it rouses it to inspired expression in lyric and other sorts of poetry, and glorifies countless deeds of the heroes of old for the instruction of posterity. But if a man comes to the door of poetry untouched by the madness of the Muses, believing that technique alone will make him a good poet, he and his sane compositions never reach perfection, but are utterly eclipsed by the performances of the inspired madman. (48)

These views are not to be taken as inviolable truths, but rather as the stuff of which our thinking about poetry has been made. A long line of poets and theorists in the Classical and European literary traditions—including Aristotle, Ovid, Horace, Shakespeare, and Dryden, to name only a few, have pondered the relationship between inspiration and unreason. As further evidence of a cultural insistence on this connection, F. C. Prescott points out that the Old English word *wood*, meaning mad, bears an etymological relation to *woþ*, meaning song, as well as to the Latin *vates*, seer or poet (265).

In the context of the current study I have shown how, from the German romantics to the surrealists, certain influential currents of literary thought have held up various forms of irrationality (if not madness per se) as an ideal. Many romantics maintained a belief in a realm beyond that of quotidian existence, a world more "real" than the inhabited one, to which only the initiated could gain access. To this world belonged an original, divine, or absolute language, a mode of discourse that was fragmented or lost entirely with the fall. Midway through the nineteenth century, Baudelaire made famous the Swedenborgian notion of *"correspondances,"* voicing a commonly held belief in the neoplatonic analogy between macrocosm and microcosm, and highlighting the poet's capacity to link those realms. The surrealists, assimilating Freudian theory, marked the unconscious as the internal site of the mysterious realm of the Other, thus restoring the moment of creative trance to its status as sacred contact with "real" reality. In fact, it could be said that the entire surrealist project involved the cultivation of unreason within the artistic sphere. In all these movements, the poet holds a privileged position somewhat akin to that of the Delphic oracles, as Plato had argued. He or she stands on the threshold of the absolute, and may, at certain moments, glimpse a truth not revealed to the uninitiated. When the poetic voice speaks under such circumstances, it is with the voice of one possessed. The poet grasps intuitively the original or absolute language. Rational discourse and its goal, communication, are discarded in favor of irrational speech that is not likely to be fully understood by those who hear it. It is not difficult to see how madness fits into this picture. If the ravings of madmen were traditionally held to be sacred, or if, as in the case of Cassandra, the oracular voice can lead to madness, this fundamental connection between the irrational and the truthful may not be easily dismissed, even in a century that "knows too much about madness."

Where does this leave us in the attempt to approach the work of a contemporary writer who has not only lived the modern experience of mental illness, but whose work clearly bears witness to that experience? To begin with, literary analysis must eschew any attempt to distinguish between lucidity and delirium as psychological states "producing" one or another type of text. In this I follow Breton, who concluded that "The well-known lack of frontiers between *nonmadness* and madness does not induce me to accord a different value to the perceptions and ideas which are the result of one or the other" (*Nadja* 144; emphasis in original). This said, we are still left with the sense that certain works of art are capable of opening up a space in which a profound and disturbing *otherness* continues to exist. Though little credence may be given to the romantic notion of an invisible reality, and still less, in postmodern thought, to the belief in an original language or an absolute truth, something in the words of the poet-madman may cause us momentarily to doubt the rock-hard solidity of discursive reason.

In spite of her adherence to surrealism and its romantic precursors, Olga Orozco does not ascribe in any discernible way to the ethos that links poetry to madness. Although her speaker avidly questions the faculty of reason and searches for ways of accessing the "other side" that eschew cold logic, it is difficult to find traces in her work of true unreason. A writer highly conscious of her craft, she rejects outright the tendency to view both madness and suicide as "elementos prestigiosos" in the literary and artistic world (qtd. in Sefamí 130). She outlines the romantic notion of transgression in which poets take their place alongside "true" madmen and other outcasts:

> Para la sociedad corriente, el mundo se divide entre los que están dentro del reglamento y los que están fuera, los transgresores. Los transgresores son siempre los criminales, los locos, los leprosos y, en fin, los tipos que han transgredido, de uno u otro modo, por pasiones o desarreglos extremos, las reglas establecidas. Foucault los enumera. (Qtd. in Sefamí 130–31)

> [For ordinary society, the world is divided between those that are within the rule and those that are outside it, the transgressors. The transgressors are always criminals, madmen, lepers, and, in sum, those who have transgressed, in one way or another, because of passions or extreme disorders, the established rules. Foucault enumerates them.]

Like Foucault, Orozco concludes that the madness of men like Van Gogh and Artaud ultimately debilitated them as artists.

Alejandra Pizarnik straddles the line between reason and unreason, in life and in literary work. Under psychiatric treatment off and on throughout late adolescence and adulthood, Pizarnik lived in fear of true insanity. (Of all those who knew her, it was Orozco with whom she shared these fears most often.)[1] Within her work, we can follow the traces of a certain discourse of madness. Chávez Silverman discusses this discourse in

Pizarnik's work with respect to its participation in an "outside/inside dichotomy" identified by Foucault and Felman ("Discourse" 274–81). She points out that Pizarnik's writing reveals certain "symptoms" that conflate neurosis and traditional, learned female behavior. Chávez Silverman further identifies these aspects of a discourse of madness in Pizarnik's work: "the absence or silence(ing) of the work of art; Foucault's notion of the mad literary speaking subject experiencing *vertige,* loss of meaning and loss of control over meaning; the search for another, frequently magic language which leads to the abandonment of (or being abandoned by) 'normal' human language; 'recovery,' comprising the discovery of a significant Other (outside the speaking subject) and this, in turn, leading to a perceived empowerment of the Logos; finally, the act of writing as a palliative, a diagnosis and even—rarely—a cure, a way to interpret/dominate one's own madness" (277).

While acknowledging each of these aspects as present in Pizarnik's work, I would emphasize that this rhetoric is part of the author's chosen *stance,* her conscious decision to situate herself within the literary tradition that honored poetic unreason. Such a stance is evident in lines such as "Me deliro, me desplomo" [I am delirious, I collapse], in which the "delirium" is a romantic conceit (57). The long prose poem "Extracción de la piedra de locura," which I cited extensively in chapter 4, points rather directly to states of mental imbalance. At first glance, this piece may appear to approximate a true rhetoric of madness, at least in the sense of withdrawal of logical connections between images: the poem skips from "cuerpos luminosos que giraban en la niebla" [luminous bodies that would spin circles in the mist] to "una reina loca que yace bajo la luna" [a mad queen lying under the moon] to "muñecos sin cabeza" [headless dolls] (*Obras* 134–36). But is this the representation of a mad discourse, or simply the surrealist technique of surveying an oneiric landscape? The speaker, addressing a "tú" that is another facet of herself, provides an important clue: "No obstante, lloras funestamente y evocas tu locura y hasta quisieras extraerla de ti como si fuese una piedra, a ella, tu solo privilegio" [Nevertheless, you cry banefully and evoke your madness and you would even like to extract it from yourself as if it were a stone—madness, your only privilege] (135). Madness, in other words, is *evoked* by a perfectly lucid subject. The final image—alluding to the poem's title—recalls the medieval belief that madness was lodged in a stone that could be surgically removed from the brain—a practice immortalized by Hieronymus Bosch's painting *The Cure of Folly.* In "Extracción," madness is a kind of object to be manipulated by the poet: it becomes, in this way, a privilege. I would argue that rather than representing a true discourse of madness, Pizarnik is participating in the romantic/surrealist project of loosening the constraints of rationality in order to give freer rein to the poetic imagination.

In the context of twentieth-century Argentine poetry, I would argue that it is not Orozco or Pizarnik but Jacobo Fijman (1898–1970) who stands out as one of the most provocative and disturbing manifestations of "the life of unreason."[2] Born to Jewish parents in Bessarabia (Russia), at the age of four Fijman immigrated with his family to Argentina. In his twenties, he began to distinguish himself as a poet of the avant-garde, moving in the literary circles in Buenos Aires that included such well-known figures as Jorge Luis Borges, Leopoldo Marechal, Oliverio Girondo, and Macedonio Fernández. Although literary historians would later classify him as a member of the Argentine Generation of 1922 (also known as the *Martinfierristas*),[3] Fijman was too much of an iconoclast to integrate himself consciously into any literary school or movement. Francine Masiello maps out Fijman's ex-centric position with respect to his contemporaries, suggesting that he came to occupy the position of *poeta maldito* of the Argentine avant-garde:

> Mientras los demás afirmaban su sentido del yo dentro de alianzas grupales y la alegría general de la época, Fijman se retrajo hacia un espacio privado, íntimo, alienado de la vida cultural argentina y de las gozosas prácticas de la aventura. Ocupó la posición de *poète maudit* de la vanguardia rioplatense, exiliado conspicuamente de las amenidades sociales de la cultura literaria. (*Lenguaje e ideología* 136).[4]

[While the others were affirming their sense of self within group alliances and the general optimism of the times, Fijman withdrew into a private, intimate space, distanced from Argentine cultural life and from the pleasant practices of that adventure. He assumed the place of the *poète maudit* of the Río de la Plata avant-garde, conspicuously exiled from the social amenities of the literary culture.]

Having had little formal education, Fijman set about studying on his own, exploring such diverse fields as law, medicine, philosophy, astrology, mathematics, classical languages, and French. He worked for a short time teaching French in a private school in Buenos Aires, but was soon discharged from his duties because of his eccentric behavior. After this,

Fijman did not hold any formal jobs for the rest of his life. Having taught himself to play the violin, he spent some years traveling through the provinces of Argentina, earning a scant living as a wandering musician.

In 1921, at the age of twenty-three, Fijman suffered a breakdown that involved a violent physical confrontation with the police in Buenos Aires, and was hospitalized for several months. (According to his own account, Fijman, suffering blows at the hands of the policemen, shouted several times that he was "The Red Christ."[5]) Seven years later, in 1928, Fijman traveled to Paris, where he became acquainted with several important surrealists of the day, including Breton, Paul Eluard, Robert Desnos, and Jules Supervielle. Fijman's brief account of his encounter with Antonin Artaud, a literary figure with whom critics have compared Fijman,[6] is perhaps indicative of the thin line between reason and unreason that he walked in that period of his life: "A Artaud lo conocí en un café, La Coupole, donde tomamos un vaso de vino blanco. Estuvimos a punto de pelearnos, yo me identificaba con Dios y Artaud con el Diablo. Sin embargo le tengo aprecio" [I met Artaud in a café, La Coupole, where we had a glass of white wine. We almost came to blows: I was identifying myself with God, Artaud with the Devil. But I still respect the man] (qtd. in Zito Lema 66). Continuing his travels in Spain, Fijman was befriended by the Spanish avant-garde writer Ramón del Valle Inclán.

After returning to Buenos Aires, Fijman appears to have made another trip to Europe in 1929 or 1930 (biographical accounts are inconclusive), traveling through France, Belgium, Italy, Portugal, and Spain. In Belgium he attempted to enter a monastery, but was turned away. This incident apparently triggered an emotional crisis for Fijman; shortly thereafter, he returned to Argentina, where he would remain until his death. In 1930 he converted to Catholicism—a process that appears to have been unfolding over several years. Little is known of his life over the next decade, except that he had by that time lost all contact with his family and enjoyed only sporadic friendships. Living in rented rooms and with few possessions to his name, Fijman spent long hours in the libraries of Buenos Aires, studying, among many other subjects, the works of Thomas Aquinas and other Christian Scholastic thinkers. With virtually no income, he lived on the charity of friends and strangers. In 1942, at the age of forty-four, he suffered another acute mental crisis and was placed in an asylum, where he remained until his death in 1970.

Fijman's reputation as a poet was largely built on his first volume, *Molino rojo* [Red mill], published in 1926. The technique of this book may be loosely termed avant-garde, and shows definite affinities with the French surrealist aesthetics.[7] (It is interesting to note that Breton's first *Surrealist Manifesto* went into circulation in 1924, only two years prior to the publication of *Molino rojo*.) His other volumes of published poetry followed soon after: *Hecho de estampas* [Made of images], written in 1929 while Fijman was living in Paris, was published in Buenos Aires in 1930; *Estrella de la mañana* [Morning star], his third and last collection of poems, was published in 1931.

Fijman is often referred to simply and conclusively as "the author of *Molino rojo*"; almost without exception, critics gravitate toward the rhetorical force of this first volume.[8] We may ask why the reputation of a poet who lived and continued writing until the age of seventy-two rests on his first book, published when he was twenty-eight years old? In the first place, it is important to note that while Fijman continued to write, he appears to have lost all interest in compiling or disseminating his work after the publication of *Estrella de la mañana*. Vicente Zito Lema and others attest to the fact that, during his years in the psychiatric hospital, he would write poems on scraps of paper and give them away to visitors. This apparent lack of concern for publishing is no doubt tied to his material situation: during the last four decades of his life, Fijman lived a marginal existence, lacking the financial or social resources necessary to promote himself as a poet.

A second important consideration is the fact of Fijman's conversion to Catholicism, soon after the publication of *Molino rojo*, certainly affected his reception in Buenos Aires literary circles. An examination of the three texts leads to the clear conclusion that a Christian mystic discourse characterizes to some degree *Hecho de estampas* and, in an even more pronounced fashion, *Estrella de la mañana*. This discourse, while it may have attracted a certain readership not previously drawn to Fijman's work, excluded him to some extent from the larger readership that had appreciated his previous eclectic and avant-garde style. Comparing the three volumes, Lindstrom observes that "*Molino rojo* . . . stands out among his collections by the subordination of all religious elements to the generation of secular meanings," particularly those meanings related to alienation and madness ("Fijman" 92). Ruth Fernández claims—and in this I concur—that the poet of *Molino rojo* and that of the other two volumes are complementary, not contradictory, facets of the same authorial personality. Nevertheless, the rhetorical distance between *Molino* and *Estrella* is vast. In my reading of Fijman, it is a certain complexity and sense of enigma, later partially suppressed by the Christian mystic vision and its often conventional diction, that lends *Molino rojo* a greater originality, plasticity, and rhetorical force.

What place does Fijman hold, overall, in the world of Argentine letters? In short, he has been both the object of great admiration and, in the words of Raúl Gustavo Aguirre, "el gran olvidado" [the great forgotten one] (429). In an article whose title bears this epithet, Aguirre summarizes the situation of Fijman's literary reception: "Tras un placer morboso por las anécdotas 'delirantes' que de Jacobo Fijman todos conocemos, se oculta el desconocimiento casi absoluto de una obra que, por mérito propio, debe figurar junto a las más altas de la poesía argentina y latinoamericana" [Hidden behind a morbid pleasure in the "crazy" anecdotes that we all know about Jacobo Fijman, there lies an almost total ignorance of a work that should figure, on its own merits, among the best of Argentine and Latin American poetry] (qtd. in Calmels 195). Masiello characterizes him as "a somewhat pitiful and lonely figure in Argentine letters, whose conflict with others is consistently defined by his quest of an irrefutable authority of knowledge"; she goes on to observe: "He thus appears among the avant-garde writers as a singularly marginalized being, estranged from the joyous pursuits of adventure that defined Argentine cultural life in the 1920s" ("Ex-Centric Odyssey" 34). Early in his life, as we have seen, Fijman enjoyed the company of many well-known literary figures of his day, both in Argentina and in Europe. But his career as a published poet is like a flare that rises into the night sky and quickly fades away. For an entire decade, between 1932 and 1942, no one seemed to have known of his existence. Then, for three decades more, Fijman lived out his life in the almost unimaginable silence of a state psychiatric hospital. In 1968, two years prior to his actual death, the Buenos Aires literary journal *Revista Capítulo* announced that he had passed away (Zito Lema, "Pensamiento" 91).

This fall into obscurity is checked only in the last years of Fijman's life, when the younger poet Vicente Zito Lema learned of his whereabouts and began to visit him on a regular basis, urging the literary community of Buenos Aires to provide some basic financial assistance. In 1969, the Buenos Aires literary journal *Talismán* dedicated an entire number to Fijman. The publication of Zito Lema's book *El pensamiento de Jacobo Fijman, o El viaje hacia la otra realidad* [The thought of Jacobo Fijman, or Journey toward the other reality] in 1970, the year of Fijman's death, marked the beginning of a slow process of renewed awareness of his life and work. The first complete edition of Fijman's poetry saw the light in 1983.[9] In the past decade, two book-length studies have appeared in Buenos Aires: Bajarlía's *Fijman: Poeta entre dos vidas* [Fijman: Poet between two lives] (1992) and Daniel Calmels's *El Cristo rojo: Cuerpo y escritura en la obra de Jacobo Fijman* [The red Christ: Body and writing in the work of Jacobo Fijman] (1996). Finally, in 1998, Fijman's stories were collected and published under the title *San Julián el Pobre* [Saint Julian the Poor], and the poems were reedited in a two-volume edition called *Jacobo Fijman: Obra poética*.

Fijman's work has merited superlative terms of praise from respected contemporaries such as Manuel Gálvez, Aldo Pellegrini, Francisco Luis Bernárdez, and Enrique Molina.[10] And yet the renewed interest in his work in the last two decades would indicate that Fijman has been held in higher esteem by subsequent generations of readers than he was by his own. It is evident, however, that in spite of recent publications, there is still a general dearth of solid critical work on Fijman's poetry. Fijman's life story is a compelling one, and he was, by all accounts, a man of tremendous charisma. Understandably perhaps, readers and critics tend to gravitate toward the emotive aspects of his life when discussing the work: terms such as *locura, manicomio, soledad,* and *silencio* [madness, insane asylum, solitude, silence] seem to hover over most discussions, hindering a broad appreciation of his literary contributions. It is my intent, in the present chapter, to examine Fijman's early poetic work as objectively as possible in light of the esoteric traditions that we have examined thus far, particularly with regard to the problematic of madness/mental illness as outlined by Foucault. The question of the vatic or prophetic voice will take on particular significance in Fijman's poetry. The issue of madness, as I see it, is not one to be avoided in a discussion of this poetry; rather, it is to be approached from two angles, both of which forbear any biographical argument about Fijman's own mental states. First, madness—*demencia* or *locura*—is a thematic concern of several of the most powerful poems of *Molino rojo*. Second, as was argued in the case of Pizarnik, madness may be examined as a type of discourse the poet chooses to adopt.

A nucleus of poems in *Molino rojo*—"Canto del cisne" [Swan's song], "Feria" [Fair], "Subcristal" [Under glass], "El 'Otro'" [The "other"], "Vísperas de angustia" [Evensong of anguish], and "Cena" [Supper]—take as their major concern the situation of being a mental patient. The perspectives of these poems are varied and complex: some reflect a speaker who recognizes and agonizes over his own mental illness; some reflect the experience of living as a more or less lucid being in the environment of the asylum; some stand on the threshold of the religious mystical experience that will come to characterize all the poems of *Estrella de la mañana*. As Carlos Riccardo points out in his preface to the 1983 *Obra poética*, the self that is projected onto these poems is multiple: "Fijman el niño, el hombre, el poeta; Fijman el loco, el vidente, el santo" [Fijman the child, the man, the poet; Fijman the madman, the seer, the saint] (9). What emerges from the collection of poems as a whole, however, is an overwhelming sense of alienation. The speaker is not a coherent, unified subject in control of his own destiny. He is, simultaneously, the rational observer of the insane world around him and the *other*, the patient seated next to the "tree of good and evil" in the patio of the asylum who is the object of ridicule.[11]

Fijman's most often quoted lines of poetry are the epigrammatic first verses of *Molino rojo*'s initial poem: "Demencia: / el camino más alto y más desierto" [Dementia: / the highest and most deserted road]. *Dementia*, meaning literally "out of the mind," stands at the threshold of the book. The title of this poem, "Canto del cisne," identifies it as a death-song, a final creative act. Such a title takes on a kind of poignant irony when we consider that it was, more accurately, the first creative act of a poet who was to live many decades after its publication in relative silence and anonymity. I cite the poem here in its entirety:

Demencia:
el camino más alto y más desierto.

Oficios de las máscaras absurdas; pero tan humanas.
Roncan los extravíos;
tosen las muecas
y descargan sus golpes
afónicas lamentaciones.

Semblantes inflamados;
dilatación vidriosa de los ojos
en el camino más alto y más desierto.

Se erizan los cabellos de espanto.
La mucha luz alaba su inocencia.

El patio del hospicio es como un banco
a lo largo del muro.

Cuerdas de los silencios más eternos.

Me hago la señal de la cruz a pesar de ser judío.

¿A quién llamar?
¿A quién llamar desde el camino
tan alto y tan desierto?

Se acerca Dios en pilchas de loquero,
y ahorca mi gañote
con sus enormes manos sarmentosas;
y mi canto se enrosca en el desierto.

¡Piedad!

(*Obra* 33–34)

[Dementia:
the highest and most deserted road.

Occupations of absurd masks, yet so human.
Deviations snore;
grimaces cough
and voiceless lamentations
deal violent blows.

Inflamed faces,
glassy dilation of the eyes
on the highest, most deserted road.

Terror makes the hair stand on end.

Abundant light praises their innocence.

The asylum courtyard is like a bench
that runs the length of the wall.

Chords of the most eternal silences.

I make the sign of the cross though I am a Jew.

Who will hear me?
Who will hear if I call from the highest
and most deserted road?

Here comes God dressed like a ward attendant
to wring my gullet
with his huge and sinewy hands.
My song coils up in the desert.

Have mercy!]

The poem that opens *Molino rojo* situates its speaker within the company of madmen, and the very personal anguish it represents is also a shared anguish. Here we have realistic details from the day-room of a mental ward: red, swollen faces; glassy, dilated eyes; snores and coughs; and "los silencios más eternos." All of this constitutes the trade or occupation ("oficio") of the insane, a "craft of masks" that are seen as absurd and at the same time very human. The physical space of the hospital is represented in the curiously flat line "El patio del hospicio es como un banco / a lo largo del muro." This verse takes on significance only when it as recognized as marking the liminal space that characterizes the social position of the mentally ill. The patients, having no true occupation, spend their time sitting on the bench that runs the length of a wall that is both literal and metaphorical.

One of the dangers of presenting mental illness in its social parameters is the risk of sentimentalizing, an approach that might win the reader's pity at the expense of literary quality. Fijman avoids sentimentalizing in most instances by using a number of distancing techniques. The first of these is a simple externalization of the scene of suffering: although this poem is ultimately about the poet/speaker and his own experience, the reader's gaze is also directed outward toward the other patients. The "camino más alto y más desierto," which appears to allude to the totalizing subjectivity of suffering, is in fact a shared road. This is indicated in the third stanza by the placement of the phrase immediately after the most direct references to the other patients (such as "semblantes inflamados").

The second distancing technique used by Fijman is a sort of dehumanizing metonymy. The speaker's hospital companions are not represented as full human beings but as fragments, from body parts ("ojos," "cabellos") to abstractions such as "extravíos." The speaking voice verges on the sentimental when he tells us that the patients' faces are "tan humanas," but the poem tells us that in fact it is not the faces but the masks that appear as human. This technique is repeated several times in the second stanza: snores emanate not from men but from *extravíos*, grimaces cough, and lamentations deal blows.

If humans are dehumanized in this poem, God is likewise undeified: "Se acerca Dios en pilchas de loquero, / y ahorca mi gañote." By using the term *gañote* [gullet], with its animal associations, the speaker places himself in the same dehumanized category as his companions. But the striking image of this line is that of God in the garb of an asylum attendant, strangling the patient with huge, gnarled hands. In keeping with the metonymical approach of earlier images, it is not the whole human who is the object of this action, but only his song, which "coils up" in the desert. To reiterate an earlier point, it is ironic that this withering away of song stands, in fact, at the very beginning of Fijman's career as a published poet. More than a statement of his situation at the time of writing, it portends his eventual (and chronologically early) silencing.

Finally, I would argue that this poem desentimentalizes its subject matter by locating itself rhetorically within a respected literary/cultural tradition. I refer to the Hebrew scriptures, in particular the Book of Job and the Psalms. The parallel with Job (which rises to the surface with the word *lamentations*) manifests itself generally in the figure of the suffering speaker who seems singled out by God to undergo a series of nearly unbearable trials. The psalmic "¿A quién llamar? / ¿A quién llamar desde el camino / tan alto y tan desierto?" functions as a kind of litany in the poem and adds a quality of lyric beauty to the desolate complaints of the speaker.

There is undoubtedly a kind of blasphemy inherent in the first poem's characterization of God as a murderous "loquero." Another key poem, "Subcristal," moves closer to an articulation of that blasphemy:

Zarpas monótonas
amarillentas de las horas
de Otoño,
en las cifras muy lentas de mi hastío.

Tonalidades;
respuestas y llamadas de motivos
en una discordancia de apariencias.
Brilla el cristal de mi locura.
Efervencencias bruscas;
ojos endemoniados de un molino
junto al enorme zueco
de una carreta que relincha.
Cascan mis dientes piedras de blasfemia.

(*Obra* 55)

[Monotonous yellow
paws: the hours
of autumn
in the slow cipher of my tedium.

Musical tones,
responses and calls of motifs

in a discordance of appearances.
The crystal of my madness shines.
A sudden effervescence:
The possessed eyes of a mill
next to the huge wooden shoe
of a wagon that neighs.

I grind stones of blasphemy between my teeth.]

Although this poem is not situated as obviously within the physical space of the hospital as was the previous poem, several terms—"discordancia de apariencias," "locura," "ojos endemoniados"—suggest that mental illness is a major concern here as well. As in numerous other poems in this collection, images of blankness, monotony, and boredom predominate. The poem seems to suggest that *hastío,* akin to the well-known ennui of the fin de siècle poets, is the only subjective response possible in an autumnal atmosphere devoid of color or movement.

The second stanza focuses on the internal perceptions of the speaker, as if his mind's processes were the scene under the glass—"subcristal"—that he and the reader were observing simultaneously. The stanza, composed of two extended noun phrases that hinge on the single verb *brilla,* functions principally as a list of perceptions. These perceived phenomena range from the musical or artistic ("tonalidades") to the auditory ("respuestas y llamadas") to the visual/tactile ("efervencias bruscas"). These phenomena, which could be grounded in an empirical reality, dissolve into hallucinatory or oneiric images: the possessed eyes of a mill next to the huge wooden shoe of a neighing wagon. The entire stanza is, in fact, a "mill of images,"[12] a textualizing of what the speaker perceives as "una discordancia de apariencias." In the center stands the phrase "Brilla el cristal de mi locura." The phrase is sharply ironic, since the image of clarity suggested by "cristal" typically represents reason and not madness. The irony, however, may operate as a kind of rebellious vindication of unreason. This poem presents an alternative view of mental imbalance, asking the reader to consider the possibility that the true "light of wisdom" may belong to the one who experiences the world as irrational.

"Subcristal" concludes with a haunting image of mute rebellion against God: "Cascan mis dientes piedras de blasfemia." The blasphemous characterization of God as a violent psychiatric attendant in "Canto del cisne" has been expanded here to represent any authority figure. The image of the teeth crunching stones gives the strong impression of fury divested of power, of anger imploding. In her analysis of *Molino rojo*, Masiello touches on this dynamic when she observes that "este sujeto desprecia primero lo que se considera como autoridad, y luego resiste a la posibilidad del silencio" [this individual first scorns what is considered authority, and then resists the possibility of silence] (*Lenguaje* 136). An interesting contrast arises in this context with the first-person narrator of "Dos días" [Two days], Fijman's largely autobiographical account of the days leading up to his first admittance to a mental hospital. In numerous instances the story's narrator defends his state of mind and his "ex-centric" behavior, insisting on his own authority within a sacred realm: "Soy el Cristo Rojo" [I am the Red Christ] (*San Julián el Pobre* 26). He refuses to recognize his own father, emblem of patriarchal authority, and begins to call another man "mi verdadero padre" [my real father] (32). When he arrives at the hospital, a policeman announces "'Aquí traemos a un individuo que dice ser el Cristo Rojo y que padece del mal de la anarquía'" [We've got a guy here who says he's the Red Christ, and who's suffering from the illness of anarchy] (38). For the speaker of the poems of *Molino rojo*, however, these rebellious and anarchical tendencies have been turned inward. If the hospital guard is equivalent to God, and one cannot rage against God, then the rage of the patient is reflected back upon himself (or even upon his fellow patients). This is the story told by many of the poems in this collection.

"Feria" is the poem that best captures the tone of impotent defiance. Although Naomi Lindstrom sees this poem as the "angered depiction of an open-air festival" ("Fijman" 94), as the title might suggest, I read it as yet another "asylum poem." I make this argument in part because "Feria" belongs to an informal grouping of poems whose numerous allusions to mental illness are more or less direct. These poems are strategically placed near the middle of *Molino rojo*, constituting the core of a book whose first word is "Demencia." The text of "Feria" reads as follows:

Organillos de misa; hacinamientos;
sacos de gritos de la mañana.

En la lentitud confusa
sorda algaraza de las obsesiones.

¡Las máscaras estúpidas
de los atormentados!

Rasguños en el quicio de la puerta
por la luz más intensa.

Bosque de soledades.

¡Ésta es la pausa
más nueva de mi vida!

Mantas de fuego
sobre los agrios soplos
de mi locura.
Feria maligna de rostros tostados;
un estanque de tiempos.

¡Máscaras en la luz más intensa y más sorda!
Agrios soplos de la locura.

(*Obra* 57)

[Hand organs for Mass; things in heaps;
bags full of cries in the morning.

A mute uproar of obsessions
in jumbled sluggishness.

The stupid masks of the tormented!

Scratches on the door jamb
by the most intense light.

Forest of solitudes.
This is the newest pause
of my life!
Blankets of fire
over the sour gusts
of my madness.
Malignant fair of sunburned faces;
stagnant pond of time.

Masks in the most intense and most muted light!
Sour gusts of madness.]

If Fijman is not referring here to a literal festival scene, he is making metaphorical use of the images typically associated with such a scene in order to depict the chaos surrounding him in the mental ward (as well as his own internal chaos). Even more than the previous poem, "Feria" is constructed as a "mill of images." There is one verb in the entire poem, the predicative *es* [is]. It is located approximately at the center of the poem, in a phrase that pauses the flow of images in order to speak of an existential pause: "¡Ésta es la pausa / más nueva de mi vida!" It is hard not to see this pause as an allusion to the situation of psychiatric confinement, which is perceived as a "bosque de soledades."

The enumeration of images that precedes and follows this key statement, creating the very piling-up or stacking effect suggested by word *hacinamientos,* is structured almost exclusively as a series of prepositional phrases beginning with *de:* "de gritos de la mañana," "de las obsesiones," and so forth. There are a total of thirteen such phrases in this short poem. The effect is indeed one of *obsession,* a word whose original meaning refers to the state of being besieged, particularly by evil spirits. This is certainly the sense of the second couplet ("En lentitud confusa / sorda algaraza de las obsesiones"), in which the speaker seems overcome by the confused tumult of his own thoughts. The quality of slowness (which would not be characteristic of the tumult of a festival crowd) recalls the first stanza of "Subcristal," with the yellow monotony of the hours and the "cifras muy lentas de mi hastío." It also points ahead to the phrase "estanque de tiempos," in which time, fragmented into discrete "tiempos," ceases to flow and becomes a stagnant pool.

The tone of impotent defiance that characterizes the description of this odd carnival inheres in the general sense of the speaker's disgust with what he sees ("Feria maligna de rostros tostados"), and particularly in the judgmental diction of the important third couplet: "¡Las máscaras estúpidas / de los atormentados!" We recall that in "Canto del cisne" the other patients were seen as wearing "máscaras absurdas" (33). The speaker of that poem reminded the reader that these masks were also "so human," but in this case the speaker, less sympathetic, sees the masks as stupid and those who wear them as tormented souls. Visually, the scene approaches Bosch's painting *Ship of Fools,* with its rudderless vessel, its masklike faces, and its allusions to moral depravity.[13]

The reference to masks is repeated in the final stanza of the poem: "¡Máscaras en la luz más intensa y más sorda!" Extremely bright light is an image that surfaces in several poems of this collection, and its meanings can vary. Earlier in this same poem, the intense light is seen as coming through a door marked with scratches. A metaphysical or spiritual reading of this image is certainly possible: the glimpsed light is sacred, and represents release from captivity or the passage into "the other side." Yet the masks of the final stanza of "Feria" are simply located *within* a light that is intense but, more significantly, mute. The spiritual function of the light gives way here to a profane one, perhaps alluding to the perpetual artificial light of the hospital, a light that is mute and that serves to silence those who live within it. The poem's final line, "Agrios soplos de la locura," reiterates imagistically the bitterness felt by the speaker toward the "carnival" of the mentally ill in which he finds himself.

In two other poems from this same subsection of *Molino rojo*, the speaker's gaze is turned away from his surroundings and focused intensely inward. In my reading of them, "El 'Otro'" and "Vísperas de angustia" are the poems in which the speaker judges most harshly his own mental and emotional states. "El 'Otro'" relies almost entirely on a technique whereby these states are personified, within a dialectic of sleeping and waking:

Tarde de invierno.
Se desperezan mis angustias
como los gatos;
se despiertan, se acuestan;
abren sus ojos turbios
y grises;
abren sus dedos finos
de humedad y silencios detallados.

Bien dormía mi ser como los niños,
y encendieron sus velas los absurdos!

Ahora el Otro está despierto;
se pasea a lo largo de mi gris corredor,
y suspira en mis agujeros,
y toca en mis paredes viejas
un sucio desaliento frío.

¡La esperanza juega a las cartas
con los absurdos!
Terminan la partida
tirándose pantuflas.

Es muy larga la noche del corazón. (*Obra* 56)

[Winter afternoon.
My anxieties stretch and yawn
like cats;

they awaken, lie down again,
open their murky gray eyes;
they spread their delicate fingers
finely etched in dampness and silences.
My spirit was sleeping deeply like a child
when the absurd ones lit their candles.

Now the Other has awakened;
he wanders down my gray hallway,
sighs into my holes
and touches a dirty and cold dejection
on my old walls.

Hope is playing cards
with the absurd ones!
The game ends with all of them
throwing slippers.

How long is the night of the heart.]

The first stanza rather unremarkably compares the speaker's "angustias" to cats that sleep, awaken, stretch, and so forth. In the second stanza more striking figure is introduced, that of the "absurdities" who light their candles and, in so doing, wake the self ("mi ser") that had been sleeping peacefully. This fragment of a scene, with its rather obvious psychological implications, also suggests a real occurrence within the psychiatric ward, where sleep is disturbed by the unpredictable, irrational actions of other patients. The fourth stanza utilizes the same technique in a more developed fashion: here, the personified absurdities are represented as playing cards with the allegorized figure of Hope. Again, a psychological interpretation is possible: the speaker's hope of release, of return to a more normalized life perhaps, is engaged in a game of chance with the irrational side of his existence. But I am struck by the more concrete implications of this image, as a reconstruction of a scene which Fijman could certainly have witnessed during his hospitalization. The card players end the game by coming to blows: not violently but pathetically, throwing slippers at each other. The visual power of this scene allows the reader to grasp on an emotive level what the speaker means by *the absurd*.

The personification of "El 'Otro'" is worked out exclusively in the poem's third stanza. The figure of the "Other" created here is the familiar doppelgänger, whose literary origins date at least to the German romantics (with the gnostic spiritual twin being an even more ancient precursor). But Fijman's *Otro* is not a fantastic projection of the ego or a Borgesian metaphysical double. This figure is more sinister and disturbing, more evocative of the terror of the disintegration of the self. In a vision of true paranoiac dimensions, the *Otro* is seen pacing the hall in front of the speaker's room, breathing or sighing into "his" holes. The speaker and the room he occupies become conflated in this image: the Other is literally at the edges of the self. This conflation is reaffirmed in the next line, in which the Other touches "mis paredes viejas." In the final line of the stanza, a curious substitution underscores the negative emotional quality of the experience. What the Other touches on the walls is "un sucio desaliento frío." The expected noun in this phrase, following the verb *suspirar*, is *aliento*: a dirty, cold breath would be a fitting image in this scenario. The term *desaliento*, however, while preserving the sense of breath, shifts the semantic focus away from life-sustaining breath: *desaliento* is discouragement, dejection, despondency.

The awakening of the irrational self, the loss of hope, the siege by the sinister Other, all lead the speaker to the simple, heavily charged final statement: "Es muy larga la noche del corazón." Like other tropes in this poem, the "long night of the heart" evokes the real situation of seemingly endless nights in a hospital bed, but works on a more abstract level as well. Read in this second sense, the phrase contains an unmistakable allusion to the well-known "dark night of the soul" of the sixteenth-century Spanish mystic poet San Juan de la Cruz. It is one of the early indications of the radical shift toward mystical vision and diction that Fijman's poetry will take in *Estrella de la mañana*.

The poem "Vísperas de angustia," whose title could refer temporally to the eve of an event, or musically to an "Evensong," offers an almost clinical perspective on the speaker's psychic states, coupled with a first-person "rhetoric of madness."

> Atmósferas de marasmo despedazan mis ademanes.
> Pasos furtivos
> en los malditos huecos de mi ser;
> desolaciones alteradas.
>
> Azar; ideas fijas.
>
> Revolotear de músicas celestes.
> ¿Vísperas de una nueva angustia?

Sospechas.
Soy de los que no vuelven, hermanos míos.

Atmósferas de marasmo
en torno del más fragante pino.

Amor, alégrame el camino.

¡Los fuegos fatuos!
¡Quebrantaré la vida por mi vida
por el imposible contacto de la eternidad!

Pasos furtivos
en el hueco de mi ser;
yo soy el prometido, el anunciado.

Revolotear de músicas celestes.

(*Obra* 58)

[Atmospheres of marasmus shatter my gestures.
Furtive steps
in the cursed hollows of my being;
agitated desolations.

Chance; fixed ideas.

Fluttering of heavenly melodies.
The eve of a new anxiety?
Suspicions.
I am of those who do not return, my brothers.

Atmospheres of marasmus
around the most fragrant pine.

Love, make joyful my road.

Fatuous fires!
I will break life for my life
for the impossible contact with eternity!

Furtive steps
in the hollows of my being;
I am the promised one, the heralded one.

Fluttering of heavenly melodies.]

Like "Subcristal" and "Feria," this poem is structured principally as a series of noun phrases without obvious connectors. The majority of these phrases are attempts to name or characterize the mental processes experienced by the speaker. The first of these phrases, "atmósferas de marasmo," bears close examination. *Marasmus* (from the Greek *marasmos*, "a wasting away") is a medical term that can refer to paralysis, atrophy, or to "a wasting of the flesh without fever or apparent disease; a condition of progressive emaciation."[14] Psychologically, it can signal a generalized apathy, and constitutes an effective metaphor for the "wasting away" of the self, without apparent physical symptoms, experienced by the chronically mentally ill. The first instance of *marasmo* in this poem connects it with the verb phrase "despedazan mis ademanes," in which the speaker perceives his gestures as being fragmented. The gesture, as an outward manifestation of the inner self, does not survive intact the assault of the disease. The second occurrence of the term is situated in the exact middle of the poem: "Atmósferas de marasmo / en torno del más fragante pino." The fragrant pine could be a metaphor for the self or the spirit. The positive, vital sense of this image is worth noting: though surrounded by a paralyzing atmosphere, the tree/spirit is left standing, so to speak, in the center of the poem.[15]

The "pasos furtivos" of the first stanza recall the marauding presence of the Other in "El Otro"; these footsteps are heard in the damned or wretched hollows of the self. On the same semantic level, as a perceived phenomenon (whether real or imaginary) is the phrase "Revolotear de músicas celestes," introduced in the third stanza and reiterated as the last line of the poem. Although a positive spiritual value could be given to this image, the verb *revolotear* undermines such a value by its connotations of instability: this is not music simply heard, but music that flutters through or swirls around the mind. The various perceived phenomena mentioned here share the quality of being outside the rational control of the speaker. He is visited by them, one could say. The poem makes explicit this conclusion in the line "Azar; ideas fijas." *Idée fixe* is another name for obsession; like the word "sospechas" in the third stanza, it marks an internal mental occurrence that is no more under the speaker's conscious control than the "revolotear de músicas celestes."

The enumeration of perceptions in this poem is broken by a simple wish-statement—"Amor, alégrame el camino"—and by the exclamatory phrases of the subsequent stanza: "¡Los fuegos fatuos! / ¡Quebrantaré la vida por mi vida / por el imposible contacto de la eternidad!" The ignis fatuus, or fatuous fire, is a light seen moving across swamps or marshes, believed to be caused by gases arising from decaying organic matter. As in the case of *marasmo*, Fijman has chosen a scientific term with strong suggestive qualities for the experience of mental illness. The implication of decaying organic matter creates a semantic link to *marasmo*, implying the wasting away of the patient's body or mind. This slow decay produces false or illusive images, that is, the products of the diseased imagination. This figure, full of complex associations, leads directly into the speaker's enigmatic statement that he will "break life" for his own life, for the "impossible contact with eternity." The verb *quebrantar* implies more than a simple splitting or fragmentation. It carries the semantic weight of violence done to something (crushing, grinding, desecrating, or defiling), and can be used to refer to broken health or a broken spirit. The phrase "quebrantar la vida por mi vida" points to an "experiencia límite," perhaps to the kind of violence that Bataille associates with hypermorality. When coupled with the notion of "contact with eternity," this experience of violence toward life is tied to the quest for the absolute, which we have seen as a premise of the esoteric traditions and of literary movements from romanticism through surrealism.

Terms such as "ideas fijas," "sospechas," and "marasmo" are generated from a self-critical perspective that employs the language of medicine and psychiatry. Two key verses, however, provide a striking counterpoint to this perspective: "Soy de los que no vuelven, hermanos míos," and "yo soy el prometido, el anunciado." Is the speaker a mental patient suffering from atrophy, obsessions, and paranoia, or is he one of the spiritual *élu*, a messianic figure destined to transcend the profane world by means of his suffering? The issue here, of course, is not the reader's evaluation of the particular human being whose voice is heard in these poems. It is, rather, a broader question of our approach to unreason as a whole and, especially, to its manifestation in works of literature.

The romantic aesthetic exalted the figure of the artist as a solitary individual, alienated from the human community he or she inhabited. In the twentieth century, the notion of alienation became a commonplace in artistic expression and in our thinking about the human condition in general. The transition from one conception of alienation to another, however, implied a significant shift. Whereas the romantic artist faced the exterior world from an essentially coherent subjective position, the modern or postmodern artist maintains a splintered subjectivity.[16] Madness, both in its premodern conception with ties to the sacred and transcendent, and in its modern conception as mental illness, can operate in literature as a metaphor par excellence for the condition of human alienation. In the poems by Fijman examined thus far, we have seen numerous instances of both the speaker's sense of profound separateness from his surroundings and his terror at the disintegration of his own psyche. The poem "Cena" portrays, more vividly than any other, the alienation experienced by the mental patient and its possible links to the act of writing poetry. The poem's title points to the central metaphor of the supper, the traditionally shared meal that is in this case consumed in isolation:

Cenas de mi soledad en hosco abatamiento;
eterna como Dios, profunda de universo.
¡He sido el más ausente: el juntador de formas!

Cenas de mi soledad . . .
El sudario más frío es uno mismo.
. . . .
Ir; pero no ir nunca;
en algodón de olvido sumir todos mis días.

Anuncios que se deslizan;
canción de gallos en la mañana azul de mi esperanza
continuación de tiempos fundamentados en dolor.

Fui un desaparecido, el más ausente:
el juntador de formas.

Amanecer desentonado . . .

(*Obra* 71)

[Suppers of my solitude in gloomy dejection;
eternal as God, deep as the universe.
I have been the most absent: the gatherer of forms!

Suppers of my solitude . . .
The coldest shroud is oneself.
. . . .
To leave, but to never go away;
to immerse all my days in the cotton of oblivion.

Signs that slip away;
cock's crow in the blue morning of my hope;
continuum of times founded in sorrow.

I was a missing person, the most absent:
the gatherer of forms.

Awakening out of tune . . .]

This poem is a tour de force in the poetics of human alienation. Like other poems of *Molino rojo*, it considers the psychological or metaphysical implications of a concrete, daily act for the isolated individual, in this case, the act of eating alone. One of the most striking metaphoric constructions of the poem—"El sudario más frío es uno mismo"—reminds us that the deadliest alienation is that of the self divided from itself. The particular situation of the chronic patient, removed from society but unable to make the final leap into death, is portrayed in the lines "Ir, pero no ir nunca; / en algodón de olvido sumir todos mis días." If we recall that the poems of this collection were written when Fijman was still a young man, many years before the beginning of his twenty-eight-year hospitalization, we sense a haunting quality of personal prophecy in these lines.

Although the speaker does not provide a clear referent for the "Anuncios que se deslizan," one strong possibility is the allusion to the annunciatory quality of his own previous existence. The prophetic certainty of "Yo soy el Cristo Rojo" is experienced as "slipping away" in this poem. This leads, in turn, to the complete disappearance of the self: "Fui un desaparecido, el más ausente." The term *desaparecido* ("missing," "late," "deceased") ties the experience of alienation directly to death. Significantly, however, this self-characterization is followed (in both occurrences in the poem) by the epithet "el juntador de formas." The phrase is ambiguous, but I submit that it refers to the function of the poet. The one who disappears loses his own form, his individual presence in the world, but he recuperates *being* through the act of "gathering forms." The poems of *Molino rojo* could stand as proof that the extreme alienation voiced by the speaker is partially mitigated by the act of gathering together, in the coherent form of poems, the otherwise fragmented images of his existence.

Alluding to Novalis's aphorism predicting the future convergence of the poet and the priest, the critic Victor Redondo arrives at the following conclusion regarding Fijman's poetry:

El futuro demostró que *no sucedió* la reunificación del sacerdote con el poeta, del mago con el cantor, pero que en algunos casos sólo esa *antigua* situación sirve para explicar a ciertos poetas (hombres que por breves chispazos destructores dejan hablar al genio poético) y para darles su verdadera dimensión—es decir, que incluye también el fracaso de una obra. (15; emphasis in original)

[The future showed that the reunification of the priest with the poet, of the magician with the bard, *did not occur,* but that in some cases only that *ancient* situation serves to explain certain poets (men who in sudden, destructive sparks let their poetic genius speak), and to grant them their true dimension—that is, the one that also includes the failure of a work].

Fijman's work, in its broad dimension, is perhaps best considered in light of that "antigua situación" which I have loosely defined as the esoteric tradition, in which the poet's voice is analogous to that of the priest or the magician. That ancient configuration, as Redondo points out, allows us to move beyond the necessary but relatively narrow conceptualization of rhetorical strategies, and to consider the poet's work in its entirety, up to and including its very failure. It seems to me that Fijman's work, though it crosses through the territories of mysticism and madness is, like that of Hölderlin or Artaud, "forever irreducible to those alienations that can be cured" (Foucault 278). I have attempted to show in this chapter that Fijman's earliest work presents the reader with a double perspective on the general problematic of reason and unreason. The prophetic voice, with its ties to the tradition of the *vates,* is undermined by a more modern, exteriorized, and critical "voice of reason." The messianic "Cristo Rojo," seen from this critical perspective, becomes a "cristo amarillo" who speaks with a "wounded" voice. Stated in other terms, poetic madness in Fijman's early work is represented alternately as sacred inspiration and as modern neurosis.

Fijman's slender second volume, *Hecho de estampas,* is constructed around the poet's attempt to come to terms with mortality. From this point forward, the poetic voice ceases to represent itself as wounded or alienated, and shifts into a Christian visionary idiom that will characterize entirely the poems of *Estrella de la mañana.* I would argue that this move from heterodoxy to orthodoxy, or from self-alienation to integration, in fact resulted in a certain compromising of rhetorical force. In terms of published work, it also resulted in a long-term silence. It is as if Fijman, uncomfortable with the multiply transgressive position of poet, Jew, and indigent in the conservative and largely Catholic social milieu of Buenos Aires in the late 1920s, chose a transcendent religious path that provided him with a sense of internal stability as well as a rationale for his continued displacement to the margins of that society. The following chapter will examine the text that allows us to hear Fijman's voice four decades after the publication of his last book of poems, a voice in which the heterodox strain was, in fact, never silenced.

6

The Dreams of Drowned Men

Jacobo Fijman and Vicente Zito Lema

> To speak about madness is to speak about the difference between languages: to import into one language the strangeness of another; to unsettle the decisions language has prescribed to us so that, somewhere between languages, will emerge the freedom to speak.
>
> —Shoshana Felman, *Writing and Madnesss*

Jacobo Fijman's poetic persona, his eccentric, exalted, and even disturbing voice, gained more widespread recognition in Buenos Aires with the publication in 1970 of *El pensamiento de Jacobo Fijman, o El viaje hacia la otra realidad* [The thought of Jacobo Fijman, or Journey toward the other reality]. This book, written by the contemporary Argentine poet Vicente Zito Lema (b. 1939), is a hybrid text that defies simple classification. It consists of two principle segments. The first, "Los fuegos mentales" [Fires of the mind] is a transcription of a Fijman monologue; the second, "Viaje hacia la otra realidad" [Journey toward the other reality] is an extensive text in which several interviews with Fijman, all conducted by Zito Lema, are merged into one. These two juxtaposed texts are framed by Zito Lema's prologue (itself a hybrid text, a combination of straightforward, journalistic presentation and highly poeticized prose) and a final brief biographical section.

Zito Lema's book deserves a detailed analysis within the context of the present study for two reasons. First, and most simply, Zito Lema gives us Fijman as no other writer has done. This book presents readers interested in Fijman's poetry with a view of the poet—albeit in his last years, and several decades after the publication of his own works—as a literary figure of considerable merit. In the ironic ways of the literary world, we could say that Fijman as a poet came alive only as he approached death, precisely because in that latter moment there was a critical apparatus in place to comprehend him. Second, Zito Lema's unusual book is in itself a manifestation of what I have called the orphic voice in Argentine poetry, with a particularly contemporary flavor. As Lindstrom observes, this text is Fijman's "Delphic self-account" ("Fijman" 90). The book as a whole situates both poets within the tradition of poetry as revelation that I have examined throughout the course of this study; it is, as the title suggests, a journey into another reality.

The hybrid character of the book, like certain of Pizarnik's later works, bears witness to a postmodern fragmentation of the literary text. *El pensamiento de Jacobo Fijman* freely crosses boundaries between types of discourse (monologue/dialogue/interview/oral verse) and literary genre (prose/poetry/essay/autobiography). It deconstructs any notion of monolithic authorial subjectivity with its blending of voices. In particular, it calls into question the basic assumption that the interviewer is to be taken as a source of rational and structured discourse. This is perhaps the most noteworthy characteristic of "Viaje hacia la otra realidad," the interview section of the book. Zito Lema's questions, as I will show, seem to operate out of a madness of their own. All of this leads me to conclude that *El pensamiento de Jacobo Fijman* suggests a way to "read" madness that is entirely unique within the corpus of Latin American literature. Shoshana Felman, in her book *Writing and Madness*, claims that what is at stake in Foucault's *Madness and Civilization* "is in fact the philosophical search for a *new status of discourse*, a discourse which would undo both exclusion and inclusion, which would obliterate the line of demarcation and the opposition between Subject and Object, Inside and Outside, Reason and Madness" (42; emphasis in original). In this chapter I offer a reading of *El pensamiento de Jacobo Fijman* that situates it within this transgressive or border-crossing discourse.

I am guided in my analysis by a series of questions that arise from the reading of this text: In what ways does *Pensamiento* reflect an esoteric worldview, and how does this affect the way in which madness is considered? What are the relative functions of reason and unreason as modes of discourse here, and how do they interact?[1] How does the reader grapple with the fluid boundaries that characterize this book? That is, what is the dynamic arising from the blending of the two voices, and how can we make sense of issues of originality and authority in this context? Finally, what is the understanding of poetry that emerges from both the monologic and the dialogic voices?

The reader does not have to look far to discover in *Pensamiento* a conscious attempt to tie Fijman's work to the line of poets we have seen thus far as forming the literary paternity of writers like Orozco and Pizarnik. In his prologue Zito Lema tells us that "Jacobo Fijman eligió por propia voluntad, con total conciencia de sus actos, la experiencia de Nerval, de Lautréamont, de Artaud. Era convocar las esencias de lo eterno, los castigos, la soledad" [Jacobo Fijman chose, of his own will, and with full consciousness of his actions, the experience of Nerval, of Lautréamont, of Artaud. This meant to call forth eternal essences, punishment, solitude] (9). Notably, this commentary focuses less on the poetic production of these writers than on their *experiencia vital*—the act of living in such a way that the writer suffers and is alienated from others in his quest for "lo eterno," or the absolute. Fijman's own formation, says Zito Lema, led him to "la búsqueda absoluta de Dios. A querer 'ver' a Dios. A sentirse Dios" [an absolute search for God. A desire to "see" God. To feel himself to be God] (11).

Significantly, Zito Lema characterizes not only Fijman's but also his own quest in terms that fall under the rubric of *lo esotérico*:

> Desde hace años, extrañas fuerzas me impulsan a frecuentar los hospicios, a pasar días y días con los llamados enfermos mentales. Presentía—y anhelaba comprobar—la existencia de otra realidad. Donde cada objeto, cada ser, cada murmullo, recobren su naturaleza inicial; donde las cosas y el hombre se integren en total armonía; donde se expandan sin límites la imaginación, el pensamiento, las soberbias de la belleza mental. Y es que nuestro mundo, nuestra realidad articulada por la razón, por el imperio de la lógica, es incompleto, falso, desintegrado.... En consecuencia, sólo sería posible el arribo a la otra realidad . . . entregándonos por completo a las exaltantes potencias de la no razón. (11)

[For years now, strange forces have driven me to visit hospitals, to spend day after day with the so-called mentally ill. I sensed—and longed to prove—the existence of another reality. Where each object, each being, each murmur, would recover its first nature; where things and man would unite in total harmony; where the imagination, thought, and the splendors of mental beauty could expand without limits. The fact is that our world, our reality as it is articulated by reason, by the rule of logic, is incomplete, false, unconnected. . . . Consequently, an approach to the other reality can only become possible by surrendering ourselves completely to the exalting potency of nonreason.]

Not surprisingly, the terms Zito Lema uses to convey his convictions regarding the existence of another, more authentic, reality coincide with certain basic surrealist premises: that rational thought is fragmentary, false, and untrustworthy; that the imagination, freed from the fetters of rational thought, can tap into a kind of originary psyche; that this more primitive psyche is both beautiful and "exalted." Zito Lema has all this in mind when he applies the term *pensamiento* to Fijman's discourse.

In a footnote to the prologue, Zito Lema outlines the structure of his book and the curious generation of its contents:

> En primer lugar, hay un texto, *Los fuegos mentales,* que he escrito en base a los pensamientos que Fijman volcara en una cinta magnetofónica, sin mayor orden, espontáneamente, completándolo luego con apuntes donde he anotado, durante largo tiempo, aquellas frases, aquellos hechos de su vida que Fijman reiteraba con mayor insistencia. Finalmente, se incluye un extenso diálogo, *Viaje hacia la otra realidad,* bajo las formas de reportaje. . . . Hubo tal identidad en la tarea realizada, incluso tanto afecto, que en muchos casos la respuesta es anterior, impulsa la pregunta; y el que pregunta responde, y así se confunden, se identifican ambos roles. (13)

> [In the first place, I have written a text called *Fires of the mind* that is based on the thoughts that Fijman recorded on tape, not following any particular order, spontaneously, completing it afterwards with notes in which I have recorded, over a long period of time, those phrases, those facts about his life that Fijman would repeat insistently. Finally, I have included an extensive dialogue, *Journey toward the other reality,* written in a journalistic mode. . . . There was such a mutual identification in the task we carried out, so much affection, that in many cases the answer precedes the question, propels the question, and he who asks responds, and so the two merge, and both roles become identical.]

I am struck by Zito Lema's candidly unorthodox approach to the presentation of his material. He explains that "Los fuegos mentales" is not a word-for-word transcription of Fijman's monologue, but rather a text that he himself has compiled based on Fijman's taped words. Furthermore, Zito Lema has "completed" this text by the interpolation of material gathered in the form of notes taken over an unspecified period of time. In a similar vein, he clarifies that "Viaje hacia la otra realidad" is not an interview per se, but rather a creative piece presented "bajo las formas de reportaje." It seems to me that we cannot question Zito Lema's sincerity in this project. His intention is far from that of falsifying or twisting Fijman's meaning in any way; in fact, his purpose is to present "una aproximación al pensamiento exteriorizado de J.F." [an approximation to the exteriorized thought of J.F.], acknowledging that anything closer than an approximation to another's thoughts is frankly impossible (13). In short, what is at stake here is nothing so simple as the "accuracy" or the "authenticity" of the text. To ask "Did Fijman really say these things?" is to miss the point. Zito Lema presents himself not as a journalist but as a poet employing, in a rather loose and imaginative fashion, certain journalistic techniques. Perhaps his most significant statements in the prologue are those regarding the mutual understanding and affection between the interviewer and interviewee, a subjective interaction that leads to an admitted confusion of roles and, thus, to a degree of "identidad en la tarea realizada" (13). He is very clear on this point: the text that emerges is a product of the blending of voices.

This sort of approach, though unorthodox, is not unusual within the parameters of the surrealist aesthetic, which questioned the reality of individual ego boundaries and affirmed the creative act as an exploration of the collectively shared unconscious or dream world. This was the premise behind certain literary experiments such as the "exquisite cadaver," in which a poem was produced through a kind of group automatism. The very notion of individual authorship, or of the artist as an exceptional being, was discarded by the surrealists as an outmoded remnant of bourgeois culture. The reader of *Pensamiento* is asked to accept the words on the page not as a verbatim transcription of an exchange between two men, but as a poetic rendering of that exchange in which the "yo" and the "tú" cohabit the same verbal space.

"Los fuegos mentales" is Fijman's life story, told in the first person. The task of analyzing it as a literary text, beyond the question of authorship discussed above, presents numerous difficulties. It obeys no formal rules of composition (least of all the basic chronology of autobiography), and it freely mixes rhetorical styles and levels of diction. I have identified three principle modes of expression in this piece as a whole, which I will describe and illustrate here briefly. First, there is straightforward autobiography: "Vine a la Argentina cuando tenía seis años. Nací en Urif, Besarabia" [I came to Argentina when I was six. I was born in Urif, Bessarabia] (23). It is worth noting that even in this supposedly factual account a discrepancy occurs between Fijman's chronology and that of official records, which indicate that the family arrived when the boy was four years old.

Second, Fijman uses anecdotal fragments as a basis for self-characterization. I cite a fairly lengthy example:

> Años después me golpearon a varazos, me estiraron en el suelo, desnudo, y me castigaron con una vara, en las manos, en las rodillas, en la cabeza. Se ve que estaban confabulados. Habían decidido mi destrucción. Por envidia. Asombro. Es incomprensible la reacción ante la Luz. . . . Y es que me veían siempre extasiado. Ajeno. (33)

> [Years later they beat me with sticks, they stretched me out on the floor, naked, and they punished me with a stick, on my hands, on my knees, on my head. Obviously there was a conspiracy. They had decided to destroy me. Because of envy. Amazement. Our reaction to the Light is incomprehensible. . . . It's that they always saw me in a rapture. Outside myself.]

This passage reveals a great deal about Fijman's troubled relationships with figures of authority; it also shows, in psychological terms, both paranoia and delusions of grandeur. Fijman identifies himself here with a spiritual light, reflecting several other passages of "Los fuegos mentales" in which he appropriates such terms as *santo, sacerdote, Sabio,* and *ministro divino* [saint, priest, Wise Man, divine minister]. On two occasions he states that he exists in a state of grace (31, 33). It is worth noting that the term *grandeur* applies only in a spiritual sense; Fijman's attitude toward worldly power is generally one of passive resignation.

Finally, Fijman provides present-tense editorial commentary on larger issues as they relate to his own life. These can be categorized principally as commentaries on religious belief and practice (particularly mystic or ascetic practices) and commentaries on mental illness and the situation of the chronically mentally ill. The latter category is fascinating to consider in light of what we have already seen of Fijman's poetic production and its relation to madness. One passage, in which Fijman describes the nocturnal activities of the other patients, serves as a somewhat disturbing gloss on the line "Es muy larga la noche del corazón" [How long is the night of the heart] from the poem "El 'Otro'":

> Por las noches, aquí las noches son interminables, burlan la vigilancia y se encuentran en los baños. Es como un descenso a los infiernos. Fuman, beben ... se masturban ... hasta aúllan. Sí; los oigo. Esa es toda mi relación con ellos. Es gente de instintos bestiales. Han llevado una vida depravada. La mayoría, desde luego, han sido pederastas. ... Todos los internos tienen problemas sexuales. Agravados con enfermedades nerviosas. A veces hasta lloran. Es para tenerles lástima. (22–23)

> [At night—the nights here are interminable—they sneak by the guards and get together in the bathrooms. It's like a descent into hell. They smoke, drink, masturbate ... they even howl. They do—I can hear them. That's the extent of my relationship with them. They're like animals. They've led depraved lives. Most of them have been pederasts. Every patient here has sexual problems. Exacerbated by nervous illnesses. Sometimes they even cry. It's enough to make you pity them.]

Fijman's lucid testimony stands in stark contrast to the "bestiality" of his fellow patients. A poignant irony arises here: in this context, Fijman is the voice of reason who separates himself from the unreasonable *others*, judging them and pitying them as he himself has been judged and pitied. In several other passages, Fijman situates himself (though ambivalently) as an outsider within the confines of psychiatric hospital:

> Vivo en un hospicio. Debo estar enfermo. Estoy, me siento enfermo. Estoy aquí porque no tengo donde ir. ... Es que soy un enfermo que podría vivir en su casa. Si la tuviera. No tengo nada. Sin embargo, no soy como los otros. Aquellos que gritan y blasfeman. ¿Adónde podría ir? ... No soy enfermo. Me han recluido. Me consideran un incapaz. Quiénes son mis jueces. ... Quiénes responderán por mí. Y sigo aquí. Rodeado, Dios, por aquellos que te niegan. Compañeros de hospicio. Mis iguales. A los que sólo Dios perdona, ama. Y que hoy aún me aterran. (27)

> [I live in an asylum. I must be sick. I am, I feel sick. I'm here because I have nowhere else to go. ... I'm a sick man who could live in his own home. If I had one. I haven't got a thing. But I'm not like the rest. Not

like the ones who shout and curse. Where could I possibly go? I'm not a sick person. They've put me away. They think I'm incompetent. Who are my judges. . . . Who will answer for me. So here I stay. Surrounded, God, by those who deny you. Fellow patients. Just like me. The ones only God forgives and loves. The ones who terrify me, to this day.]

In these two passages Fijman identifies the most troubling issues surrounding mental illness, discussed at length by Foucault in *Madness and Civilization,* that is, the distinction between the madman and the criminal, on the one hand, and between the madman and the indigent, on the other. Fijman saw himself as sane and ethical, even saintly, but always *ajeno.*

The Fijman of "Los fuegos mentales" is an unreliable narrator who invites the reader to share in his fundamental distrust of language. In one anecdote, he tells of a visit to a priest in which he confessed to having committed "sins of the tongue." "Al hablar siempre se abusa," he explains, "O se miente" [When speaking, one always commits abuses, or lies] (19). With wry humor, he goes on to relate the priest's inane response to Fijman's sense of sin: "Y él me contestó: 'Sí, pero eso no es pecar. Pecar es con otro y con otra. . . .' Yo: No hice ni con otro ni con otra. 'Bueno, pero hasta que no haga con otro y con otra no vuelva más aquí.' De lo que se deduce que el [cura] que estrujaba el pañuelo era un miserable. Y que, indiscutiblemente, es una obligación la pederastía" [And he answered me, "Yes, but that's not sinning. Sinning is with another man or a woman...." Me: I didn't do anything with another man or a woman. "Fine, but until you've done something with another man or a woman, don't come back." All of which leads me to conclude that the one who wrung his handkerchief was a wretch. And that pederasty, beyond all doubt, is a moral obligation] (19).

Masiello has observed that Fijman was a man "whose conflict with others is consistently defined by his quest for an irrefutable authority of knowledge" ("Ex-Centric Odyssey" 34). The above passage opens with Fijman's "confession" that language—his own and that of others—is false or abusive by nature, that is, not to be trusted as a source of authority (a position that will be called into question in the "Viaje" section). It becomes evident here that, in spite of his conversion to Catholicism, Fijman regarded the authority of the Church as suspect, both in terms of doctrine and of the men who represented it. Sensing his intellectual and ethical superiority over the priest, Fijman can only respond with biting sarcasm. In a later passage, he clarifies that his relationship to the established church is strictly a spiritual and ethical one: "Yo soy sacerdote. Pero no admití las órdenes de la curia.... Es que no quería seguir esa carrera para lucrar. Sino realmente para hacer una vida espiritual" [I am a priest. But I never took the vows of priesthood.... I didn't want to enter that profession in order to get rich—I really wanted to lead a spiritual life] (*Pensamiento* 23).

Fijman's eccentricity, his sui generis spirituality, his difficult relationship with any sort of established authority, are all condensed into one striking and poignant phrase: "Hice conducta de poesía" [I conducted my life as poetry] (24).[2] He goes on to explain: "Sentí de pronto que tenía que cambiar la vida. Alejarme del mundo. Y me aislé. Me fui de todos, aún de mí.... Pero seguí escribiendo y pintando. En silencio. En soledad. En los sacrificios. Era una verdadera necesidad" [There came a time when I knew I had to change my life. Distance myself from the world. So I went into seclusion. I went far away from everyone, even from myself.... But I kept writing and painting. In silence. In solitude. In sacrifices. It was an absolute necessity] (24).

Writing poetry, for Fijman, is not a profession or a pastime, but a way of life, a total ethical pursuit. Consciously or not, he refers to Rimbaud's injunction for the poet to *changer la vie* [change life], and he intuits the relationship of poetry to this change. Most significantly, perhaps, he is able to situate his state of isolation from others (silence and solitude) within a framework of personal will and necessity dictated by his sense of himself as an artist. Even his own social and psychic alienation ("Me fui de todos, aún de mí") is given a sense of larger purpose. The prophetic breadth of this conceptualization of the self-as-poet is echoed in the final lines of "Los fuegos mentales," lines which need no further commentary:

> En un antiguo texto de Nostradamus, figura, en acróstico, mi
>   nombre. Aquel día, cuando lo leí, sentí detrás mío un puñal.
> Y supe entonces de los sufrimientos que me aguardaban.
> Pero nunca he querido ser dictador. Ni matar a nadie.
> El símbolo de mi vida es la cruz.
> Pero a veces me despierto y grito *Cuervos, Cuervos*.
> Y me agarro de la punta de los pelos. (34)

> [In an ancient text by Nostradamus, my name appears in an acrostic. That day, when I read it, I felt a knife behind me.
> And I knew at that moment that suffering was in store for me.

But I have never wanted to be a dictator, or to kill anyone.
The cross is the symbol of my life.
But sometimes I awaken shouting *Crows! Crows!*
And I grab my hair hard with my hands.]

The interview section of *Pensamiento*, "Viaje hacia la otra realidad," could be characterized as a surrealist reworking of the Platonic dialogue. Clearly, Zito Lema approaches Fijman as a philosophical mentor, and the latter's responses at times are sober and thought-provoking lessons in life. At other times, however, the Socratic teacher-disciple relationship is deconstructed. This may occur, for instance, when Zito Lema's questions carry more philosophical weight than Fijman's responses, or when Fijman's responses are fascinating but ultimately unintelligible. This text also undermines the Platonic assumption that philosophical inquiry is fruitful only when directed by one who knows. Fijman is the wise older mentor, but he also suffers from delusions and maintains an idiosyncratic worldview that resists systematization. As in the case of Breton's inquisitive friendship with the mad Nadja, whom he calls "a free genius" (*Nadja* 111), wisdom is sought in this case from one whose relationship to the rational, ordered world is unstable and spontaneously creative. In a modern context, "Viaje" also functions as a kind of parody of the journalistic approach to writers and their work, exploding certain assumptions that the journalist, the writer, and the reader bring to the interview as text. As interviewer, for example, Zito Lema does not anchor the exchange in any way: there is no visible order to the questions, no follow-through from one answer to the subsequent question, no attempt to elucidate unclear responses or to draw conclusions based upon them. In fact, as I will show, Zito Lema's questions are often more self-consciously surreal, more irrational than Fijman's responses. In the following pages I will examine the curious text that results from this dialogue between poets that often reads as the chronicle of a double dream.

If "Los fuegos mentales" is presented as a direct transcription of Fijman's words in which Zito Lema's collaboration remains invisible, "Viaje hacia la otra realidad" represents the younger poet's voice as well; in fact, it is the interweaving of these two voices that gives this work its distinctive flavor. My intent here is to examine the various modes in which the participants in this dialogue exchange ideas, memories, metaphysical speculations, and, at times, a language that resists classification entirely. To read "Viaje" is to be reminded of Foucault's crucial observation that "Madness, in the classical sense, does not designate so much a specific change in the mind or in the body, as the existence, under the body's alterations, under the oddity of conduct and conversation, of a *delirious discourse*" (Foucault 99; emphasis in original).

It should be noted, initially, that certain of Zito Lema's questions follow a conventional interview pattern, in which Fijman is approached as a master writer with the potential to shed light on his own work. In the vast majority of cases, however, the questions reveal a poetic, even surrealistic, content. Zito Lema asks, for example: "¿El devenir de las estaciones, puede ser interrumpido sin prejuicio de la armonía universal?" [Can the course of the seasons be interrupted without detriment to universal harmony?] (*Pensamiento* 45). Some questions draw on a Zen tradition: "Encerrado en una habitación, con paredes totalmente negras y una vela, ¿puede un hombre llegar a comerse una mano?" [Can a man enclosed in a room with black walls, where there is a single candle, be driven to eat his own hand?] (59); others border on the purely absurd: "¿Qué papel le corresponde al arco-iris, dentro de una visión del mundo como obra de un loco desesperado?" [What is the role of the rainbow within a vision of the world as the work of a desperate madman?] (69).

Fijman appears to be acutely aware, at several points in the text, of the interview as a constructed or artificial exchange. He calls attention to the questionable nature of the questions themselves on more than one occasion, thus creating an ironic distance between himself and his interlocutor. Zito Lema's first question reads as follows: "Si los opuestos determinan lo mayor en la imagen, ¿debe considerarse al negro necesariamente un opuesto?" [If an image is largely determined by the play of opposites, should black necessarily be considered an opposite?] (37). Fijman provides a long and varied response, and then concludes with these words: "Además, aquél que así pregunta ya sabe, es poeta. Para qué difundir lo que los dos sabemos" [Anyway, whoever asks that kind of question already knows; he's a poet. Why expound upon what we both know?] (37). This is a remarkable commentary on the interview process as a whole, particularly given its placement as the initial response in the text. Fijman acknowledges Zito Lema's role in the interview as that of a poet, and expresses doubt about the purpose of this staged conversation in which the two discuss what they already know. Given the enigmatic nature of the question and its response, the allusion to shared knowledge may reflect the standard esoteric assumption that truth is meant exclusively for the initiated.

On another occasion, Fijman points to an inherent inadequacy in a complex question by Zito Lema regarding the term *culture:* "La contestación es difícil. La propia pregunta configura toda una representación parcial, pero no por ello menos válida, de la verificación del mundo" [That's difficult to answer. The question itself presupposes an entire biased conception of the substantiation of the world—though such bias makes it no less valid] (39). He then proceeds to respond to the question in an utterly lucid fashion, employing sociological terminology at one point, and making reference to the etymology of the term *culture:* "debe reconocérsele que deriva de *culto,* entendiéndolo no solamente en un sentido religioso sino fundamentalmente ético" [we should recognize that *culture* is derived from *culto*— worship, adoration—taking this not merely in a religious sense but in a profoundly ethical sense] (39). Fijman concludes solidly: "Lo real es que nuestra cultura es un concepto abstracto" [In reality, our culture is an abstract concept] (39). In this exchange, Fijman presents himself as a sober and self-possessed man of penetrating intelligence. He expresses a critical view of the question before attempting a response, thus controlling the nature of the interaction.

This self-conscious participation in the interview process assumes a more perplexing character in the following exchange:

> *Zito Lema:* Mis abuelos de niño me contaban que la lengua de los ahorcados tiene mil colores, aunque predomina el negro, y es inconmensurable. ¿Usted ha visto esa lengua?
>
> *Fijman:* Sus abuelos eran gente sabia. Ahora deben estar, con los míos, en algún convento.
> En el hospital he visto muchos ahorcados. Todos tenían lengua. . . .
> Asombra verlos colgados de los árboles . . . Tan altos. . . .
> Algunos se suicidan para evitar los interrogatorios de los médicos. Son espantosos.
> Usted me pregunta; yo le contesto. Yo le pregunto; usted me contesta. Pero, ¿qué relación tengo yo con un médico? (75–76)

> [*Zito Lema:* When I was a child, my grandparents told me that the tongue of a hanged man has a thousand colors, although black predominates, and that it is enormous. Have you seen that tongue?
>
> *Fijman:* Your grandparents were wise people. They're probably in some convent now, with my grandparents.

In the hospital I've seen many hanged men. All of them had a tongue.
. . .
It's shocking to see them hanging from the trees . . . So high . . .
Some of them commit suicide to avoid questioning by the doctors.
They're frightening.
You ask me; I answer you. I ask you; you answer me. But what do I
have to do with a doctor?]

The final lines are unexpected, but we can follow a certain thread of associations. The question about hanged men leads Fijman to recall patients in the asylum who have hanged themselves. Several, he says, have committed suicide in order to avoid questioning by the doctors. Although this seems unlikely, the crucial point here is the sense of extreme desire to elude interrogation. Having come this far in his pattern of associations, it seems inevitable that Fijman would connect the experience of these alleged suicides to his own immediate experience. Like a doctor with his patient, Zito Lema is "interrogating" Fijman. The latter recognizes, however, that the exchange in this case is two-way: his self-conscious role in the interview process makes him as much a "doctor" as Zito Lema. But if this is true, Fijman is disconcerted by the implications. "¿Qué relación tengo yo con un médico?" he asks, as if disturbed by his own complicity in the interrogation, which he associates with victimization. Answering his own question, he concludes his response with these thoughts:

Los pobres ahorcados quedan lívidos; sin sangre.
A uno lo bajaron del árbol, lo pusieron en el suelo.
Y lo toqué. . . .
Nadie entiende lo que es un sentido. (76)

[The poor hanged men end up very pale, bloodless.
They brought one down from the tree and laid him out on the ground.
And I touched him. . . .
No one understands what the senses are.]

In keeping with his apparent desire to participate self-consciously in the interview process, Fijman always attempts a response that, to one degree or another, honors the question. Rather than doubting the legitimacy of a question or refusing to answer, Fijman tends to simply deflect the question. When Zito Lema asks, "¿Para un suave, hermoso guante de piel humana, cuántos culpables se necesitan? [How many guilty men does it take to produce a smooth, lovely glove of human skin?], Fijman answers succinctly (and ironically), "Eso se estudia en la antropología" [They study that in anthropology] (61). In some instances, the response even functions as a kind of grounding for a question that is, in itself, a flight of ideas.

> *Zito Lema:* Los viajes a las regiones extrañas, los grandes descubrimientos de los navegantes, ¿estuvieron signados por algún demonio?
>
> *Fijman:* No. Eran materias estudiadas. Se guiaban por las cartas de los geógrafos florentinos. (80–81)
>
> [*Zito Lema:* Do you believe the journeys to strange regions, the great discoveries of the navigators, were the result of some pact with some devil?
>
> *Fijman:* No. They were simply subjects of study. The navigators were guided by the charts of Florentine geographers.]

In the question just cited, Zito Lema draws on a medieval view of the world; in other instances, his questions may recall a folk tradition or superstition: "En ciertas circunstancias se escuchan sus ruidos . . . sus voces. . . . ¿Quiénes viven en el fondo del río?" [In certain circumstances you can hear their noises . . . their voices. . . . Who lives at the bottom of the river?] (80). In either case, Fijman ignores the irrationality of the query; his answer is immediate and direct: "Los ahogados. Ellos viven en el fondo. Son seres castigados" [Drowned men. They live at the bottom. They are castigated beings]. The direct response, however, typically dissolves into a free association of thoughts or images triggered by the question. In this case, Fijman follows with a fantastical anecdote:

> Una noche, siendo niño, viajaba en un barco. Se me acercaron dos princesas rusas, de largos vestidos, y me preguntaron qué opinaba de ellas. Yo les dije: prostitutas.
> Y ellos me contestaron: "Sí, es cierto". . . . Y se tiraron al agua.
> Muchos años después, cuando me mataron, las volví a ver. Estaba investigando cómo es el sueño de los ahogados. Me confesaron que sufrían mucho. Que tenían los pies atados a una roca. Y se despidieron de mí diciendo: "Adiós . . . adiós, Jacobo Fijman." (80)
>
> [One night, when I was a child, I was traveling in a boat. Two Russian princesses wearing long dresses came up to me, and they asked me

what I thought of them. I told them: prostitutes. And they answered, "Yes, it's true".... And they threw themselves in the water. Many years later, when I got killed, I saw them again. I was researching the nature of the dreams of the drowned. They confessed that they suffered a great deal. That they had their feet tied to a rock. And then they took leave of me, saying "Goodbye, goodbye, Jacobo Fijman."]

Fijman's attempt to participate lucidly in the interview, or even to impose a logical structure on it, is complicated at all points in the text by a discourse that is not easily classifiable as rational or irrational. In the following question, Zito Lema hovers between a hermetic classification and a surrealist juxtaposition of unrelated items: "¿Puede hablarse de coincidencias elementales entre la puesta del sol y una partida de cartas?" [Can one speak of elemental coincidences between the sunset and a card game?]. Fijman's answer appears to take the form of a logical syllogism:

A los sacerdotes les está prohibido tocar las cartas.
La puesta del sol en el occidente simboliza la muerte.
Los sacerdotes representan la muerte de Cristo. (61)

[Priests are forbidden to touch cards.
The sun setting in the west symbolizes death.
Priests represent the death of Christ.]

The first two propositions, in and of themselves, are basically true. The relationships Fijman establishes might be schematized as follows: If priests (A) are forbidden to touch cards (B), and if the sunset (C) symbolizes death (D), then priests (A) represent death (D). Formally, there is a type of logical development here, but the actual content deconstructs any sense of meaning. Taken together, priests, cards, sunsets, and the death of Christ have no logical relationship beyond the loosely associative. The reader is free to dismiss such a passage as pure delirium, and yet the mock-syllogistic structure hints at some encoded meaning, one that only the initiated reader will grasp.

It is impossible to know whether Fijman intended the above-cited passage to be a parody of syllogistic reason. What we can affirm, however, is that the dynamic interplay between reason and unreason does operate on a conscious level in several places in this text. Not surprisingly, Fijman's critique of the rational faculty is couched in religious terms: "La razón humana no puede demostrar a Dios. La razón humana nos prohibe conocer a Dios; o aspirar entonces a convertirnos en lo que no se conoce" [Human reason cannot demonstrate the existence of God. Human reason prohibits us from knowing God, or from aspiring to become what we do not know] (47). He speaks here of the age-old desire to experience the unknown or the absolute, but the notable word in this context is "convertirnos." Fijman's dream of the absolute involves not only knowing, but becoming and being, and it is the faculty of reason that he sees as obstructing this path to transcendence. The notion of "becoming what is unknown" leads to a striking conclusion:

> A nadie se le ocurre aspirar a Dios.
> Sólo a mí.
> Yo soy Dios. Jacobo Fijman es Dios. (47)

> [It doesn't occur to anyone to aspire to become God.
> Only to me.
> I am God. Jacobo Fijman is God.]

Is this yet another version of "Soy el Cristo Rojo" and "Soy el anunciado"? It would appear to be, and as such, would be identifiable from a psychiatric point of view as delusional thought. Yet this facile interpretation calls for a caveat. As Raúl Gustavo Aguirre suggests, "Un psiquiatra honesto se acercará reverentemente—como era común entre los pueblos antiguos—a estos hombres en quienes lo Sagrado adquiere una voz" [A psychiatrist will approach reverently—as ancient peoples commonly did—those men in whom the Sacred acquires a voice] (Aguirre 434). Working backwards through the segment in which the above passage occurs, we can see Fijman struggling to shed some rational light on this apparent display of extreme irrationality. "Aspirar a Dios no configura necesariamente soberbia" [Aspiring to be God does not necessarily point to arrogance], he claims; and prior to this: "Dios hace otro Dios en la persona que quiere" [God creates another God in the person he chooses] (*Pensamiento* 46). By casting the question of identity with God in divine terms that point beyond all human will, Fijman displaces the question of his own dementia: God is the one who has chosen to make another god of him. In a similar passage he claims, "Soy amigo de Jesucristo, como lo soy de Dios, el Padre. Incluso he comido con ellos. Todo es misterio" [I am a friend of Jesus Christ, as I am of God the Father. I have even eaten with them. Everything is a mystery] (57–58). The troubling aspect of each of these declarations, from a rational point of view, is Fijman's leap from metaphor or analogy into absolute identity. When he says he is God's friend he does not seem to refer to a close spiritual relationship with God, but to a here-and-now, flesh-and-blood acquaintance. He has eaten with God. Of course, this last statement bears relationship to the communion rite, the Christian metaphor par excellence. Is Fijman simply intensifying the sense of this metaphor, or does he mean something else? His answer is simply that these things are beyond human grasp: "Todo es misterio."

The "delirious discourse" that forms an undercurrent throughout the text of "Viaje" becomes a direct thematic concern in certain exchanges worthy of examination. Leaving aside his poetic method of questioning, Zito Lema asks Fijman abruptly: "¿Por qué está internado en este sitio?" [Why were you put in this place?]. Fijman's answer is a mixture of denial, rebellion, and epigrammatic wisdom:

Según los médicos debido a que estoy enfermo. Trastornos mentales.

Yo creo, sin embargo, que la mayoría de la gente padece de trastornos mentales, incluso los propios médicos. ¿O acaso la mayoría de los que están en los almacenes y en las tiendas es gente de razón? ¡Ninguna! Y los médicos, por ejemplo, el que más o el que menos padece de psicosis. ¿Y es que alguien sabe lo que es el alma, lo que es el intelecto? (78)

[According to the doctors, because I'm sick. Mental disorders. But I believe that most people suffer from disorders of the mind, even doctors themselves. Or is it possible that most of those who work in warehouses and stores are people of reason? Not a one! And doctors, for instance, all suffer from one degree or another of psychosis. Does anyone really know, after all, what the soul is, what the intellect is?]

This response goes directly to the heart of the question What is madness? How valid are our conventional distinctions between spirit and intellect, and how do we know what to classify as disease in either? Is the common shopkeeper or the educated professional, in particular the psychiatrist, less prone to "unreason" than the indigent individual? Fijman, by posing these very questions, places himself at a critical distance from the discourse of madness.

In another passage, Zito Lema formulates a general and open-ended question regarding the nature of madness: "¿Qué es el delirio? ¿Cuál su causa? ¿Hasta dónde . . . ?" [What is insanity? What is its cause? To what degree . . . ?], to which Fijman responds:

> Hay un delirio poético. Del que padecen los poetas, los artistas.
> Delirio es como salirse del surco. Como si un arado se saliese del surco.
> Pero este delirio corresponde a lo que los Tribunales llaman "del tercer grupo."
> Ellos clasifican a los enfermos en tres categorías.
> Primer Grupo: el de la fatuidad (imbéciles, idiotas).
> Segundo Grupo: de los frenéticos.
> Tercer Grupo: de insanía.
> A mí me consideran en el tercer grupo . . .
> El delirio viene por vicios, o por manías, o por voluntades . . .
> El delirio son instantes. Puede durar toda la vida. (54–55)

> [There is such a thing as poetic madness. Poets and artists suffer from this madness.
> Delirium means going out of the groove. Like a plow leaving the furrow.
> But this delirium corresponds to what the Courts call "the third type." They classify patients in three categories:
> First Group: fatuousness, foolishness (imbeciles, idiots).
> Second Group: the frenzied, distracted ones.
> Third Group: insanity.
> They put me in the third group . . .
> Madness comes from vice, or from manias, or by choice . . .
> Delirium is momentary. But it can last a lifetime.]

When asked pointedly to speak about delirium, Fijman does so with lucidity. He provides an accurate etymology of delirium: *de-* + *lira* = "out of the furrow," recalling the agricultural metaphor that gave rise to the term. He lists three categories and three internal causes or origins of madness. Fijman's third category of madness, "insanía" or "delirio poético," parallels Plato's third category as explicated in the Phaedrus: "The third type of possession and madness is possession by the Muses. When this seizes upon a gentle and virgin soul it rouses it to inspired expression in lyric and other sorts of poetry, and glorifies countless deeds of the heroes of old for the instruction of posterity" (Plato 48). Although Fijman attributes this classification to "the Courts" and does not mention Plato, it seems evident that he has familiarized himself to some degree with classical theories of unreason. Significantly, Fijman does not evade the issue of his own mental illness. Rather, he provides an external evaluation of his condition ("A mí me consideran..."), thereby placing himself in the third category. In this way, Fijman indirectly classifies his mental own state as a "poetic delirium," encouraging his interlocutor (and the reader) to view his expression within the Platonic framework of "the noble effect of heaven-sent madness" (48).

Although the dialogue of "Viaje" embraces several themes, from sexuality to crime and punishment to urban decadence, I would argue that the relationship between poetry and madness, and the nature of artistic expression in a broader sense, are its fundamental concerns. Zito Lema formulates a straightforward question about the degree to which mental illness can influence a work of art, to which Fijman responds:

> En cuanto a mi obra, los médicos dicen que no hay en ella signos de enfermedad.
> Y yo lo creo; ya que no hay en mi poesía nada en contra de la gramática.
> En Artaud, la enfermedad influyó en contra de su obra.
> Pero él no podía alejarse de la locura.
> Porque era la locura de Satán.
> Si Artaud hubiera estado sano, estudiaría la escolástica.
> Hay que estudiar.
> El Conde de Lautréamont era un loco. Yo leía su obra y supe de su vida estando en el Uruguay. Era un hombre pésimo. Se dedicaba a los vicios. Y hacía poesía con ello. Era un monstruo. Sólo en él había locura.
> Nerval, en cambio, era bueno. Pero se ahorcó en un farol. Le gustaban las manzanas.
> Lautréamont y Artaud me angustian. Su psicología es la de los vagos. Yo estaba atraído a ser como ellos, pero me salvé con la misa y los libros santos. El sufrimiento de los viciosos no es noble. Es muy alejado al de los mártires. (82–83)

[With regard to my work, the doctors say that there are no signs of sickness in it.
And I believe that, since there is nothing in my poetry that goes against grammatical norms.
Artaud's mental illness was a negative influence on his work.
But he couldn't manage to get away from madness.

Because his madness belonged to Satan.
If Artaud had been healthy, he would have studied Scholasticism. One must study.
The Count of Lautréamont was a lunatic. I read his work and learned about his life when I was in Uruguay. He was a terrible man. He threw himself into vice. Then he made poetry with it. He was a monster. There was only madness in him.
Nerval, on the other hand, was a good man. But he hung himself from a lamppost. He liked apples.
Lautréamont and Artaud distress me. Theirs was a psychology of tramps. At one point I was tempted to be like them, but I saved myself with going to Mass and with holy books. The suffering of the depraved is not noble. It is a far cry from the suffering of martyrs.]

Fijman is certain that his work, because it adheres to grammatical norms, displays no signs of mental illness. This seems an odd commentary, given his presumed familiarity with European avant-garde literary movements that proposed a total revolt against the inherited conventions of literary language. In other words, Fijman was well aware that to write "en contra de la gramática" was a conscious, rational decision made by many of his contemporaries. If we take this commentary at face value, it seems to point to a rather limited notion of the ways in which mental imbalance might be manifested in a work of literature: Fijman recognizes this strictly as a matter of style or structure.

This superficially aesthetic focus, however, shifts when he discusses the work of Artaud, Lautréamont, and Nerval. When Fijman comments that mental illness influenced Artaud's work negatively, he seems to echo Foucault's contention that "Artaud's madness does not slip through the fissures of the work of art; his madness is precisely the *absence of the work of art*" (*Madness* 287). Fijman, however, is speaking from an ethical perspective that distances him markedly from Foucault, and, I might add, from Bataille and Pizarnik. His critique of the other writers is grounded in a kind of Manichean view of madness, which pits the "viciosos" against the "mártires." In this view, Artaud's madness belonged to Satan, and Lautréamont was a monster. Interestingly, this type of madness is discussed in William James's *The Varieties of Religious Experience* as "diabolical mysticism, a sort of religious mysticism turned upside down" (426).[3] Fijman recognizes the fascination that the work of Lautréamont and Artaud holds for many readers, but insists that his conscious choice was to steer clear of the path of depravity that these figures represented for him. His divergence from the stance taken by Bataille and Pizarnik is striking: for them, the basest of human interactions (such as pederasty or sadism) presented a valuable liberation from stifling bourgeois norms, at least inasmuch as these interactions could be compellingly represented in the literary text. For Fijman, the "literature of evil" is simply and utterly reprehensible. And yet, in spite of his ethical clarity on this matter, Fijman confesses that Lautréamont and Artaud provoke distress or anguish in him. He seems to intuit that no dismissal of these writers on moral grounds can alter the impact of their work.

Fijman's convictions regarding the fundamentally ethical nature of poetry surface in a passage that, consciously or not, produces marvelously comical effects:

> Los mendigos, en los caminos de España, recibían pan y sopa en los conventos. Y otorgando en respuesta una pleitesía.
> Dios, en cambio, me ha dado personalmente el pan.
> Pan francés. Con fiambre. Era exquisito. Sin pedir nada.
> Premiando simplemente mi bondad.
> Ello prueba la existencia de la poesia. (*Pensamiento* 46)

> [On the roads of Spain, beggars used to be given bread and soup in the convents. And they would pay some homage in return.
> God, on the other hand, has given bread to me personally.
> French bread. With cold cuts. It was delicious. I hadn't asked for a thing.
> He was simply rewarding my goodness.
> This proves the existence of poetry.]

Fijman's unique spirituality once again expresses itself in terms of a literally personal relationship with God, in this instance with concrete evidence of the miracle: French bread and cold cuts. He relates this event directly to his own ethical comportment, his *bondad,* and to his view of himself as existing in a state of grace. In contrast to the convent beggars, Fijman received his sustenance directly from God, as a reward for his goodness. From all this he infers the existence of poetry.

The understanding of poetry we see emerging could be traced to the German romantics' conviction that poetry was not merely a verbal form of artistic expression, but a way of being in the world, a conviction that the surrealists took entirely to heart. To the notion of poetry as a total ethical pursuit Fijman adds an idiosyncratic mystical element, connecting the poetic intuition to a state of grace. It is in this light that he affirms that "Mis obras prueban que no sólo soy hombre de razón, sino de razón de gracia" [My works prove that I am a man not only of reason, but of the reason of grace] (84). He intimates here that human reason is not a quality to be considered independently of spirituality; rather, reason is enhanced by divine grace. When asked "Cómo siente la poesía?" [How do you feel poetry?], Fijman responds:

> Es un estado de ánimo, antes de la reflexión.
> En cuanto a lo demás, me remito a la obra poética de Aristóteles.
> Esto es un secreto de estado.
> Yo he tenido una infancia poética.
> Desde niño me llamaban el poeta. (63)

> [It is a spiritual state, prior to reflection.
> As for the rest, I turn to the *Poetics* of Aristotle.
> This is a state secret.
> I had a poetic childhood.
> Even as a child, they called me *the poet.*]

Again, Fijman distinguishes between the purely rhetorical or aesthetic, the craft of writing that one might learn from studying Aristotle's *Poetics*, and the deeper and more primordial "estado de ánimo," a state in which poetry is associated with childhood and prerational thought. (Bataille's comments on the poetic—that is, savage and sacred—childhood of the protagonists of *Wuthering Heights* seem especially pertinent to recall here.) Fijman's distinction is interesting to consider in light of his above-cited statements regarding grammatical norms as a standard of measure for the "insanity" of a text. His commentary implies that true mental illness would result in the writer's inability to manipulate the rhetorical or linguistic surface of his work. The "delirio poético" from which he and certain other artists suffer, however, is something altogether different, something with profound ethical and spiritual implications.

Although Fijman published nothing after 1930, he continued to write poetry and to draw and paint until his death. His answers to Zito Lema's questions "¿Para qué escribe? ¿Para qué pinta?" [Why do you write? Why do you paint?] provide a final insight into his views regarding the nature of artistic creation:

Lo hago para que mis actos se ordenen a Dios.
Buscando la verdad y no la oscuridad. Y escribo para Dios y para mi perfección.
Y Dios sencillamente lo aprueba.
Y esto dicho en lengua baja. Para que todos me entiendan.
Entre mi pintura y mi poesía hay una misma mano.
Las mismas concepciones.
De niño me dijeron que sería un gran pintor.
Y entonces lo quemé todo.
Ahora lo hago para purificar mis sentidos, externos e interiores. Sólo de esa forma es válido pintar o escribir.
Y hasta que los que se dicen pintores o escritores no lo entiendan, deberían dejar esas cosas. Porque están mintiendo.
El arte tiene que volver a ser un acto de sinceridad. (77–78)

[I do it so that my acts can be ordered in the eyes of God.
Looking for truth, not darkness. And I write for God and for my own perfection.
God simply affirms my acts.
And I say this in a simple tongue, so everyone will understand me.
Between my painting and my writing there is a single hand.
The same conceptions.
As a child they told me I would be a great painter.
That's when I burned everything.
Now, I do it to purify my senses, both the external and the internal.
Only in this way is it valid to paint or to write.
And until those who call themselves painters or writers understand this, they should leave those things aside. Because they are lying.
Art must become once again an act of sincerity.]

This testimonial forces Fijman's readers to reconsider the assumption that madness was the point where his work became impossible or fell silent. What Fijman expresses here is, rather, an unequivocal disregard for any external approval of his work; that is, a conscious decision to write or paint exclusively for the purification of his own senses. His purpose for writing or painting is stated in unequivocally transcendental terms. Worldly pride in his artistic talent stood in such contradiction to Fijman's notion of a truly ethical existence that he burned his paintings as a child and, as an adult, left his poetry to enter the world on scraps of paper handed to visitors.

What conclusions can be drawn from this reading of *El pensamiento de Jacobo Fijman*? What can be said about the fluid lines that mark both the internal and external boundaries of the text? What is the relationship between Fijman's published volumes of poetry and the monologic and dialogic voices heard in this book (separated by a period of almost forty years)? In what way is this text a "journey toward another reality," as its title suggests, and what meaning could such a journey hold for Fijman's readers? Finally, what does this book tell us about the nature of poetry as Zito Lema and Fijman conceive it?

First, the hybrid structure of the book as a whole demands that the reader discard certain assumptions upon approaching its contents. Although the book was compiled by Zito Lema in an attempt to bring the reader as close as possible to the thought of Jacobo Fijman, the text that is produced bears the mark of both writers, one ultimately indistinguishable from the other. When Zito Lema speaks in his preface of the identification between himself and Fijman, the sense of a shared task so strong that the two roles merged into one (13), we sense a curious tension between the younger man's devotion to a revered older poet whose oracular voice fascinates, and the modernist dissolution of the writer-as-subject. *Pensamiento* brings us a sort of journalistic account of one man's thought, but as readers we have no way of knowing to what extent that thought has been recast by the journalist himself. As I pointed out previously, Zito Lema makes no attempt to disguise his manipulation of the materials gathered from his conversations with Fijman. From the notes taken over hundreds of hours of dialogue, Zito Lema has fashioned what appears to the reader to be a single seamless interview. Its odd juxtapositions and unexpected leaps are equally the result of Fijman's free-associative verbal techniques and Zito Lema's conscious—that is, artistic—questioning and editing strategies.

After relinquishing the certainty that Fijman's author-figure in this text is a stable and univocal presence, the reader must also discard the assumption that the interviewer is a source of rational, well-ordered, and clearly articulated statements and questions. Quite the contrary: as I have demonstrated in numerous examples, Zito Lema's voice in the dialogue that constitutes "Viaje" is whimsical, nonsequential, and sometimes virtually incomprehensible. One of the most unusual and attractive features of this text, it seems to me, is Fijman's recognition of the interview as a constructed text, and the way in which he repeatedly steers Zito Lema's questions back into rational territory—only to veer off again into a pattern of free association whose logic is purely poetic.

This said, I believe it is important to recognize the true lyric beauty achieved in many passages of both "Los fuegos mentales" and "Viaje." It is interesting, in this respect, to reconsider Fijman's trajectory as a poet in light of the verbal poetry he produces in *Pensamiento*. In Chapter 5, I argued that the shift toward a Christian mystical rhetoric characterizing *Estrella de la mañana*, Fijman's last published book of poetry, had a somewhat immobilizing effect. The reliance on a handful of adjectives and symbolic nouns, cast in highly repetitive syntactical structures, gives this poetry a kind of one-dimensionality that will disappoint the reader not fully attuned to the religious concerns of the book. Fijman's poetic voice in *Pensamiento*, however, seems to have recuperated the original force and dynamism that characterized *Molino rojo*. The religious convictions have been strengthened, if anything, in the years elapsed between *Estrella* and *Pensamiento*, but the conventional symbolism now alternates with fresh, unusual, and sometimes disturbing imagery. One could cite many instances in "Viaje" in which Fijman leaps from one type of language to another without blinking:

> La concepción de la virgen es immaculada.
> Esto es también un secreto de estado. Vía de Cristo.
> Cristo es rubio. Pero un día fue negro. Y otro verde. (68)

> [The virgin's conception is immaculate.
> This is another state secret. Christ's Way.
> Christ is light-skinned. But one day he was black, and another, green.]

In a passage such as this, the Christian devotee meets the surrealist rebel, the priest meets the madman. *Pensamiento* is a journey into another reality not only because there are repeated flashes of delusional thought, but because that thought inhabits the same space as a sort of haunting wisdom.

With Zito Lema's rendering of Fijman's voice we have come full circle, returning to the ancient principle of poetic madness. The curious interplay in *Pensamiento* between transgression and transcendence, between delusion and wisdom, is, finally, a matter of language. "The marvelous logic of the mad," says Foucault, seems to mock that of the logicians, "because at the secret heart of madness, at the core of so many errors, so many absurdities, so many words and gestures without consequence, we discover, finally, the hidden perfection of a language" (Foucault 95). It is this notion of poetic language—secret, primordial, marvelous, perfectible—that I wish to take up in my Conclusion. It is what draws Orozco, Pizarnik, and Fijman together in a common dream and in a common recognition of the impossibility of the dream.

Conclusion

A Talisman in the Darkness

> Esas sílabas rotas en la boca fueron por un instante la palabra.
> [Those broken syllables in the mouth were, for a moment, the word.]
> —O. Orozco, "Rehenes de otro mundo" [Hostages from another world]

The three poets examined in this study represent three different moments in twentieth-century Argentina's literary history. Their work has been examined from three distinct (though overlapping) perspectives: the rhetoric of the occult, the rhetoric of evil, and the rhetoric of madness. As we have seen, the patrimony represented by the esoteric line of poets, from the German romantics to the surrealists, has been interpreted in various ways by Olga Orozco, Alejandra Pizarnik, and Jacobo Fijman. What, then, is the common thread, the conviction that leads to a shared poetics?

I would argue that the focal point for these poets constitutes, above all, a theory of poetic language. Orozco, Pizarnik, and Fijman share a concern for the efficacy of the poetic word, a concern arising from the belief in poetry as revelation, and in the poet as seer or *vates*. It is as if these Argentine writers had taken upon themselves the project of completing the masterpiece that Mallarmé envisioned but never executed: "An Orphic Explanation of the Earth." Several interrelated concepts suggest themselves as soon as we take the vatic or orphic mode as the premise from which these three poets depart and to which they return. First, the world is viewed from the mythical perspective of a lost golden age, the fragmentation of a universe that formed, *in illo tempore*, a coherent whole with the divine or absolute. The human fall from grace, as the basic condition of existence, necessitates positive action whose purpose is to restore, to the highest degree possible, the primal unity. The various means employed toward this purpose can be conceptualized as moving in two directions: the transcendent, embodying Novalis's notion of "the raising of mankind above itself," and the transgressive, the crossing of boundaries into forbidden, potentially dangerous zones. By implication, the individuals who achieve true movement above or beyond ordinary consciousness possess extraordinary powers and extraordinary knowledge: they become initiates. The vision granted to these individuals often centers on the analogous nature of the universe: they see certain correspondences between microcosm and macrocosm, between human consciousness and absolute reality, which are hidden from less perceptive persons. Rimbaud articulated the role of poet as visionary in these now-famous terms: "The Poet makes himself a *seer* by a long, gigantic and rational *derangement* of *all the senses*. . . . Unspeakable torture where he needs all his faith, all his super-human strength, where he becomes among all men the great patient, the great criminal, the one accursed—and the supreme Scholar!—Because he reaches the *unknown*!" (307; emphasis in original). Orozco articulates strikingly similar notions as the basis of her own poetics:

> Los poetas siempre andamos en búsqueda de revelaciones, siempre tratamos de desenterrar misterios. Algo que puede ser la palabra perdida; buscamos lo indecible. . . . [La palabra] se evapora, y además es peligroso. A veces uno se sumerge a grandes profundidades, hasta quedar unido a la superficie por nada, por un hilo. Yo he tenido temores de no poder retornar y supongo que eso les pasará a muchísimos: quedarse enredado en esos enigmas que hay en las profundidades. Es el buceo en lo desconocido. (Qtd. in Sefamí 106)

> [We poets are always seeking revelations, we're always trying to unearth mysteries. Something that could be the lost word; we're searching for the unspeakable. . . . [The word] evaporates away, and moreover, it's dangerous. Sometimes you sink to great depths, until you're tied to the surface by nothing, by a thread. I've been afraid of not being able to come back, and I suppose that happens to many people: getting tangled up in those enigmas that lie in the depths. It's diving into the unknown.]

Thus, the literary tradition which Orozco, Pizarnik, and Fijman take as their chosen heritage identifies the poet as the supreme occult initiate. Like Orpheus, the poet travels into a territory fraught with dangers, seeing and experiencing what the surrealists will identify as "the marvelous." (Beginning with Baudelaire, that territory had become the human psyche itself.)

The poet thus acquires a powerful *gnosis,* and returns to sing an uncanny song. Poetry, in this view, may be connected to the profane world, but its purpose is to reveal the essential ties between that world and the absolute. Poetic language, as the primary vehicle for this revelation, is sacred, magical, potent in and of itself.

What are the origins of this view of the language of poetry? Medieval and Renaissance reformulations of ancient esoteric beliefs placed great emphasis on the sacred qualities of language. This was especially true of the hermetic worldview, with its central analogue of "as above, so below": human language was seen as perfectible, moving ever closer to divine language. As conceived by thinkers such as the fifteenth-century Giovanni Pico della Mirandola or the sixteenth-century Giordano Bruno, "our visible universe is but the reflected image of an invisible, and each has subtle and practically unlimited power over the other. The key to that power is words" (Thorndike 21). Harold Bloom, who bases much of his literary theory on perceived conjunctions between gnostic and cabalistic thought, points out that, in the Cabala, theories of divine emanation were also theories of language. The *sefirot,* internal qualities or attributes of the deity, were "complex figurations for God, tropes or turns of language that substitute for God" (*Kabbalah* 25). This set of beliefs thus embraced a "magical theory of language," a theory, Bloom contends, that most strong poets have shared secretly with the Cabalists (76).

The analogical conception of the universe that centered on a belief in poetry as magic, as voiced by Novalis and the romantic poets, was later reformulated by Baudelaire, Rimbaud, and Mallarmé. These writers' thoughts on language reflected a nineteenth-century revival of the works of Emanuel Swedenborg, who is generally credited with popularizing the notion of an original or absolute language, as well as the doctrine of correspondences which was to become crucial for many writers, most notably Baudelaire. Enid Starkie, examining Swedenborg's influence on Baudelaire, summarizes the beliefs of Swedenborg's followers in this way:

> Swedenborgians are convinced that material objects exist in this world only because they have their origin in the world of the spirit, and the hidden relation between things here below and in the invisible world they call *correspondences.* . . . Everything in the world is merely a symbol, and these symbols are the language of nature, a hieroglyphic language in which every material form expresses an idea, and this language existed long before the languages which human beings now speak were evolved. . . . The true thinker will be the

man who can decipher the hidden writings of nature, and interpret the mysterious book of the universe. (227–28)

This eighteenth-century doctrine was to have profound ramifications for European poetry in the nineteenth and twentieth centuries. As a whole, romantic poets came to identify themselves within the context of Swedenborg's "true thinker," who could decipher the text of the world. Rimbaud, who follows much of Baudelaire's aesthetic closely, will declare prophetically: "A language must be found. Moreover, every word being an idea, the time of a universal language will come!" (309).

Ultimately, the Swedenborgian belief in a primal or universal language became one of the organizing principles for twentieth-century surrealist poetry. The modern association between the poetic word and occult powers, explains Bays in *The Orphic Vision*, constituted a merging of the Homeric tradition, which stressed poetry's hypnotic effects, with the Platonic tradition, which associated poetry with Bacchic frenzy. Thus, whether raised to an ecstatic height or lowered to infernal depths, the poet is thought to achieve, ephemerally, an otherworldly consciousness in which language takes on a life of its own. Thus, language, in particular the language of lyric poetry, is exalted not as a means of describing the universe, but as a means of knowing it intimately, of achieving gnosis. Poetry becomes, for the surrealists and their followers, one of the least-fallible means of returning to a state of mythic origins.

Jacobo Fijman arrives, via an orphic excursion into the rhetoric of madness, at a mystical conception of poetry. His particular brand of mysticism relies on tropes of verbal language: praying, praising, singing—all magnificently condensed in the line "Mi boca grande de oración derrama vuelos" [Great with prayer, my mouth pours out flights] (*Obras* 115). Although he avoids the self-referentiality so characteristic of the work of Orozco and Pizarnik, Fijman repeatedly metaphorizes poetic language as *canto* or *voz*, and thus explores its possibilities not only for human expression, but also for communication with a sacred realm. In the earlier poems of *Molino rojo*, as we have seen, the *yo lírico* represents himself as fragmented and alienated, "herido en mi canto" [wounded in my song] (110). The voice of the later poetry, in contrast, strives toward "la oración profunda" [the deep prayer] (122). He achieves a truly oracular quality in certain poems, in which he affirms the vatic power of the poet not only to see but also to name:

Tuve profundo canto, voz de mi muerte bajo los vuelos,
voz de mi gracia sobre los vuelos.
Tuve profundo canto:
nombré los días, nombré las noches con su nombre.

(*Obra* 131)

[I had a profound song, voice of my death beneath flights,
voice of my grace over flights.
I had a profound song:
I named the days, I named the nights with their name.]

In the interview text of *El pensamiento de Jacobo Fijman*, chronologically much later than his published work, Fijman's ties to esoteric principles of language become even more patent. Following a prompt by Zito Lema regarding the relationship between poetry and knowledge, Fijman affirms: "La poesía es ciencia. Algunos la consideran categoría inferior. Y sin embargo, ella fundamenta todas las ciencias. La química sin poesía se convierte en nada" [Poetry is science. Some people consider it an inferior category, but in fact it is the foundation of every science. Chemistry without poetry becomes meaningless] (43). After exploring this notion further, Fijman concludes: "Pero el Padre, el Hijo, y el Espíritu Santo son poetas" [But the Father, the Son, and the Holy Spirit are poets] (43). Notably, his response places poetry at the origin of both sacred/arcane and profane knowledge.

In a later passage, a conjecture by Zito Lema regarding the truth value of poetic expression elicits a response from Fijman that affirms the biblical notion of the divine word as source of all creation. Zito Lema asks: "¿Hay equilibrio entre su poesía y al que le cortan la lengua por no mentir?" [Is there some balance between your poetry and the man whose tongue is cut out so he won't lie?], to which Fijman responds: "Sí. En primer lugar, por aquello de 'al principio fue el verbo . . .' Y quise dar con ello" [Yes. In the first place, due to the matter of "In the beginning was the Word . . ." And I wanted to discover it] (63). His task as a poet, he seems to say, is to discover—uncover, recover—the *logos* that marks all origins. In another passage, Zito Lema asks Fijman if it is possible to reduce all human language to ten words. Fijman's reply, characteristically enigmatic, ends with the following enumeration: *Dios, Alma, Ángel, Piedra, Planta, León, Hombre, Psiquis, Espíritu,* and *Pneuma* [God, Soul, Angel, Rock, Plant, Lion, Man, Psyche, Spirit, and Pneuma]. We recall that *pneuma*—meaning *breath* in Greek—was the term used by the gnostics to speak of the particle of deity housed within each human soul. The goal of gnostic ritual was to free the *pneuma* from its earthly confines and allow it to be reunited with the original spirit from which it emanated. Although Fijman does not make allusion to this doctrine here, it is significant that he includes *pneuma* among the "essential ten words" of human language.

Fijman's most transparent testimony to the potential of language occurs in response to the question "¿Cómo describiría la ciudad ideal?" [How would you describe the ideal city?]:

> ... La ciudad estará glorificada. Y todos los objetos serán blancos. Y su lengua será no el latín o el castellano sino la lengua de Jacobo Fijman. Los hombres se entenderán de un modo tan notable que estarán muy cerca del conocimiento de los ángeles. El idioma será enseñado por Dios mismo.... Va a ser una lengua no sólo política y filosófica sino divina.
> No habrá nadie que cometa un solo error. Tal es su perfección, y de tal modo será enseñada.
> Dios y yo enseñaremos la verdad.
> Cuando la resucité, aquella mujer me dijo: "Yo ya sé tu lengua...."
> Hay una lengua fijmaniana, pero aquí, en esta ciudad, no se habla.
> (50)

> [... The city will be glorified. All the objects will be white. And its language will not be Latin or Spanish, but the language of Jacobo Fijman. Men will understand each other in such a remarkable way that they will come very close to the knowledge of the angels. This language will be taught by God himself....
> It will be a language that is not only political and philosophical, but divine.
> No one will commit even a single error. Such will be the perfection of this language, and thus it will be taught.
> God and I will teach the truth.
> When I revived her, that woman said to me: "I have already learned your language...."
> There is a Fijmanian language, but here, in this city, it is not spoken.]

This is Saint Augustine's City of God with a particularly linguistic twist. Apart from the detail specifying the whiteness of objects, Fijman's vision of the ideal city is described entirely in terms of a Swedenborgian absolute language. The perfection of this language—and the citizens' ability to master it—will allow for flawless communication on all levels. This level of communication will lead to a knowledge that is divine or semi-divine. Fijman's vision, of course, is tinged with an irrationality that transgresses even accepted spiritual norms. If language is the structure of the utopian city, it is also, as Foucault reminds us, "the first and last structure of madness."[1]

Fijman's poetics centers on the sacred origins of language and on its perfectibility as a human institution. Orozco, perpetually grappling with the *este lado / el otro lado* dichotomy, tends more toward an exploration of the magical or otherworldly properties of language. The act of writing poetry constitutes the ideal praxis for reaching across the threshold into *l'inconnu*. We have already seen how Orozco employs the rhetoric of curse or incantation in such poems as "Cartomancia" and "Para destruir a la enemiga." It is important to reiterate that these poems work out on an explicit level the question of "word magic" which in fact underlies all of Orozco's poetic production. Even in its most neutral manifestations, the *logos* in Orozco exhibits great affective powers. As the speaker of "Rara sustancia" claims,

> Basta que una palabra me atraviese de pronto lado a lado
> ....
> para que quede impresa como una quemadura hasta el subsuelo de mi anatomía.
>
> (*Noche* 28)
>
> [A word only needs to pierce me suddenly from one side to the other
> ....
> in order for it to be imprinted like a burn down to the subsoil of my anatomy.]

Here, the word is experienced as a strong and immediate physical impression, a perception gathered not by mental faculties but by the senses. In other contexts, the word takes on a more metaphysical or spiritual quality. Immured in her own solitude and silence, the speaker of "En el bosque sonoro" [In the sonorous forest] observes the almost miraculous appearance of "estas bocas que se abren en el muro, contra toda esperanza, y que musitan siempre la palabra" [these mouths that open in a wall, against all hope, and that perpetually mutter the word] (*Obra* 150). The wall, a common symbol in Orozco's work, represents all that separates human existence from the absolute. In this poem the wall is perforated, as it were, by mouths, an image that attests to the power of human language. This poem goes on to insist, however, that the poetic word is not one of easy consolation; it is a watchword allowing the Orphic journey and return: "Palabra inaudible, palabra empecinada, palabra terrible—mi mantra del ascenso y del retorno—palabra como un ángel suspendido entre la aniquilación y la caída" [Inaudible word, stubborn word, terrible word—my mantra of ascent and return—word like an angel suspended between annihilation and the fall] (*Obra* 150–51). In what is perhaps Orozco's most uncompromising declaration of the power of poetry, the metaphor points directly to the efficacy of word magic: "mis palabras, mi único talismán en las tinieblas" [my words, my only talisman in the darkness] (*Noche* 22).

Evidence for an esoteric theory of language also abounds in the work of Alejandra Pizarnik. Like Orozco, she defines the poet's trade as one dealing in the magical, incantatory power of words: "Mi oficio (también en el sueño lo ejerzo) es conjurar y exorcizar" [My trade (which I also carry out in my dreams) is to conspire and exorcize] (*Obras* 135). The vatic function of the poet is apparent in several passages, sometimes combined with a view of poetic language as otherworldly and magical: "Los sortilegios emanan del nuevo centro de un poema a nadie dirigido. Hablo con la voz que está detrás de la voz y emito los mágicos sonidos de la endechadora" [The spells emanate from the new center of a poem addressed to no one. I speak with the voice that is behind the voice and I emit the magical sounds of the mourner](167). Pizarnik's characteristic adaptation of prophetic rhetoric involves a clear sense of language as *other*. The poem "Fragmentos para dominar el silencio" [Fragments for mastering silence], for example, begins: "Las fuerzas del lenguaje son las damas solitarias, desoladas, que cantan a través de mi voz que escucho a lo lejos" [The forces of language are solitary, desolate, ladies that sing through my voice that I listen to from a distance] (123). This is clearly a modern, alienated version of the ancient theme of possession by the oracle. Rather than giving voice to the wisdom of the gods, this speaker sees herself (from an ironic distance) as being inhabited by strange female beings whom she identifies as "the forces of language." Tremendous power is accorded to language in this vision, but it is a power negatively identified as "lonely" and "desolate." The sense of language as a disembodied force that converts the speaker—apparently against her will—into an oracle is developed further in another prose poem:

> Escucho mis voces, los coros de los muertos. Atrapada entre las rocas; empotrada en la hendidura de una roca. No soy yo la hablante: es el viento que me hace aletear para que yo crea que estos cánticos del azar que se formulan por obra del movimiento son palabras venidas de mí. (*Obras* 143)

> [I listen to my voices, the chorus of the dead. Trapped among the rocks, wedged into the crack in a rock. The speaker is not me: it is the wind that makes me flap my wings so I can believe those canticles of chance formulated through movement are words springing out of me.]

The speaker's sense of alienation from her own voice (or voices) reaches an extreme degree in this passage. Her own agency as a speaking subject is virtually nil: her trapped body becomes a kind of natural siren whose song is created by the wind among the crags.

These passages in which the speaker accords a totalizing and alienating power to the forces of language are offset, in some cases, by the expression of a desire to recuperate her sense of agency with regard to the *logos*. In true surrealist spirit, Pizarnik often affirms poetic language as a way of *being* in the world. The final lines of the prose poem "El deseo de la palabra" attest to this spirit:

> Ojalá pudiera vivir solamente en éxtasis, haciendo el cuerpo del poema con mi cuerpo, rescatando cada frase con mis días y con mis semanas, infundiéndole al poema mi soplo a medida que cada letra de cada palabra haya sido sacrificada en las ceremonias del vivir. (*Obras* 156)

> [I wish I could live only in ecstasy, making the body of the poem with my body, rescuing each phrase with my days and my weeks, infusing the poem with my breath just as each letter of each word has been sacrificed in the ceremonies of living.]

Pizarnik's use of the term *éxtasis* was considered in Chapter 4 as it related to Bataille's notion of subject-object fusion in sexuality and in death. In contrast to the alienated voice of the previously cited poems, the poet/speaker here envisions fusing her own body with the poem, literally writing with the body. The poem is thus created as the gods created human beings, breathing life into them. This creation, however, is inextricably linked to destruction: each letter is immolated in the "ceremonies of living." The conclusion of this poem points to Pizarnik's struggle to separate art from life, a matter of crucial importance to her work to which I will subsequently return.

Having established the grounding of each of these poets in the esoteric principles of language, principles which affirm the sacred origins of language, its existence as a powerful force sometimes beyond the control of the human agent, and its analogous relationship to magic and other occult arts, I must now complicate the picture. The relationship of these poets to poetic language, indeed, to the very practice of their craft, is not one of blind faith but of irony, doubt, and even negation of the *logos*. By way of conclusion to my study, I will examine the highly conflicted approach to poetic language that marks a significant commonality in the work of Fijman, Orozco, and Pizarnik.

The negation of the *logos* shapes, in many ways, the modern contours of the esoteric tradition in literature. In his essay "Los signos en rotación" [Signs in rotation] Octavio Paz identifies the fundamental problem of the twentieth-century artist as the loss of an integrating *imago mundi* (314). Lacking such an image, he argues, the modern artist attempts to organize and supply meaning to a constantly shifting set of signs. As if in direct dialogue with Paz, Orozco's speaker asks: "¿Y cómo asir el signo a la deriva /—ése y no cualquier otro—/ en que debe encarnar cada fragmento de este inmenso silencio?" [And how to grasp the sign adrift /—that one and no other—/ in which each fragment of this immense silence should be embodied?] (*Mutaciones* 92). For writers from the avant-garde on, belief in the real efficacy of language maintains an uneasy balance with an ironic and critical view of language. Thus, the poet is fundamentally at odds with his or her own medium. Rimbaud was the first to capture this modern problematic in poetry. Paz makes the following observation of Rimbaud's pivotal work: "A partir de *Une Saison en Enfer*, nuestros grandes poetas han hecho de la negación de la poesía la forma más alta de la poesía: sus poemas son crítica de la experiencia poética, crítica del lenguaje y el significado, crítica del poema mismo. La palabra poética se sustenta en la negación de la palabra" [Beginning with *Une Saison en Enfer*, our great poets have made the highest form of poetry out of the denial of poetry: their poems are a critique of the poetic experience, a critique of language and meaning, a critique of the poem itself. The poetic word is sustained by the negation of the word"] (*Signos* 311).

The problem outlined here is not, as it was for mystic poets such as San Juan de la Cruz, or even for many romantic poets, the mere inadequacy of language as the expressive vehicle for a "real" experience of unity. It is, rather, a breakdown on the very level of language-as-reality, an inability to accept, as thinkers and writers of the esoteric tradition historically have, the unmediated efficacy of verbal structures as powers in themselves. Speaking again of Rimbaud's postulations on poetry and language, Paz observes that Rimbaud's *"Il faut être absolutament modern"* is an enigmatic declaration: "Whatever may be the interpretation given to this phrase, and there are many, it is evident that here *modernity* stands in opposition to *alchemy of the word* (*Bow* 237; emphasis in original).

On Latin American soil, one variant of this philosophical and aesthetic problem surfaces in the early Neruda. The visionary mode of *Residencia en la tierra,* argues Enrico Mario Santí, can be only partial and disjointed. The poem, instead of allowing a fusion of subject with object, that is, instead of engendering "the experience of infinity," temporalizes that goal and removes it from "immediate consumption" (58). Thus, the dissonance one senses in the first two volumes of the *Residencia* cycle, the disjunction between the speaker's desire for presence and his experience of difference, can be traced to "the counterpoint of expressive commitment and ironic demystification" (58). The result for Neruda (as for the three poets of this study) is that "Writing becomes . . . an agent of desire: Tantalus' water and fruit" (58). For poets who align themselves with the esoteric tradition, the object of desire is above all a reintegration of the fragmented word/world. The twentieth-century poet can only represent that reintegration as a frustrated or failed endeavor.

I have already spoken at length of Jacobo Fijman's trajectory as a poet, the brief flare of his appearance on the literary scene of Buenos Aires, followed by decades of silence. This is in fact a double and conflicting trajectory, as I argued in Chapter 5. To read Fijman's work chronologically is to follow his lyric voice from one who is "wounded in [his] song" to one who sings "the deep prayer." In several poems from his third and last volume, the poem-prayer is represented as a positive act set in motion against the agonies of the world. And yet this poet who had, in conjunction with his religious conversion, "found his voice," is the same poet who—at least from an exterior perspective—succumbs to silence.

Is there perhaps another way of conceiving silence, not as failure but as the ultimate object of desire, a state beyond language? Ernst Cassirer provides a possible way to consider this problematic with regard to Fijman: "It is especially the cult of mysticism, in all ages and among all peoples, that grapples again and again with this intellectual double problem—the task of comprehending the Divine in its totality, in its highest inward reality, and yet avoiding any particularity of name or image. Thus all mysticism is directed toward a world beyond language, a world of silence" (74). For the most part, Fijman's texts invite us to read his final silence (that is, his decision not to publish) in this way. In one of his earliest poems, silence is represented as oppressive and stultifying: "En el horno apagado del silencio / mis frutos maduraron / estérilmente" [In the cold oven of silence / my fruits ripened, / sterile] (*Obras* 35). Soon, though, he moves toward a conception of silence as plenitude: "Mana silencio de mi pecho; / mi silencio tan viejo como el mundo. / ¡Alegría de invierno!" [Silence flows from my breast; / my silence old as the world. / Joy of winter!] (78). Interestingly, Orozco also delineates the two types of silence to which these lines allude. The first is seen in negative terms, as something to overcome: "uno es el silencio como cerrazón, como balbuceo" [one is the silence of obstinacy, like a stammering]; the second approximates a mystical state: "ese silencio que es la plenitud total y que debe ser la plenitud final, que hace innecesaria la palabra" [that silence which is complete plenitude and that may be the final plenitude, the one that makes the word unnecessary] (qtd. in Sefamí 115). Is it possible to explain Fijman's retreat into silence as the achievement of a state in which language became, for him, unnecessary?

In an interview published in 1969 in the literary journal *Talismán*, Vicente Zito Lema poses the question of Fijman's literary silence directly: "¿Por qué dejó de publicar su poesía?" [Why did you stop publishing poetry?][2] Fijman's initial response is a pragmatic one: he could not afford the expenses involved. He then goes on to give deeper reasons: after the publication of *Estrella de la mañana*, he chose to "cambiar la vida" [change his life] dedicating himself exclusively to the study of scholastic and patristic texts. His concluding remark is noteworthy: "Pero fundamentalmente, por miedo a perderme en la literatura y alejarme de Dios" [But fundamentally, out of fear of losing myself in literature and distancing myself from God]. Fijman seems to be positing an unbridgeable gap between the spiritual life and the literary one. Bataille's contention that literature "is guilty and should admit itself so" seems appropriate to recall here. Literature inspired fear in Fijman; he stopped publishing poetry not because he had achieved that final plenitude that makes language unnecessary, but rather because literary language—sacred and perfectible as it might be—continued to plunge him into supremely uncomfortable dilemmas. Literature became for him a trap, something in which to lose himself, and in so doing to distance himself from God.

There is one word that surfaces in Fijman's poetry, *blasfemia*, that serves as a marker for the poet's conflicted relationship with language. The final line of "Subcristal" (a poem analyzed in Chapter 5) reads: "Cascan mis dientes piedras de blasfemia" [My teeth grind stones of blasphemy] (*Obras* 54). This is one of the "asylum poems" in which the speaker decries the monotony of confinement, the vague, slow, muffled sights and sounds of his environment set against "el cristal de mi locura" [the crystal of my madness]. In this context, blasphemy—stones cracked by the teeth—represents the response of language to oppression. It is a curse muttered under the breath, but a powerful, rock-hard curse, expressed in quiet violence. Blasphemous speech is antisacred speech; it intends to profane, to mock, to vilify. As a trope, it occupies a place opposite that of "la oración profunda." The place of blasphemy among the final poems of *Estrella de la mañana*, therefore, presents an interesting paradox. Immediately following a poem of spiritual reintegration whose speaker calmly affirms "este llanto dichoso de mi alma" [this joyful weeping of my soul], Poem XXXVII states:

Ojos de niño
donde el cielo vuelve a encontrar la desnudez de las estrellas,
golpeamos llenos de horror
las voces que enlazan las palabras,
noches visibles
en nuestras manos sordas y en nuestros cuerpos alimentados de
  muerte.

Respiramos los gritos
de la piel de los ríos que hieden desesperanzas
y corazones lúcidos del frío
que arrastran el agua obscurecida de la blasfemia.

(*Obras* 147)

[A child's eyes
where the sky rediscovers the nakedness of the stars, horrified, we
  pound
the voices that link words,

visible nights
in our deaf hands and in our bodies nourished by death.

We breathe the cries
of the skin of rivers that reek of hopelessness
and hearts lucid with cold
that drag the darkened water of blasphemy.]

This enigmatic poem presents a dark and violent vision that is directly related to language. The plural speaking subject, who is "horrified," is discharging blows against certain *voices*. Significantly, these are voices that on some level integrate or reintegrate language: they link words. The subjective *we* cannot hear or perceive the world in any way, as they have "deaf hands." They do, however, breathe in the cries of the rivers' skin. Rather than being the rivers of life, these are rivers stinking of hopelessness. Finally, there are "hearts lucid with cold" that drag water "darkened by blasphemy." Fijman's rhetoric is rarely as brutal or negative. If the line "Cascan mis dientes piedras de blasfemia" speaks of language's violent response to oppression, Poem XXXVII seems to present a violence carried out against language as oppressor. After lashing out against the unidentified voices, the deaf subject is essentially stripped of agency, reduced to the action of breathing in the cries of others. In sum, this poem complicates any facile conclusion that Fijman "found his voice" toward the end of his short publishing career, or that his religious conversion led to a mystical silence. Blasphemy was always the threat hiding behind the affirmations of a sacred language. Perhaps Orozco intuited this in a poem she dedicated to Fijman, Artaud, and Van Gogh, whose first lines read:

Fue una chispa sagrada en el infierno,
la ráfaga de un cielo sepultado en la arena,
la cabeza de un dios que cae dando tumbos entre un rayo y el
    trueno.

(*Mutaciones* 33)

[It was a sacred spark in hell,
the gust from a sky buried in the sand,
the head of a God who falls tumbling between lightning and thunder.]

Orozco, as we have seen, affirms the power of the poetic word by calling it her "talisman in the darkness." In constant counterpoint to the affirmations of verbal potency, however, the reader finds a questioning, an undermining, or an outright denial of the authority of the poetic word. She explores different modes of poetic discourse, that is, the prophetic or the mystical, elaborating certain configurations of poetic symbols and images and drawing constantly on the esoteric worldview embodied in gnosticism, hermeticism, and the occult arts. In each case, however, Orozco's lyric speaker reaches an impasse. The oracle remains silent, or the powers of prophetic speech fail her. The grounding in gnostic belief systems, in the final analysis, serves mainly to reinforce the disintegration of human existence and its utter alienation from the absolute. In sum, Orozco subjects the poetic word to acts of intense scrutiny, and the faith that remains after such scrutiny is not a facile one.

Certain critics have observed the ambivalent relationship to language in Orozco's poetry. Lindstrom notes that several poems of *Mutaciones de la realidad* and *La noche a la deriva* reveal "[una] ansiedad insegura por parte de la invocadora, que llama a un muerto sin confiar en su habilidad de comunicarse con él" [an anxious insecurity on the part of the voice that invokes, that calls to someone dead without trusting in her ability to communicate with him] (774). Thorpe Running, referring to Orozco's later work, claims that her allusions to a mysterious or fundamental word are overshadowed by stronger textual evidence verifying, to the contrary, that "ella ha perdido toda certeza con respecto al lenguaje" [she has lost all certainty regarding language] (14). Noting her distance from the surrealist revival of belief in the primordial power of language, Running underscores the irony in the fact that Orozco "usa el elemento clave de los surrealistas—la imagen—para poner en duda la eficacia del lenguaje" [uses the surrealists' key element—the image—to place in doubt the efficacy of language] (14).

In her early work, as we have seen, Orozco shows a fascination with the "dangerous games" inherent in the radical potentialities of the poetic word; these possibilities, however, are denied as soon as they are named. The tarot reader's vision, couched in messianic terms, dissipates immediately: "Pero nada ha llegado. / Nada que fuera más que estos mismos estériles vocablos" [But nothing has arrived. / Nothing that might be anything but those same sterile words] (*Obra* 84). The heightened consciousness surrounding the expectation of a poem that would reunify the fragmented world is deflated by an acknowledgment of the impotence of language. On an even larger scale, the entire poetic endeavor that makes up *Cantos a Berenice* draws to a close with a profound skepticism: "Tal vez sea imposible mi cabeza, ni un vacío mi voz, / algo menos que harapos de un idioma irrisorio mis palabras" [Perhaps my own head is impossible, my voice not even a void, / my words something less than the tatters of a derisory language] (184).

In numerous instances, particularly in Orozco's later work, a precarious balance is maintained between word and silence.[3] The magical power of naming is discredited by the speaker of "No hay acceso" [No access], who sees illusory "espejismos del verbo en cada nombre" [mirages of the word in every name] (*Noche* 15). In another poem, the clairvoyance promised to the poet whose words are "vidrios transparentes" [clear glass] is spoiled when those very transparencies are "trizados contra un muro" [shattered against a wall] (35). In the elegy written for Pizarnik, whose suicide was an acute personal loss for Orozco, the speaker's outrage at the young poet's death is directed at poetry itself. Language here is invested with a terrible power: "¡Ah los estragos de la poesía cortándote las venas con el filo del alba . . . !" ["Oh, the havoc wreaked by poetry, cutting your veins on the sharp edge of dawn] (*Mutaciones* 76). But in counterpoint to this, the image of "esos labios exangües sorbiendo los venenos en la inanidad de la palabra" [those bloodless lips sipping the poison from the pointlessness of the word] deprives poetic language of any real efficacy (76).

Among her later poems, "En el final era el verbo" [In the end was the word] stands as the clearest testament to Orozco's continuing struggle with the illusions and disillusions of language. It is a consummate example of what Paz calls the "critical poem," that is, "that poem that contains its own negation and that makes of that negation the point of departure for the song" (*Bow* 250). The title, "En el final era el verbo," establishes an immediate distance between the poem and biblical affirmation that "In the beginning was the Word" (John 1:1). Even after the demise of the word, Orozco's title seems to suggest, there remains a tenaciously regenerated word.

The poem's opening lines reiterate the ephemeral, ungraspable nature of language: "Como si fueran sombras de sombras que se alejan, las palabras" [As if words were shadows of shadows that withdraw] (*Revés* 113). The mythical identity between thing and name provides yet another cause for the speaker's skepticism: "Entonces, ¿no habrá nada . . . que se confunda con su nombre desde la piel hasta los huesos?" [Is there nothing, then . . . that merges with its name from skin down to bones?] (113). The poet-speaker, retrospectively considering her allegiance to the word, finds herself at an ironic distance from her own past:

Y yo que me cobijaba en las palabras como en los pliegues de la
  revelación

o que fundaba mundos de visiones sin fondo para sustituir los
   jardines del edén
sobre las piedras del vocablo.

(*Revés* 113)

[And I, who sheltered myself with words as in the folds of revelation
or who founded worlds made of bottomless visions to replace the
   gardens of Eden
on the rocks of the word.]

This passage appears to erode the very foundations of a belief in poetry as revelation, and of the poet as seer-prophet. In fact, the poem goes on to suggest, language may belong to a realm that excludes the subjective voice entirely: the speaker imagines each word as existing "a imagen de otra luz ... pero dispuesta a tejer y a destejer desde su propio costado el universo / y a prescindir de mí hasta el último nudo" [in the image of another light ... but willing to weave and unweave from its own side of the universe / and to dispense with me down to the last knot] (113).

The dramatization of the poet's impasse regarding language, in sum, is Orozco's fullest expression of a gnostic worldview that places human life at a virtually unbridgeable distance from the absolute. Each possibility embraced by the speaker for passing through what she calls the wall of the visible—magic and divination, the constant reconfiguration of the self, and ultimately, the symbolic transformation of the world through language—ultimately fails. In her last published volume, Orozco's *yo poético* declares her defeat unreservedly: "No te pronunciaré jamás, verbo sagrado" [Never will I pronounce you, sacred word] (*Boca* 9). Nevertheless, her vocation as a poet, an authentic calling that returns her unremittingly to the act of writing, demands a circular process, rather than an end.

As virtually every critic has pointed out, Pizarnik constructed for herself a world that consisted almost entirely of language, of poetry.[4] Although her orientation was not religious in any discernible way, her faith in the power of language surpassed that of Orozco or Fijman. In Orozco's own words,

Alejandra había hecho un refugio en la palabra, no en la vida. Su biografía se acababa, no contaba ya; era la palabra. Ves que la palabra se convierte en el sujeto de sus poemas. El lenguaje termina por ser de una manera absorbente el único motivo del poema. Es decir, ya no hay más que la palabra. Y la palabra no sirve de techo, tampoco. La palabra, si no transmite otra cosa, se vuela. (Qtd. in Sefamí 129)

[Alejandra had fashioned a refuge for herself in the word, not in life. Her biography was running out, it no longer counted; it was the word. You can see that the word becomes the subject of her poems. Language ends up being, in an all-engrossing way, the only motive for the poem. That is, nothing is left but the word. But the word cannot provide shelter. The word, if it transmits nothing else, flies away.]

The final allusion here is to Pizarnik's own image: "Cuando a la casa del lenguaje se le vuela el tejado y las palabras no guarecen, yo hablo" [When the roof flies off the house of language and words no longer shelter, I speak] (*Obras* 123). More than a talisman, the poetic word for Pizarnik is the very roof under which she dwells, or even "mi única patria" [my only homeland] (153). When this house/homeland fails to provide a protective space for her, the response is unforgiving. Almost from the beginning, Pizarnik enters into a combative and defensive position with regard to "[las] perras palabras" [doggish words] (220). This becomes particularly evident in her later work, in which she virtually abandons the lyric poem in favor of various experimental prose forms whose linguistic content is increasingly transgressive. The text "Toda azul" [All blue] offers an image for the writer's attempt at total transgression: "Mostré, uno a uno, los dedos de una de mis manos.—El lujurioso, el voluptuoso, el lúbrico, el mórbido, y el lascivo. Mi mano es el espejo de la matadora" [I showed, one by one, the fingers of one of my hands.—The lecherous one, the voluptuous one, the lubricious one, the morbid one, and the lascivious one. My hand is the mirror of the assassin] (210). As Bataille prescribed, the hand that writes stands as emblem for the perversely sexual, the morbid, and the violent.

Speaking of Pizarnik's unruly social behavior in the last years of her life (her propensity for obscene jokes and raucous laughter), as well as the frenetic verbal quality of texts like "La bucanera de Pernambuco o Hilda la polígrafa" [The bucaneer of Pernambuco, or Hilda the polygraph], Piña comments that "En este sentido, lo que angustia más allá de la carcajada que a veces surge, es la percepción de una especie de *venganza* exasperada contra el lenguaje por no ser esa 'patria' que se ha buscado" [In this sense, the distressing thing, apart from the momentary bursts of laughter, is the perception of a kind of exasperated *vengeance* against language for not being that "homeland" that was sought] (*Alejandra Pizarnik* 229; emphasis in original). In an early lyric poem Pizarnik had spoken of "la palabra inocente" [the innocent word], but she comes to realize, with Bataille, that literature is essentially guilty. Embracing that notion, and with writers like Baudelaire and Lautréamont as her models, Pizarnik initially felt compelled to produce powerful texts such as *La condesa sangrienta*. But with time, even the transgressive model of poetry lost its efficacy, leaving Pizarnik at an impasse that was both literary and existential.

Several texts written in the last years of her life (1970–72) elucidate the nature of this impasse. In "Tangible ausencia," the sense of homelessness is patent:

> No sé donde detenerme y morar. El lenguaje es vacuo y ningún objeto parece haber sido tocado por manos humanas. Ellos son todos y yo soy yo. Mundo despoblado, palabras reflejas que sólo solas se dicen. Ellas me están matando. Yo muero en poemas muertos que no fluyen como yo, que son de piedra como yo, ruedan y no ruedan, un zozobrar lingüístico, un inscribir a sangre y fuego lo que libremente se va y no volvería. Digo esto porque nunca más sabré destinar a nadie mis poemas. (*Obras* 207)

> [I don't know where to stop and dwell. Language is vacuous, and nothing seems to have been touched by human hands. They are everything, and I am I. Uninhabited world, reflecting words that only by themselves can speak themselves. They're killing me. I'm dying in dead poems that don't flow, as I don't, that are made of stone like I am, roll and don't roll, a linguistic shipwreck, an engraving in blood and fire of what escapes and won't come back. I say this because never again will I know how to address my poems to anyone.]

The sense of existential orphanhood—indeed, the lifeless condition of her entire world ("mundo despoblado")—is linked directly to the vacuousness of language. Again, words take on a life of their own ("sólo solas se dicen"). We have seen in earlier poems how the forces of language exist apart from the alienated speaker, sometimes forcing an oracular stance upon her. In this later poem, even the oracle is dismantled; the words do not merely invade, they kill. The entire linguistic project founders. The final line of the piece is significant, in that Pizarnik seems to be saying that the link between poet and reader has been severed. One of the guiding principles of Bataille's *Literature and Evil* is that literature is communication (*Litera-*

ture viii). Pizarnik seems to intuit here that her increasing desperation at the failure of language's presumably sacred powers, her move in the direction of greater and greater linguistic transgression, would eventually leave her unable to communicate. "Un instante ilícito se paga con años de silencio opaco" [One illicit moment is paid for by years of opaque silence], says the speaker of "Toda azul," in a telling hyperbole (*Obras* 211). The breakdown of communication is associated with the envisioned moment of death: "A la hora de morir uno canta para sí, no para los demás" [At the hour of death one sings to herself, not to others] (220).

Orozco and Fijman both struggled against the force of silence that represented, if not the failure to emit the spoken or written word, then the failure of that word to transmit meaning to others. Comparing Orozco's work to Pizarnik's, Kuhnheim observes: "We see inanimate objects speak as speaking subjects become mute or lose the 'power' of speech. This last phrase signals an important difference between the two authors, for while Pizarnik calls upon the force of silence, Orozco continues to acknowledge language's strength against silence" (71). Particularly in her later work, Pizarnik does ascribe a positive value to silence, enacting something akin to a poetic death-wish. The speaker of "Una traición mística" [A mystical betrayal], referring to an unnamed other, declares: "Yo me arrojo en su silencio; yo, ebria de presentimientos mágicos acerca de una unión con el silencio" [I hurl myself into her silence; I, drunk with magical premonitions about union with silence] (*Obras* 212). The unfulfilled human relationship dissolves imperceptibly into a relationship with silence:

> Recuerdo. Una noche de gritos. Yo subía y no tenía posibilidad de arrepentirme; subía cada vez más alto sin saber si llegaría a un encuentro de fusión o si me quedaría toda la vida con la cabeza clavada en un poste. Era como tragar olas de silencio, mis labios se movían como debajo del agua, me ahogaba, era como si estuviera tragando silencio. En mí éramos yo y el silencio. Esa noche me arrojé de la torre más alta. (212)

> [I remember. A night of shouting. I was rising, and I had no chance of repenting; I rose higher and higher without knowing if I would achieve fusion, or if I would spend the rest of my life with my head nailed to a post. It was like swallowing waves of silence; my lips moved as if under water, I was drowning, it was as if I were swallowing silence. I and silence were both inside me. That night I hurled myself from the highest tower.]

This passage is remarkable in that it employs the rhetoric of mysticism to deconstruct the experience of mystic union. Terms like "presentimientos mágicos," "cada vez más alto," "encuentro," "unión," and "fusión" combine the esoteric qualities of language with a quasi-religious epiphany. The epiphany breaks down on two levels, however. First, the desired union is not with God or a sanctified lover, but rather with silence itself. An impossible circularity is set up: were the union to take place, the written text would not exist. The poem does exist as a space of representation, however, in which the mystic ascent can be formulated. Here the second failure of the epiphany occurs, with the speaker's precipitous descent: with silence inside her, she hurls herself from the highest tower. These are the passages that have led Pizarnik's critics to speak of the blurred line between life and art.

Silence for Pizarnik is both an object of desire, an entity with which the speaker strives to meld her own self, and "el lugar peligroso" [the dangerous place] from which she seeks to extricate herself (*Obras* 213). This is not a rhetorical choice for Pizarnik, or even a profoundly spiritual one, as it was for Fijman. It is a matter of life and death: "Estoy muriendo porque alguien ha creado un silencio para mí" [I am dying because someone has created a silence for me] (213). Ultimately, Pizarnik's disillusionment with language reaches an extreme from which she, as author, cannot retreat—although, in pointed irony, the poem still survives as vehicle for her desperation. "En esta noche, en este mundo" [In this night, in this world], published only months before her death, gives a glimpse of the darkened corner of language into which she had backed herself.[5] I cite here the first stanza:

en esta noche en este mundo
las palabras del sueño de la infancia de la muerte
nunca es eso lo que uno quiere decir
la lengua natal castra
la lengua es un órgano de conocimiento
del fracaso de todo poema
castrado por su propia lengua
que es órgano de la re-creación
del re-conocimiento
pero no el de la resurrección
de algo a modo de negación
de mi horizonte de maldoror con su perro
y nada es promesa

> entre lo decible
> que equivale a mentir
> (todo lo que se puede decir es mentira)
> el resto es silencio
> sólo que el silencio no existe

(*Obras* 239)

> [in this night in this world
> the words of dream of childhood of death
> never is that what one means to say
> the mother tongue castrates
> the tongue is an organ of knowledge
> of the failure of all poems
> castrated by their own tongue
> which is the organ of re-creation
> of re-cognition
> but not that of the resurrection
> of something by way of negation
> of my horizon of Maldoror with his dog
> and nothing is a promise
> among the sayable
> which is the same as lying
> (everything that can be said is a lie)
> the rest is silence
> except that silence doesn't exist]

This poem works on the level of an *ars poetica* for a poet who no longer believes in the art. The esoteric tenet of language/poetry as an "organ of knowledge," stated explicitly by Fijman, is given an ironic twist by Pizarnik: the knowledge obtained is that of the failure of all poems. While acknowledging poetry's capacity to "re-create" and "re-cognize" the world, Pizarnik faults it for being incapable of *resurrection*, the ultimate power that her early, unmitigated faith had granted to it.

In the foregoing analyses I have attempted to demonstrate that the shared poetics of Orozco, Pizarnik, and Fijman is structured as a tensional relationship between belief in the sacred nature of the *logos*, in the efficacy of the praxis of poetry as a means of transgression and transcendence, and a critical distancing from or negation of this same praxis. Strong literary

Conclusion: A Talisman in the Darkness   171

models exist within the esoteric traditions, particularly in their nineteenth-century German and French reformulations, for ascribing to poetry the ability to transform the world by the reintegration of dispersed fragments into a meaningful whole. Without question, literary/philosophical influence has been a powerful factor in shaping the worldview of these three writers. The importance of surrealism in particular, a movement contemporary with Fijman's published writings and foundational for the work of Orozco and Pizarnik, is not to be underestimated.

The faith of these authors in the transformational powers of language may thus be attributable to the legacy of the romantic movement that spilled over into certain facets of the European and Latin American avant-garde. But "the word" is never simply and exclusively "the poetic word." It is possible to argue that early in this century, language was broadly viewed as transformative. The buoyant mood that accompanied the end of the First World War was also, for many Argentines, the result of decades of relative prosperity, with its inherent promise for an open, progressive, and democratic future. The surrealists' characteristic optimism and the propensity of avant-garde writers in general to highlight the ludic qualities of writing reflect the general spirit of the times.

But the fall from grace had long before been set in motion. Paz's notion of the critical poem, which he sees as an authentic response to the loss of a true *imago mundi* that characterizes twentieth-century art, actually has its beginnings in Rimbaud and its full development in Mallarmé. Paz elaborates: "Poetry, conceived by Mallarmé as language's only possibility of identification with the absolute, of being the absolute, denies itself each time it is realized in a poem . . .—unless the poem is simultaneously a criticism of that attempt (*Bow* 250). It is following this line of reasoning that Pizarnik concludes that "todo es posible / salvo / el poema" [everything is possible / except / the poem] (*Obras* 241), and Orozco speaks of "el triunfo del vocablo, con la lengua cortada" [the victory of the word, with the tongue slashed] (*Boca* 9). In sum, it appears that an uncritical belief in the poetic endeavor had become impossible, even from a purely literary point of view, since before the turn of the century. The conflictive relationship with language that we have seen represented in texts from all three authors is, to some degree, an inherited conflict.

However, to speak of a purely literary point of view, or a relationship with language solely patterned on literary models, would be to imply a naively simple set of explanations. In the introduction, I raised the question of the "retreat into literature" that characterizes to a large degree (though in distinctive modes) the lives of Fijman, Orozco, and Pizarnik. In the case of Fijman and Pizarnik, the retreat from public life into literature eventually led to extreme forms of silence. Were there factors characterizing the Argentine political situation that would help us to develop a more comprehensive picture of poetry's engagement with its broader milieu? Several speculative approaches to this question are possible.

First, we might examine these poets' attraction to certain esoteric principles, such as that of an original divine unity that was splintered at some catastrophic moment in the mythical past. Historians often speak of the period from 1880 to 1914 as Argentina's "Golden Age" (Skidmore and Smith 73). This period was coming to its close in Jacobo Fijman's adolescent years. The political and social agitation that characterized the decade of the teens in Buenos Aires caught up the young Fijman, who participated for some time in anarchist activities. The peak period of strike activity, 1918–19 (79), coincides with violent altercations with the police that Fijman experienced, subsequent to which he abruptly dropped out of active political life. In his late teens and early twenties, Fijman lived the very personal experience of watching his country's Golden Age come to an end. Orozco, born in 1920, inherited a social and political atmosphere permeated with a sense of loss and pessimism about the future. And for Pizarnik's generation, Argentina's former grandeur was truly a part of a quasi-mythical past, not to be mourned so much as distrusted.

The belief in the sacred origins and the potency of the written or spoken word can likewise be examined in light of the cultural and political milieu in which these writers have moved. It seems rather evident that such a belief, in twentieth-century Europe or Latin America, reflects a fervent desire more than a solid faith. In a poem called "La palabra que sana" [The healing word], Pizarnik creates a scenario of hope and impossibility: "Esperando que un mundo sea desenterrado por el lenguaje, alguien canta el lugar en que se forma el silencio" [Waiting for a world to be unearthed by language, someone sings the place where silence is shaped] (*Obras* 163). Discussing the way in which nineteenth-century writers embraced the Swedenborgian vision of cosmic correspondences, Wilkinson suggests deeper (though perhaps unconscious) political motivations: "The notion of a hidden but absolute order seems inevitably to carry with it the potential for criticizing the corrupt institutions of society. And a belief in a universal language that corresponds both to the structures of human consciousness and the world provides a means for individuals, however isolated, to imagine themselves as part of a whole, or what Marxist historians often call a totality" (3–4). Such an explanation seems at least partially applicable to the situation of the Argentine writers who have been the focus of this study. The perception of an unchanging divine order, a more authentic "elsewhere" on whose threshold the poet stands, reflects a profound discomfort with an unstable and untrustworthy temporal order. Correspondingly, a universal or perfectible language can be posited as the basis for an ideal social order. As political language in particular came to be perceived as less and less bound to any unchanging truth (witness Pizarnik's claim that everything that can be said is a lie), a sacred poetic language comes to represent the only possibility for a return to coherence on any level.

Wilkinson's thesis hits upon the idea of *belonging*, which points to the final speculative conclusions I will draw about Fijman, Orozco, and Pizarnik. The romantic notion of the poet as supreme outsider can be applied to the author-figure of each of these writers. The insider/outsider dialectic was exacerbated in Argentina by the situation of immigration in the early decades of the century (and later, in the 1960s and 1970s, by that of political exile). The immigrant's dream of a more prosperous and just society undoubtedly contributed to the myth of a semiutopian Argentina, and may be one of the forces behind the trope of *el otro reino* [the other realm]. But the brutal realities of immigrant life in these decades led to a disillusionment that coincided with the weakening of political and social structures both in Argentina and in Europe. Discussing the work of Gérard de Nerval, Wilkinson sees Swedenborgian principles at work in "the attempt to recover, through writing, an experience of wholeness which is unattainable, except in the writer's dreams" (141). Not surprisingly, Jrade identifies the same dynamic in the poetry of the Spanish American *modernistas* who stood at the threshold of the twentieth century: "The Modernist author deals with feelings of fragmentation and alienation by attempting to rediscover a sense of belonging and 'wholeness.' In doing so, he or she stands squarely in the mainstream of modern literary currents, the source of which is English and German Romanticism" (4).

In short, a desired return—via literary paradigms—to mythical, cosmic, occult orders seems entirely plausible for writers living under the historical conditions that shaped twentieth-century Argentina. Yet this return constitutes, as we have seen, a theory of language, a symbolic imaginary, and not, as the surrealists would have it, a way of being in the world. Ultimately, the defeat of language as means for a return to wholeness is patent in all three writers. In a poem that functions as a kind of epitaph for the entire poetic endeavor, Orozco concludes:

> Nuestro largo combate a muerte fue también un combate a muerte con la muerte, poesía.
> Hemos ganado. Hemos perdido,
> porque ¿cómo nombrar con esta boca,
> cómo nombrar en este mundo con esta sola boca en este mundo con esta sola boca?

(*Boca* 9–10)

> [Our long fight to the death was also a fight to the death with death, Poetry.
> We have won. We have lost:
> for how can you name with this mouth,
> how can you name in this world with this only mouth in this world with this only mouth?]

For poets like Orozco, the struggle with language is a struggle against death itself: poetry is a life-giving activity. Like Pizarnik, who cautiously affirms the potential of writing even as she discards her faith in the poem as artifact, or like Fijman, who opened chinks in his silence by giving away poems written on scraps of paper, Orozco declares her defeat by writing yet another poem. Honoring the extreme complexity of her art, she poses the mythic question of how to *name*—how to link word with thing, language's most sacred function—as a problem not of cosmic proportions, but of earthly, immediate ones.

Notes

Introduction

1. Jrade's most recent book, *Modernismo, Modernity, and the Development of Spanish American Literature* (1998), traces the legacy of *modernismo* in later twentieth-century Spanish American poetry and fiction. She reiterates the importance of occultist thought to the ideological foundations of *modernismo*, and briefly examines the manifestation of this thought in poets such as Argentina's Leopoldo Lugones, Uruguay's Julio Herrera y Reissig, and Mexico's Amado Nervo.

2. Mention should also be made of García Terrés's book *Poesía y alquimia: los tres mundos de Gilberto Owen* (Mexico City, 1980).

3. Breton himself, in a September 1950 interview with José M. Valverde, commented that "the Spanish-language poet who most touches me is Octavio Paz" (*Conversations* 242).

4. The terse, almost skeletal style to which I refer is characteristic of the majority of Pizarnik's lyric poems, the work for which she is best known. In contrast, many of the texts she wrote late in life, published posthumously as *Textos de sombra y últimos poemas* [Shadow texts and other poems] (1982), take the form of prose poems or short dramatic pieces, and tend toward a loosely constructed, neobaroque style.

5. The long segment of *Man Facing Southeast* in which the enigmatic mental patient named Rantes directs a production of Beethoven's Ninth Symphony is based directly on a scene from Fijman's autobiographical story "Dos días" [Two days]. Other than this scene, there is little explicit connection between Rantes and Fijman.

6. For a more in-depth examination of the oracular poetic voice in Orozco, see my article "From Sibyl to Witch and Beyond: Feminine Archetype in the Poetry of Olga Orozco," *Chasqui: Revista de Literaturea Latinoamericana* 27.1 (1998): 11–22.

7. *Dementia* is the initial word of Fijman's first and most well known book of poetry, *Molino rojo* [Red mill] (33).

8. Latin American poets have always held Edgar Allan Poe and Walt Whitman in high esteem. However, it is only in recent decades, with Alberto Girri (b. 1918) and,

in a more contemporary vein, Diana Bellessi (b. 1946), that poets in Argentina have considered poets from the United States as a source of literary inspiration.

9. The surrealists, many of whom led public lives and initiated various forms of engagement with their social and political milieu, must be cited as an exception to the model of romantic detachment from society.

10. Two books considered essential reading by Pizarnik could provide the framework for a study of the esoteric traditions in French poetry: Raymond's *From Baudelaire to Surrealism* (1933) and Béguin's *L'Ame romantique et le rêve* (1939). Of the latter, Piña comments that it was "[un] libro que prácticamente todos los que conocieron a Alejandra señalan como uno de sus grandes amores" [a book that practically everyone who knew Alejandra points to as one of her great loves] (*Alejandra Pizarnik* 81).

11. One group of contemporary writers in Argentina, centered around the literary magazine *Ultimo Reino* (first published in 1979), is interested in maintaining the neoromantic or esoteric approach outlined in this study. Included in this group are Luis Benítez, Gustavo Margulies, Mario Morales, Víctor Redondo, Eduardo Alvarez Tuñón, Susana Villalba, Horacio Zabaljuáregui, and Jorge Zunino. For further commentary on this and other contemporary trends in Argentine poetry, see especially Zanetti, "Brechas del muro" and Piña's introduction ("Estudio preliminar") to *Poesía argentina de fin de siglo*.

Chapter 1. The Esoteric Tradition in Literature

1. For a more comprehensive treatment of the esoteric traditions, especially as they relate to nineteenth- and twentieth-century literature, see especially Balakian's *Literary Origins of Surrealism*, Bays's *The Orphic Vision: Seer Poets from Novalis to Rimbaud*, Béguin's *L'Ame romantique et le rêve*, Raymond's *From Baudelaire to Surrealism*, and Paz's *Children of the Mire*. Roger Shattuck also provides a concise account of "The Occult" in Appendix II of his book *Forbidden Knowledge* (339–42).

2. The Illuminists, or Illuminati, were participants in an anticlerical, deistic society founded in Bavaria in 1776. By extension, the term *illuminati* can refer to persons who possess extraordinary knowledge or enlightenment.

3. Breton, "The Art of the Insane," 220. The essay is a vindication of the art produced by the mentally ill, and a denouncement of the critical establishment that has ignored such art. Breton states: "I am not afraid to put forward the idea, a paradoxical one only at first sight, that the art of those who are presently categorized as mentally ill represents a store of mental health" (220).

Chapter 2. Gnostic and Hermetic Discourse in the Poetry of Olga Orozco

1. Biographical details are taken from Sefamí's book of interviews, *De la imaginación poética*, 96–101.

2. In the interview with Sefamí, Orozco makes explicit the line of literary influence in which she places her own work, and upon which I have based this study.

When Sefamí inquires about the presence of romantic elements in her work, Orozco responds:

> Sí, están. Y lo están por mi propia esencia personal, aparte de las lecturas que son cosas de complementación. . . . Creo que prendieron en mí, sobre todo, los antecedentes que toma el surrealismo mismo. Es decir, todo lo que le sirvió al surrealismo, porque estaba dentro de la línea que respondía a sus mismos propósitos . . . : sueño, libertad, amor, el mundo de lo maravilloso, el mundo de lo mágico, el mundo de lo onírico y lo extrasensorial. (*De la imaginación poética* 125)

> [Yes, there are. And they are in me because of my own personal nature, apart from my readings, which are a complementary thing. . . . I think that in me, it was mainly the antecedents of surrealism that took hold. That is, everything that was valuable to surrealism, because it was in that line that responded to its own purposes . . . : dream, freedom, love, the world of the marvelous, the world of magic, the world of dream imagery and of extrasensory perception.]

3. With regard to the formal and discursive unity of Orozco's poetry, see Lindstrom, "La voz poética," 765; Luzzani Bystrowicz 227; and Running 12.

4. For Orozco's early work, I cite from the collection *Obra poética* (Buenos Aires: Corregidor, 1979), which contains the volumes *Desde lejos* (1946), *Las muertes* (1952), *Los juegos peligrosos* (1962), *Museo salvaje* (1974), and *Cantos a Berenice* (1977).

5. For a thorough discussion of female archetypal figures in Orozco's poetry, see my article "From Sibyl to Witch and Beyond: Feminine Archetype in the Poetry of Olga Orozco," *Chasqui: Revista de Literatura Latinoamericana* 27.1 (1998): 11–22.

6. For my overview of gnosticism, I rely principally on Hans Jonas's seminal study *The Gnostic Religion* (1963). Other important sources of contemporary scholarship on gnosticism include Pagels's *The Gnostic Gospels* and Perkins's *The Gnostic Dialogue*. The definitive editions of the gnostic texts themselves can be found in Layton's *Gnostic Scriptures: A New Translation* and in *The Nag Hammadi Library in English*.

7. Torres de Peralta explores at length this particular facet of gnostic myth in *La poética de Olga Orozco*, 12–14.

8. Other common variations of this formula are "este mundo/el otro mundo" [this world/the other world] and "este reino/el otro reino" [this realm/the other realm]. The phrase "la otra orilla" [the other shore] is also reiterated often in her work.

9. In her book *The Symbolist Movement,* Balakian notes the importance of the French term *gouffre*—gulf, pit, abyss—for mid- and late-nineteenth-century poets from Baudelaire forward. She explains:

> After Baudelaire this obsession with the abyss will become one of the chief characteristics of the mental attitude of what was called "decadent". . . . The "gouffre"

is the frontier between the visible and the invisible, the conscious and the unconscious, nonlife and the living; how far one can push beyond the accepted frontier and still come back to write about it, became the foremost poetic question after Baudelaire. (51–52)

10. Pellarolo, "La imagen de la estatua de sal," 41–49.

Chapter 3. The Occult as Revelation and Power of Passage in Orozco's Poetry

1. It is interesting to compare Orozco's phrase "Ya soy ajena a mí" [Now I am estranged from myself] with a strikingly similar phrase from Jacobo Fijman: "Ahora vivo detrás de mí mismo" [Now I live behind myself] (*Obra poética* 59).

2. Eighteenth-century French alchemist Dom Pernety enumerates the steps of the alchemical process as they corresponded to the signs of the zodiac: (1) calcination (Aries); (2) congelation (Taurus); (3) fixation (Gemini); (4) dissolution (Cancer); (5) digestion (Leo); (6) distillation (Virgo); (7) sublimation (Libra); (8) separation (Scorpio); (9) ceration (the waxing of a substance,or the softening of a hard substance) (Sagittarius); (10) fermentation (Capricorn); (11) multiplication (Aquarius); (12) projection (Pisces). (Coudert 199)

3. Orozco comments further on the relationship between magic and poetry:

> La magia, como la poesía, se maneja por una conversión simbólica de todo el universo. Ahora, la magia trata de convocar poderes. La poesía, en cambio, es una apuesta más allá de toda esperanza o desesperanza, y se reitera, a pesar de la frustración. (Qtd. in Sefamí 106)

> [Magic, like poetry, operates by means of a symbolic conversion of the whole universe. Now, magic tries to convoke powers. Poetry, however, is a bet made beyond all hope or desperation, and it is reiterated, in spite of the frustration.]

Chapter 4. Alejandra Pizarnik and the Literature of Evil

1. Olga Orozco, *Mutaciones de la realidad* 75–77. According to Orozco, "*Talita cumi* son las palabras que le dice Jesús a la hija de Jairo, cuando la resusita; quiere decir 'Levántate muchacha'" [*Talita cumi* are the words that Jesus speaks to the daughter of Jairus when he resuscitates her; they mean, "Rise and walk, young woman"] (qtd. in Sefamí 114).

2. Also worthy of mention are two small volumes published abroad during Pizarnik's lifetime: *Nombres y figuras* (Barcelona: Colección La Esquina, 1969), and *Los pequeños cantos* (Caracas: Árbol de Fuego, 1971). Two important volumes were published posthumously: *El deseo de la palabra* (Barcelona: Ocnos/Barral, 1975), a selection of poems that Pizarnik had planned, together with Antonio Beneyto and Martha Moia, prior to her death; and *Textos de sombra y últimos poemas* (Buenos Aires: Sudamericana, 1982), edited by Olga Orozco and Ana Becciú.

3. The figure of the child who exists simultaneously with the adult she will become is similarly evoked in Orozco's poem "Ceremonia nocturna":

En el fondo de ti hay siempre alguien que con la noche gime,
alguien que llora igual que una criatura olvidada en un bosque o en un
   desván en llamas,
alguien que humilde, tierna, desgarradoramente,
... trata de tomarse de tu mano, su propia mano en el impredecible porvenir.

(*Revés* 97)

[In your depths there is always someone who moans with the night,
someone who cries like a creature forgotten in a forest or a flaming attic,
someone who humbly, tenderly, wrenchingly,
... tries to take your hand, her own hand in the unpredictable future.]

4. Baudelaire xii. The phrase is taken from Baudelaire's "Preface to the Flowers."
5. Articles I have found useful in the discussion of Pizarnik's language-centered poetry (often, as it relates to the themes of absence and death) are Robert E. DiAntonio's "On Seeing Things Darkly in the Poetry of Alejandra Pizarnik: Confessional Poetics or the Aesthetic Metaphor?," Jill S. Kuhnheim's "Unsettling Silence in the Poetry of Olga Orozco and Alejandra Pizarnik," Francisco Lasarte's "Más allá del surrealismo: La poesía de Alejandra Pizarnik," Jacobo Sefamí's "Vacío gris es mi nombre mi pronombre: Alejandra Pizarnik," and Thorpe Running's "The Poetry of Alejandra Pizarnik." Although no critic has pinpointed Pizarnik's literary relationship to Bataille, Piña makes general mention of an association between the work of the two writers in her article "La palabra obscena" (31). In many ways, Piña's extensive essay on the element of the obscene in Pizarnik's work examines points relevant to my own, particularly with regard to "La condesa sangrienta."
6. Bordelois 242. Pizarnik's complete comment on Bataille reads as follows:

Pero mi lectura de fondo sigue siendo Georges Bataille. Ah, il faut parler de ça. ... Acaba de salir un texto póstumo de él, sobre el humor y la muerte que da justísimo en el lugar exactísimo en que la vida se abra para mostrar su parte más vivida, más vivida, más aleteante, palpitante, bueno, es cruel hablarte y que no lo leas. (242)

[But my most fundamental reading continues to be Georges Bataille. Oh, we need to talk about that. ... They just published a posthumous text of his, about humor and death, that hits right at the point where life opens up to show the most vivid, most vivid, most palpitating, throbbing, anyway, it's unfair to tell you about him and for you not to read him.]

7. The phrase is taken from Cristina Piña, *Alejandra Pizarnik* 122.
8. The few details available regarding Bataille's biography are taken from the introduction to Allan Stoekl's edition of his selected writings, *Visions of Excess* (ix–xxiii).

9. Bataille's writings are often cited as influential in the intellectual formation of Maurice Blanchot, Roland Barthes, Jacques Derrida, Michel Foucault, Julia Kristeva, and Jean Baudrillard, to name only some thinkers and writers whose own work has had a significant influence on postmodern thought.

10. Bataille maintained a complex and often hostile relationship with André Breton and many of the French surrealists of his day. He argued that the integration of the base or impure elements of life into the surrealist aesthetic was undermined by their determination to raise these elements to a new category of the spiritually transcendental. Breton, for his part, dismissed Bataille as an "excremental philosopher" and criticized his attempts to approach the heterogeneous by means of rational principles—a fundamental contradiction, according to Breton. For a more complete discussion of the polemic, see Stoekl's introduction to *Visions of Excess* (x–xv). In spite of these differences, I consider Bataille to be a spokesman for the surrealist literary aesthetic, taking into account the territory it shares with Bataille: its revolutionary tendencies and its appropriation of socially subversive values such as obscenity, perverse sexuality, and a fascination with death and morbidity.

11. In *Alejandra Pizarnik,* Piña also discusses Pizarnik's characteristic use of obscene language in social situations, which began in adolescence but apparently increased in intensity toward the end of her life (see especially 128–29 and 162–63). This matter underscores Pizarnik's desire to transgress in life as well as in literature, or her unwillingness to distinguish between the two.

12. Extensive and useful analyses of this work can be found in Foster, Negroni, and Piña ("La palabra obscena").

13. First written in 1965 and published in Mexico in that same year, *La condesa sangrienta* was not published in Argentina until 1971.

14. Foster reads *La condesa sangrienta* primarily as "a meditation on the horror of absolute power" ("Of Power and Virgins" 101). Although he presents convincing arguments for the links between Pizarnik's depiction of Báthory and the cultural and political realities of Argentina in the decades of the 1960s and 1970s, he downplays the direct concern with sexual perversity that, in my opinion, propels this text forward. My reading of Pizarnik's text assumes that she takes Báthory's sadistic acts on their own terms, rather than as a means for a meditation on power.

15. Negroni suggests that *La condesa sangrienta* can be considered "También como un gesto de apropriación, a la vez violento y sutil, de una imaginería ajena que le permite explorar tras una máscara esos vínculos escuridizos entre crueldad, sexo, placer y muerte" [Also as a gesture of appropriation, both violent and subtle, of a different imaginary that permits her to explore behind the mask those slippery bonds between cruelty, sex, pleasure and death] (109).

16. Deleuze argues that the sadist "cannot do more than accelerate and condense the motions of partial violence. He achieves the acceleration by multiplying the number of his victims and their sufferings" (29).

17. Chávez Silverman's article "The Look That Kills: The 'Unacceptable Beauty'

of Alejandra Pizarnik's *La condesa sangrienta*" proposes that we read this as a lesbian text. In this text, she claims, "Alejandra Pizarnik comes closer, perhaps, than anywhere else in her oeuvre to overcoming speechlessness . . . , in the specular representation and even, I would argue, (self) recognition of a lesbian self divided" (302). This soundly reasoned approach contrasts with my own in that it attempts to situate Pizarnik's production of *La condesa sangrienta* within fundamentally biographical parameters—as a "divided" expression of the poet's lesbian desire—rather than within the parameters of textual transgression largely derived, as I argue, from her literary obsessions.

18. According to Piña (*Alejandra Pizarnik* 127), this passage was written in Paris in 1962, though it was not published until 1968.

Chapter 5. Poetry and Madness in Jacobo Fijman

1. Orozco recounts that Pizarnik would often call her late at night, desperate with fear, and that Orozco would "certify" her sanity with an incantation such as "Yo, gran cocinero del Rey, mientras miro pasar las nubes, atestiguo por el mismo árbol que da sombra en mi balcón, que Alejandra Pizarnik está perfectamente sana" [I, great cook of the king, while I watch the clouds go by, testify by the very tree that shades my balcony, that Alejandra Pizarnik is perfectly healthy] (qtd. in Piña, *Alejandra Pizarnik*, 85).

2. Biographical details are taken from Zito Lema, *El pensamiento de Jacobo Fijman* 87–92.

3. Bajarlía, in his *Fijman, poeta entre dos vidas*, refers to Fijman as "uno de los más singulares poetas de la generación de 1922" [one of the most singular poets of the generation of 1922] (7). See also Isaacson and Urquía, who comment that "Este poeta, hoy casi olvidado, fue uno de los principales animadores de la generación martinfierrista y, en su hora, considerado entre los pares de Borges, Bernárdez y Molinari" [This poet, almost forgotten today, was one of the main enthusiasts of the "Martinfierrista" generation, and in his time was considered among the equals of Borges, Bernárdez, and Molinari] (1:196).

4. See also Masiello's article "Ex-centric Odyssey: The Poetry of Jacobo Fijman."

5. See Zito Lema, *El Pensamiento de Jacobo Fijman* 34.

6. Comparisons between Fijman and Artaud stem from the biographical facts of their confinement for mental illness and from the avant-garde nature of their work. See Bajarlía 123–37, Pellegrini 8; Zito Lema, "Poeta en hospicio" 22.

7. Bajarlía transcribes the following account by Fijman of his meeting with Breton and his ironic (and comic) appreciation of surrealism:

> Su doctrina era muy sencilla, recién ahora la entiendo. Vos hablás y no sabés lo que dijiste, pero algo salió de tu boca, una palabra, una escupida. Cada palabra es un proyectil, pero vos lo ignorás. Cuando te diste cuenta, el punto se agarra la barriga o se revuelve cuerpo a tierra. Esto se llama *automatismo*, que es algo así

como el puntillismo de la máquina Singer. El cerebro, entretanto, queda en la culata. No interviene el fusil. Después de la explicación, el franchute me leyó un poema y me atraganté. La bebida me salió por los ojos y estornudé tres veces. André Breton salió furioso y gritó: *Mon Dieu, mon Dieu!* o algo parecido, y como lo miré fijamente, agregó: *merde a Tristan Tzara!* No entendí nada, pero desde ese día supe lo que era el surrealismo. (29)

[His doctrine was very simple; only now do I understand it. You speak and you don't know what you said, but something came out of your mouth, a word, spittle. Each word is a projectile, but you don't know this. When you realize it, the point grabs its gut or rolls around in the dirt. This is called *automatism*, which is something like the pointillism of a Singer sewing machine. Meanwhile, the brain stays in the butt. The gun doesn't intervene. After this explanation, the Frog read me a poem, and I choked. My drink came out of my eyes and I sneezed three times. André Breton went out furiously, shouting *Mon Dieu, mon Dieu!* or something like that, and when I glared at him, he added, *Shit on Tristan Tzara!* I didn't understand a thing, but that day I learned what surrealism was.]

8. See Fernández 15, Calmels 95, Bajarlía 149–56.

9. Jacobo Fijman, *Obra poética*. This volume includes brief critical essays by Carlos Riccardo, Víctor Redondo, and Juan Jacobo Bajarlía.

10. See Pellegrini 6–8; Molina, "Ni un paso atrás" 4–5; and Bernárdez 77–79.

11. The reference is to Fijman's story "Dos días" [Two days], an account of Fijman's own first experience with mental breakdown and admittance to a mental hospital. At the end of the story, the protagonist, recently admitted to the asylum, points at another patient: "'¡Oh miren, un loco!' grito, señalando a un sujeto.... Allí está el árbol de la ciencia del bien y del mal" ["Oh look, a madman," I shout, pointing to one of them.... There is the tree of good and evil] ("Dos días" 37).

12. The phrase "molinos de imágines" [mill of images] occurs in the poem "Molino" (*Obra poética* 59).

13. In the poem "Sub-drama," also from *Molino rojo*, Fijman alludes to another Rabelaisian scene: "Murga carnavalesca / ¡Las risas rojas!" [Carnavalesque street band / their red laughter!]. The medieval flavor of the images recall those of "Feria": "Pasa un convoy de brujas caprichosas; / cuelgan mis extensiones deformadas" [A convoy of whimsical witches goes by; / my deformed extremities hang] (*Obra poética* 63–64).

14. *Webster's New Twentieth-Century Dictionary, Unabridged*, 2nd ed. (1975), s.v. "marasmus."

15. It is worth noting that Poem X from *Hecho de estampas* contains a similar reference to "sagrados pinos" [sacred pines] (98).

16. Kuhnheim identifies alienation as an element common to Orozco's and Pizarnik's work; she discusses "their differing constructions of a dissociated self," specifically in terms of the female-gendered speaker in the work of both poets (86–87).

Chapter 6. The Dreams of Drowned Men: Jacobo Fijman and Vicente Zito Lema

1. Felman presents the issue thus: "Madness integrated into literature immediately raises the question of how the unreadable can as such be read: How and why does nonsense produce sense?" (104).

2. Breton's companion Nadja, referring to her propensity to create stories spontaneously by free association, makes a similar observation: "I live this way altogether" (74).

3. The entire text of the passage from James (*The Varieties of Religious Experience*) reads as follows:

> In delusional insanity, paranoia, as they sometimes call it, we may have a *diabolical* mysticism, a sort of religious mysticism turned upside down. The same sense of ineffable importance in the smallest events, the same texts and words coming with new meanings, the same voices and visions and leadings and missions, the same controlling by extraneous powers; only this time the emotion is pessimistic: instead of consolations we have desolations; the meanings are dreadful; and the powers are enemies to life. It is evident that from the point of view of their psychological mechanism, the classic mysticism and these lower mysticisms spring from the same mental level, from that great subliminal or transmarginal region of which science is beginning to admit the existence, but of which so little is really known. (426)

Conclusion. A Talisman in the Darkness

This chapter's epigraph was taken from a poem that appeared in *Mutaciones* and that was dedicated to Vincent Van Gogh, Antonin Artaud, and Jacobo Fijman.

1. Foucault, *Madness and Civilization* 100. The full citation reads as follows: "*Language is the first and last structure of madness*, its constituent form; on language are based all the cycles in which madness articulates its nature" [emphasis in original].

2. All fragments cited in this paragraph are taken from Zito Lema, "Reportaje a Jacobo Fijman: Contribución a un intento de conocimiento," *Talismán* 11.

3. For a thorough examination of the function of silence in Orozco's and Pizarnik's work, see Kuhnheim 67–89.

4. An excellent discussion of Pizarnik's search for a homeland in language can be found in Laura García-Moreno, "Alejandra Pizarnik: The Poet as Hostage," *Latin American Literary Review* 24.48 (1996): 67–93.

5. It should be noted that Orozco, in homage to Pizarnik, titles her 1994 volume of poems *Con esta boca, en este mundo*.

Bibliography

Aguirre, Raúl Gustavo. "'Demencia: El camino más alto y más desierto" . . . Jacobo Fijman: El gran olvidado" ["Dementia: the highest and most deserted road" . . . Jacobo Fijman: The great forgotten one]. *Revista Iberoamericana* 37 (1971): 429–36.
Bajarlía, Juan-Jacobo. *Fijman, poeta entre dos vidas* [Fijman, poet between two lives]. Buenos Aires: Ediciones de la Flor, 1992.
Balakian, Anna. *Literary Origins of Surrealism: A New Mysticism in French Poetry.* New York: King's Crown Press, 1947.
———. *Surrealism: The Road to the Absolute.* Chicago: University of Chicago Press, 1986.
———. *The Symbolist Movement: A Critical Appraisal.* New York: Random House, 1967.
Bataille, Georges. *Death and Sensuality: A Study of Eroticism and the Taboo.* Salem, N.H.: Ayer, 1984. Trans. of *L'erotisme.* Paris: Minuit, 1957.
———. *Literature and Evil.* Trans. Alastair Hamilton. New York: Marion Boyars, 1985. Trans. of *La Littérature et le Mal.* Paris: Galliard, 1957.
———. *The Tears of Eros.* San Francisco: City Lights, 1989. Trans. of *Les larmes d'Eros.* Paris: Jacques Pauvert, 1961.
———. *Visions of Excess: Selected Writings, 1927–1939.* Ed. Allan Stoekl. Trans. Allan Stoekl, Carl R. Lovitt, and Donald M. Leslie, Jr. Theory and History of Literature Series 14. Minneapolis: University of Minnesota Press, 1985.
Baudelaire, Charles. *Flowers of Evil: A Selection.* Ed. Marthiel and Jackson Mathews. New York: New Directions, 1955.
Bays, Gwendolyn. *The Orphic Vision: Seer Poets from Novalis to Rimbaud.* Lincoln: University of Nebraska Press, 1964.
Béguin, Albert. *El alma romántica y el sueño* [The romantic soul and the dream]. Trans. Mario Monteforte Toledo. 1954. Reprint, Mexico City: Fondo de Cultura Económica, 1978.
Bernárdez, Francisco Luis. "Vaivén de Fijman" [Fijman's swaying]. In *Fijman: El poeta celestial y su obra,* ed. Ruth Fernández, 77–79. Buenos Aires: Tekhné, 1985.

Betz, Hans Dieter. "Magic in Grego-Roman Antiquity. In *Encyclopedia of Religion*, ed. Mircea Eliade, 9:93–97. New York: Macmillan, 1987.

Bloom, Harold. *Agon: Toward a Theory of Revisionism*. Oxford: Oxford University Press, 1982.

———. *The Anxiety of Influence: A Theory of Poetry*. London: Oxford University Press, 1973.

———. *The Flight to Lucifer: A Gnostic Fantasy*. New York: Farrar, Straus, Giroux, 1979.

———. *Kabbalah and Criticism*. New York: Continuum-Seabury, 1975.

Bordelois, Ivonne. *Correspondencia Pizarnik* [Pizarnik correspondance]. Buenos Aires: Editorial Planeta, 1998.

Breton, André. "The Art of the Insane, the Door to Freedom." In *Free Rein; La clé des champs*, trans. Michel Parmentier and Jacqueline d'Amboise, 217–20. Lincoln: University of Nebraska Press, 1995.

———. *Conversations: The Autobiography of Surrealism*. Trans. Mark Polizzotti. New York: Marlowe, 1993. Trans. of *Entretiens*. Paris: Gallimard, 1969.

———. *Manifestoes of Surrealism*. Trans. Richard Seaver and Helen R. Lane. Ann Arbor: University of Michigan Press, 1972. Trans. of *Manifestes du Surréalisme*. Paris: Pauvert, 1962.

———. *Nadja*. Trans. Richard Howard. New York: Grove Press, 1960.

Burckhardt, Titus. *Alchemy: Science of the Cosmos, Science of the Soul*. Trans. William Stoddart. Baltimore: Penguin, 1971.

Calmels, Daniel. *El Cristo Rojo: Cuerpo y escritura en la obra de Jacobo Fijman; Apuntes para una biografía* [The red Christ: Body and writing in the work of Jacobo Fijman; Notes for a biography]. Buenos Aires: Editorial Topía, 1996.

Cassirer, Ernst. *Language and Myth*. Trans. Susanne K. Langer. New York: Dover, 1946.

Chávez Silverman, Suzanne. "The Discourse of Madness in the Poetry of Alejandra Pizarnik." *Monographic Review* 6 (1990): 274–81.

———. "The Look That Kills: The 'Unacceptable Beauty' of Alejandra Pizarnik's *La condesa sangrienta*." In *¿Entiendes? Queer Readings, Hispanic Writings*, ed. Emilie L. Bergmann and Paul Julian Smith, 281–305. Durham, N.C.: Duke University Press, 1995.

Cirlot, J. E. *A Dictionary of Symbols*. 2nd ed. Trans. Jack Sage. New York: Barnes and Noble, 1971.

Coudert, Allison. "Renaissance Alchemy." In *Encyclopedia of Religion*, ed. Mircea Eliade, 1:199–202. New York: Macmillan, 1987.

De Costa, René. *The Poetry of Pablo Neruda*. Cambridge: Harvard University Press, 1979.

Deleuze, Gilles. "Coldness and Cruelty." In *Masochism: "Coldness and Cruelty" and "Venus in Furs."* New York: Zone Books, 1991.

Detienne, Marcel. "Orpheus." In *Encyclopedia of Religion*, ed. Mircea Eliade, 11:111–14. New York: Macmillan, 1987.

DiAntonio, Robert E. "On Seeing Things Darkly in the Poetry of Alejandra Pizarnik: Confessional Poetics or Aesthetic Metaphor?" *Confluencia* 2.2 (1987): 47–52.

Eliade, Mircea. "Alchemy: An Overview." In *Encyclopedia of Religion*, ed. Mircea Eliade, 1:183–86. New York: Macmillan, 1987.

———. *The Forge and the Crucible: The Origins and Structures of Alchemy*. 2nd ed. Trans. Stephen Corrin. Chicago: University of Chicago Press, 1978.

———. *Myths, Dreams, and Mysteries: The Encounter Between Contemporary Faiths and Archaic Realities*. Trans. Phillip Mairet. London: Harvill, 1960.

———, ed. *Encyclopedia of Religion*. 16 vols. New York: Macmillan, 1987.

Faivre, Antoine. "Esotericism." In *Encyclopedia of Religion*, ed. Mircea Eliade, 5:156–63. New York: Macmillan, 1987.

———. "Hermetism." In *Encyclopedia of Religion*, ed. Mircea Eliade, 6:293–302. New York: Macmillan, 1987.

Felman, Shoshana. *Writing and Madness: Literature/Philosophy/Psychoanalysis*. Trans. Martha Noel Evans, Shoshana Felman, and Brian Massumi. Ithaca, N.Y.: Cornell University Press, 1985.

Fernández, Ruth. *Fijman: El poeta celestial y su obra* [Fijman: The celestial poet and his work]. Buenos Aires: Tekhné, 1985.

Fernández Moreno, César. *La realidad y los papeles: Panorama y muestra de la poesía argentina contemporánea* [Reality and roles: Panorama and sample of contemporary Argentine poetry]. Madrid: Aguilar, 1967.

Fijman, Jacobo. "Dos días" [Two days]. In *San Julian el Pobre: Relatos* [Saint Julian the Poor: Stories], 19–38. Buenos Aires: Araucaria Editores, 1998.

———. *Estrella de la mañana* [Morning star]. Buenos Aires: Editorial Número, 1931.

———. *Hecho de estampas* [Made of images]. Buenos Aires: Editorial Gleizer, 1930.

———. *Molino rojo* [Red mill]. Buenos Aires: Editorial "El Inca," 1926.

———. *Obra poética* [Poetic works]. 2 vols. Buenos Aires: La Torre Abolida, 1983.

Foster, David William. *Gay and Lesbian Themes in Latin American Writing*. Austin: University of Texas Press, 1991.

———. "Of Power and Virgins: Alejandra Pizarnik's *La condesa sangrienta*." In *Violence in Argentine Literature: Cultural Responses to Tyranny*, 98–114. Columbia: University of Missouri Press, 1995.

Foucault, Michel. *Madness and Civilization: A History of Insanity in the Age of Reason*. Trans. Richard Howard. New York: Vintage-Random, 1965.

Frye, Northrop. "Charms and Riddles." In *Spiritus Mundi: Essays on Literature, Myth, and Society*, 123–47. Bloomington: Indiana University Press, 1976.

García Terrés, Jaime. *Poesía y alquimia: los tres mundos de Gilberto Owen* [Poetry and alchemy: the three worlds of Gilberto Owen]. Mexico City: Ediciones Era, 1980.

Gorski, William T. *Yeats and Alchemy*. Albany: SUNY Press, 1996.

Hole, Christina. *A Mirror of Witchcraft*. London: Chatto and Windus, 1957.

Holmyard, E. J. *Alchemy*. Baltimore: Penguin, 1968.

Isaacson, José, and Carlos Enrique Urquía, eds. *Cuarenta años de poesía argentina* [Forty years of Argentine poetry]. 3 vols. Buenos Aires: Aldaba, 1962.

James, William. *The Varieties of Religious Experience*. 1902. Ed. Martin E. Marty. Harmondsworth, England: Penguin, 1982.

Jitrik, Noé. *Las armas y las razones: Ensayos sobre el peronismo, el exilio, la literatura*. Buenos Aires: Sudamericana, 1984.

Jonas, Hans. *The Gnostic Religion: The Message of the Alien God and the Beginnings of Christianity*. Boston: Beacon Press, 1963.

Jrade, Cathy L. *Modernismo, Modernity, and the Development of Spanish American Literature*. Austin: University of Texas Press, 1998.

———. *Rubén Darío and the Romantic Search for Unity: The Modernist Recourse to Esoteric Tradition*. Austin: University of Texas Press, 1983.

Jung, Carl Gustav. *Alchemical Studies*. Vol. 13 of *Collected Works of C. G. Jung*, eds. Barbara Forryan and Janet M. Glover. Princeton: Princeton University Press, 1967.

———. *The Portable Jung*. Ed. Joseph Campbell. Trans. R. F. C. Hull. New York: Viking Penguin, 1971.

Kahane, Henry, and Renée Kahane. "Hellenistic and Medieval Alchemy." In *Encyclopedia of Religion*, ed. Mircea Eliade, 1:192–96. New York: Macmillan, 1987.

Kuhnheim, Jill Suzanne. *Gender, Politics, and Poetry in Twentieth-Century Argentina*. Gainseville: University Press of Florida, 1996.

Lasarte, Francisco. "Más allá del surrealismo: La poesía de Alejandra Pizarnik." *Revista Iberoamericana* 49.125 (1983): 867–77.

Lautréamont, Comte de [Isadore Ducasse]. *Maldoror (Les Chants de Maldoror)*. Trans. Guy Wernham. Mt. Vernon, N.Y.: Golden Eagle Press, 1943.

Layton, Bentley. *Gnostic Scriptures*. Garden City, N.Y.: Doubleday, 1987.

Lindstrom, Naomi. "Jacobo Fijman: Jewish Poet?" In *Tradition and Innovation: Reflections on Latin American Jewish Writing*, eds. Robert DiAntonio and Nora Glickman, 89–98. Albany: SUNY Press, 1993.

———. "Olga Orozco: la voz poética que llama entre mundos" [Olga Orozco: The poetic voice that calls between worlds]. *Revista Iberoamericana* 132–33 (1985): 765–75.

Luzzani Bystrowicz, Telma. "Olga Orozco, poesía de la totalidad" [Olga Orozco, poetry of totality]. In *Historia de la literatura argentina* [History of Argentine literature], ed. Ramón Mariani, vol. 5, *Los contemporáneos* [The contemporaries], 227–31. Buenos Aires: Centro Editor de la América Latina, 1982.

Mahé, Jean Pierre. "Hermes Trismegistos." In *Encyclopedia of Religion*, ed. Mircea Eliade, 6:287–93. New York: Macmillan, 1987.

Malinowski, Bronislaw. *Magic, Science, and Religion and Other Essays*. Garden City, N.Y.: Anchor Doubleday, 1954.

Masiello, Francine. "Ex-Centric Odyssey: The Poetry of Jacobo Fijman." *Hispanic Journal* 6.2 (1985): 33–44.

———. *Lenguaje e ideología: Las escuelas argentinas de vanguardia*. Buenos Aires: Hachette, 1986.
Matterer, Timothy. *Modernist Alchemy: Poetry and the Occult*. Ithaca, N.Y.: Cornell University Press, 1995.
Middleton, John. "Theories of Magic." In *Encyclopedia of Religion*, ed. Mircea Eliade, 9:82–89. New York: Macmillan, 1987.
Molina, Enrique. "La poesía de Olga Orozco" [The poetry of Olga Orozco]. *Testigo* 8 (1972): n.p.
———. "Ni un paso atrás" [Not one step back]. *Talismán: Revista Literaria* 1:1 (1960): 4–5.
The Nag Hammadi Library in English. 3rd ed. Gen. ed. James M. Robinson. San Francisco: Harper and Row, 1988.
Negroni, María. "*La condesa sangrienta:* Notas sobre un problema musical" [*The bloody countess:* Notes on a musical problem]. *Hispamérica* 23.68 (1994): 99–110.
Novalis [Friedrich von Hardenberg]. *Henry von Ofterdingen*. Trans. Palmer Hilty. New York: Frederick Ungar, 1964.
Orozco, Olga. *Con esta boca, en este mundo* [With this mouth, in this world]. Buenos Aires: Sudamericana, 1994.
———. *En el revés del cielo* [On the other side of the sky]. Buenos Aires: Sudamericana, 1987.
———. *Mutaciones de la realidad* [Mutations of reality]. Buenos Aires: Sudamericana, 1979.
———. *La noche a la deriva* [Night adrift]. Mexico City: Fondo de Cultura Económica, 1983.
———. *Obra poética* [Poetic works]. Buenos Aires: Corregidor, 1979.
———. *Páginas de Olga Orozco seleccionadas por la autora* [Pages from Olga Orozco, selected by the author]. Buenos Aires: Editorial Celtia, 1984.
———. "La poesía como juego peligroso" [Poetry as a dangerous game], afterword. In *Poemas* [Poems], by Olga Orozco, 99–102. Medellín, Colombia: Departamento de Bibliotecas, Universidad de Antioquía, 1984.
Otto, Rudolf. *The Idea of the Holy: An Inquiry into the Non- rational Factor in the Idea of the Divine and its Relation to the Rational*. Trans. John W. Harvey. 2nd ed. London: Oxford University Press, 1950.
Pagels, Elaine. *The Gnostic Gospels*. New York: Vintage-Random, 1981.
Pavitt, William Thomas, and Kate Pavitt. *The Book of Talismans, Amulets, and Zodiacal Gems*. London: William Rider, 1914.
Paz, Octavio. *Alternating Current*. Trans. Helen R. Lane. New York: Viking, 1973. Trans. of *Corriente alterna*. Mexico City: Siglo XXI, 1967.
———. *The Bow and the Lyre*. Trans. Ruth L. C. Simms. Austin: University of Texas Press, 1973.
———. *Children of the Mire: Modern Poetry from Romanticism to the Avant-*

Garde. Trans. Rachel Phillips. Cambridge: Harvard University Press, 1991. Trans. of *Los hijos del limo*. Mexico City, 1956.

———. *Los signos en rotación y otros ensayos* [Signs in rotation and other essays]. Madrid: Alianza, 1971.

Pellarolo, Silvia. "La imagen de la estatua de sal: Síntesis y clave en el pensamiento de Olga Orozco" [The image of the statue of salt: Synthesis and key in the thought of Olga Orozco]. *Mester* 18 (1989): 41–49.

Pellegrini, Aldo. "La Poesía de Jacobo Fijman" [The poetry of Jacobo Fijman]. *Talismán: Revista Literaria* 1.1 (1969): 6–8.

Perkins, Pheme. *The Gnostic Dialogue: The Early Church and the Crisis of Gnosticism*. New York: Paulist Press, 1980.

Piña, Cristina. *Alejandra Pizarnik*. Buenos Aires: Editorial Planeta, 1991.

———. Estudio preliminar [Preliminary study] to *Páginas de Olga Orozco seleccionadas por la autora* [Pages from Olga Orozco, selected by the author], by Olga Orozco, 13–55. Buenos Aires: Editorial Celtia, 1984.

———. Estudio preliminar [Preliminary study] to *Poesía argentina de fin de siglo* [Argentine Poetry at the end of the century], ed. Cristina Piña. Buenos Aires: Vinciguera, 1996.

———. "La palabra obscena" [The obscene word]. *Cuadernos Hispanoamericanos*, Supplement 5 (May 1990): 17–38.

Pizarnik, Alejandra. *Arbol de Diana* [Tree of Diana]. Buenos Aires: Editorial Sur, 1962.

———. *Extracción de la piedra de locura* [Extraction of the stone of folly]. Buenos Aires: Sudamericana, 1968.

———. *Obras completas: Poesía completa y prosa selecta* [Complete works: Complete poetry and select prose]. Buenos Aires: Corregidor, 1994.

———. *Semblanza* [Profile]. Ed. Frank Graziano. Mexico City: Fondo de Cultura Económica, 1984.

———. *Textos de sombra y últimos poemas* [Shadow texts and last poems]. Ed. Olga Orozco and Ana Becciú. Buenos Aires: Sudamericana, 1982.

Plato. *Phaedrus and Letters VII and VIIII*. Trans. Walter Hamilton. New York: Viking Penguin, 1973.

Prescott, Frederick Clarke. *The Poetic Mind*. New York: Macmillan, 1922.

Quispel, Gilles. "Gnosticism from Its Origins to the Middle Ages." In *Encyclopedia of Religion*, ed. Mircea Eliade, 5:566–74. New York: Macmillan, 1987.

Rahim, Habibeh. "Islamic Alchemy." In *Encyclopedia of Religion*, ed. Mircea Eliade, 1:196–99. New York: Macmillan, 1987.

Raymond, Marcel. *From Baudelaire to Surrealism*. London: Methuen, 1970. Trans. of *De Baudelaire au Surréalisme*. 1933.

Redondo, Victor. "Jacobo Fijman en la ciudad de la gallina mañanera, o La presencia del ausente" [Jacobo Fijman in the city of the morning hen, or The presence of the absent one], introduction to *Obra poética*, by Jacobo Fijman, 11–16. Buenos Aires: La Torre Abolida, 1983.

Riccardo, Carlos. Nota preliminar [Preliminary note] to *Obra poética*, by Jacobo Fijman, 5–10. Buenos Aires: La Torre Abolida, 1983.
Rimbaud, Arthur. *Rimbaud: Complete Works, Selected Letters*. Trans. and introd. Wallace Fowlie. Chicago: Phoenix–University of Chicago Press, 1966.
Running, Thorpe. "Imagen y creación en la poesía de Olga Orozco" [Image and creation in the poetry of Olga Orozco]. *Letras Femeninas* 13:1–2 (1987): 12–20.
———. "The Poetry of Alejandra Pizarnik." *Chasqui* 14.2–3 (1985): 45–55.
Santí, Enrico Mario. *Pablo Neruda: The Poetics of Prophecy*. Ithaca, N.Y.: Cornell University Press, 1982.
Sefamí, Jacobo. *De la imaginación poética: Conversaciones con Gonzalo Rojas, Olga Orozco, Álvaro Mutis y José Kozer* [Of the poetic imagination: Conversations with Gonzalo Rojas, Olga Orozco, Álvaro Mutis, and José Kozer]. Caracas: Monte Ávila Editores Latinoamericana, 1996.
———. "Nota introductoria" [Introductory note]. In *Con esta boca, en este mundo*, by Olga Orozco, 7–8. Mexico City: Casa Abierta al Tiempo, Universidad Autónoma Metropolitana, 1992.
Skidmore, Thomas E., and Peter H. Smith. *Modern Latin America*. New York: Oxford University Press, 1992.
Skyrme, Raymond. *Rubén Darío and the Pythagorean Tradition*. Gainesville: University Press of Florida, 1975.
Sosnowski, Saúl. *Borges y la Cábala: La búsqueda del verbo* [Borges and the Cabala: The search for the word]. Buenos Aires: Hispamérica, 1976.
Starkie, Enid. *Baudelaire*. Norfolk, Conn.: New Directions, 1958.
Stoekl, Allan. Introduction to *Visions of Excess: Selected Writings, 1927–1939*, by Georges Bataille. Minneapolis: University of Minnesota Press, 1985.
Surette, Leon. *The Birth of Modernism: Ezra Pound, T. S. Eliot, W. B. Yeats and the Occult*. Montreal: McGill-Queen's University Press, 1993.
Tacconi, María del Carmen. "Para una lectura simbólica de Olga Orozco" [Toward a symbolic reading of Olga Orozco]. *Sur* 348 (1981): 115–23.
Thorndike, Lynn. *The Place of Magic in the Intellectual History of Europe*. New York: Columbia University Press, 1905.
Tiryakian, Edward A. "Preliminary Considerations." In *On the Margin of the Visible: Sociology, the Esoteric, and the Occult*, ed. Edward A. Tiryakian, 1–15. New York: Wiley, 1974.
Torres de Peralta, Elba. *La poética de Olga Orozco: Desdoblamiento de Dios en máscara de todos* [The poetics of Olga Orozco: Unfolding of God in the mask of all]. Madrid: Playor, 1987.
Torres Fierro, Danubio. "Olga Orozco: Hacia el verso primordial" [Olga Orozco: Toward the primordial verse]. In *Memoria plural: Entrevistas a escritores latinoamericanos* [Plural memory: Interviews with Latin American writers], 197–202. Buenos Aires: Sudamericana, 1986.
Tuveson, Ernest Lee. *The Avatars of Thrice Great Hermes: An Approach to Romanticism*. Lewisburg, Pa.: Bucknell University Press, 1982.

von Franz, Marie-Louise. *Alchemy: An Introduction to the Symbolism and the Psychology.* Toronto: Inner City Books, 1980.

Wilkinson, Lynn R. *The Dream of an Absolute Language: Emanuel Swedenborg and French Literary Culture.* Albany: SUNY Press, 1996.

Willson, A. Leslie, ed. *German Romantic Criticism.* New York: Continuum, 1982.

Xirau, Ramón. *Poesía y conocimiento* [Poetry and knowledge]. Mexico City: Cuadernos de Joaquín Mortiz, 1978.

Yates, Frances. *Giordano Bruno and the Hermetic Tradition.* Chicago: University of Chicago Press, 1964.

Zanetti, Susana. "'Brechas del muro': Exilio interior y censura. La poesía en Buenos Aires de la dictadura a la democracia" ["Breaches in the wall": Interior exile and censorship. Poetry in Buenos Aires from dictatorship to democracy]. In *Literatura argentina hoy: De la dictadura a la democracia* [Argentine literature today: From dictatorship to democracy], ed. Karl Kohut and Andrea Pagni, 275–85. Frankfurt: Vervuert Verlag, 1989.

Zito Lema, Vicente, ed. "Jacobo Fijman: Poeta en hospicio" [Jacobo Fijman: Poet in the asylum]. *Talismán: Revista Literaria* 1.1 (1969): 1–26.

———. *El pensamiento de Jacobo Fijman, o el viaje hacia la otra realidad* [The thought of Jacobo Fijman, or The journey toward the other reality]. Buenos Aires: Rodolfo Alonso Editor, 1970.

———. "Reportaje a Jacobo Fijman" [Interview with Jacobo Fijman]. *Talismán: Revista Literata* 1:1 (1969): 10–13.

Zuesse, Evan. "Divination." In *Encyclopedia of Religion,* ed. Mircea Eliade, 4:375–82. New York: Macmillan, 1987.

Index

Absolute, 97, 98, 151, 154, 163, 165
Abyss, 177n.9
Acéphale (political group), 77
Aesthetic principles, 1, 6
Aguirre, Raúl Gustavo, 70, 103, 138
Alberti, Rafael, 17
Alchemy, 41–49, 55–56, 59, 65, 68; astrology and, 49, 53; reverse, 46
Aleixandre, Vicente, 17
Alienation, 47, 66, 157; from the absolute, 163; as literary theme, 20, 118, 131; of writers, 125
"Animal que respira." *See* Orozco, Olga
"Anotaciones para un autobiografía." *See* Orozco, Olga
Antonyms, use of in literature, 48–49
Árbol de Diana. *See* Pizarnik, Alejandra
Aristotle, 144
Artaud, Antonin, 71, 76, 95, 98, 101, 125, 162; mental illness of, 141–42, 143, 181n.6
Astrology, 49, 52–53
"Atavíos y ceremonial." *See* Orozco, Olga
Aurélia (Nerval), 32
Authenticity, 11
Automatic writing, 11, 17
Avant-garde poetry, 17, 70, 100, 101–2, 158, 171; French, 77; Spanish, 101
Aventuras perdidas, Las. *See* Pizarnik, Alejandra

Barjarlía, Juan Jacobo, 69–70
Bataille, Georges, 72, 76–80, 142, 143, 160, 166; Breton and, 180n.10; death and eroticism in works of, 84–85, 87, 157; essay on *Wuthering Heights*, 80, 81, 82–83, 84; on poetry, 86, 144; principle of evil in works of, 74, 80, 81–83, 87–90, 92–94. Works: *Death and Sensuality: A Study of Eroticism and the Taboo (L'erotisme)*, 78, 84, 87; *Literature and Evil*, 74–75, 77–78, 80, 87, 167; *The Tears of Eros*, 88; *Visions of Excess: Selected Writings, 1927–1939*, 77
Báthory, Erzébet, 88–91, 92
Baudelaire, Charles, 74, 79, 86, 93, 167; belief in poetry as magic, 151; on dark side of the psyche, 7, 150; doctrine of *correspondances*, 5–6, 37, 97, 151–52; on mission of poetry, 5–6; occultism as theme in works of, 5. Works: *Fleurs du mal*, 74
Bellessi, Diana, 175n.8
Benarós, León, 16
Bernárdez, Luis, 104
Blake, William, 22, 74, 85, 92
Bloom, Harold, 22–23. Works: *Kabbalah and Criticism*, 22
Boehme, Jakob, 22
Borges, Jorge Luis, 23, 100
Breton, André, 16, 93, 101, 102, 132; Bataille and, 180n.10; on existence, 28; on madness, 97, 176n.3; on reason, 11; on surrealism, 9. Works: *Manifestoes of Surrealism*, 9; *Surrealist Manifesto*, 102
Brontë, Emily, 74, 80, 83. Works: *Wuthering Heights*, 80, 81, 82–83, 84, 92, 144
Bruno, Giordano, 151

"Bucanera de Pernambuco o Hilda la polígrafa, La." *See* Pizarnik, Alejandra
Buñuel, Luis, 79

"Caída, La." *See* Orozco, Olga
Calvino, Italo, 72
Cannibalism, 85, 91
"Canto del cisne." *See* Fijman, Jacobo
"Cantora nocturna." *See* Pizarnik, Alejandra
Cantos a Berenice. *See* Orozco, Olga
"Cartomancia, La." *See* Orozco, Olga
"Catecismo animal." *See* Orozco, Olga
Celestial double (heavenly twin) concept, 31–33, 39
"Cena." *See* Fijman, Jacobo
"Ceremonia nocturna." *See* Orozco, Olga
Cernuda, Luis, 17
Chance, 11
Chants de Malador, Les (Lautréamont), 74
Charm poetry, 64–65
Chemistry, 43
Chien Andalou, Le (film), 79
Chouchy Aguirre, Ana María, 16
Christian orthodoxy and doctrines, 2, 23, 24, 45
Collège de Sociologie, 77
Communication: as function of poetry, 7; literature as, 167; rational discourse as, 97; transmundane, 27
Condesa sangrienta, La. *See* Pizarnik, Alejandra
Con esta boca, en este mundo. *See* Orozco, Olga
Conjecture, 52
Contra-Attaque (political group), 77
Correspondances (doctrine), 5–6, 37, 97, 151–52, 172
Cortázar, Julio, 72
Cosmic evil (doctrine), 23, 24–25, 30, 40
Cosmic unity, 2–3, 4, 54, 172
Critique Social, La review, 77
Curses, 63–64, 65
Cynicism, 54

Dadaism, 10
Dangerous games/zones, 12–13, 19, 41, 50, 54, 65, 75, 87, 91, 150, 163, 169

Death: alienation and, 120; as supreme object of desire, 66; as transcendence, 85, 88. *See also* Bataille, Georges; Pizarnik, Alejandra
Death and Sensuality: A Study of Eroticism and the Taboo. *See* Bataille, Georges
Delphic oracle, 96, 97, 124
"Desdoblamiento de Dios en máscara de todos." *See* Orozco, Olga
"Deseo de la palabra, El." *See* Pizarnik, Alejandra
Desnos, Robert, 101
"Despertar, El." *See* Pizarnik, Alejandra
Divination, 49–50, 52, 56, 59, 65, 165
Divine spark image, 46
Documents (review), 77
"Dos Diás." *See* Fijman, Jacobo
Dreams, 52, 55, 78, 127
Dualism: in gnosticism, 36; God as separate from the cosmos, 23, 25, 29–30; of good and evil, 26, 49; radical, 49

Eco, Umberto, 23. Works: *The Name of the Rose*, 23
Eluard, Paul, 101
Emerald Tablet, 42
Empiricism, 43
"En contra." *See* Pizarnik, Alejandra
"En el bosque sonoro." *See* Orozco, Olga
"En el final era el verbo." *See* Orozco, Olga
En el revés del cielo. *See* Orozco, Olga
"En la rueda solar." *See* Orozco, Olga
Epicureans, 54
Equilibrium (concept), 34
Erotisme, L'. *See* Bataille, Georges
Erzébet Báthory, la Comtesse Sanglante. *See* Penrose, Valerie
Esoteric tradition, 1, 14, 40, 50, 55, 72, 149, 171; gnosticism and, 163; language and, 156, 158–59; in literature, 158, 159; madness and, 95, 124; poetry and, 2, 12, 151; quest for the absolute in, 118; surrealism and, 9–10; worldview, 124. *See also specific poets*
Essential word concept, 6
Estrella de mañana. *See* Fijman, Jacobo
Evil, 40, 78, 149; cosmic, 23, 24–25, 30, 40; practices, 55–56

Existence and essence gap, 10
Existential exile, 41
"Exquisite cadaver," 127
Extracción de la piedra de locura. See Pizarnik, Alejandra

Fall from paradise, 3–4, 12, 23, 149; as defining condition of humanity, 24; gnosticism and, 28–29, 33, 36; in hermetic mythology, 39; as literary theme, 8, 28–29, 39; loss of language and, 97; principle of evil and, 95
Faust. See Goethe, Johann Wolfgang von
"Feria." See Fijman, Jacobo
Fernández, Macedonio, 100
Fijman, Jacobo, 148, 162; alienation as theme in works, 118, 119–20, 121, 125, 131; on artistic creation, 144–45; avant-garde style, 101–2, 103, 142; biographical data, 100–1, 127–28; blasphemy in works of, 108–9, 161–62; characterizations of God, 106, 107, 109, 110, 125, 138, 143; Christian mystic vision/spirituality, 102–3, 105, 121, 144, 147, 152, 160; conversion to Catholicism, 101, 102, 130–31, 142, 159, 162; critical reception, 103–4, 110, 120–21; dehumanization as theme in works, 107–8; delusional thought of, 128, 130, 132, 138, 147; disintegration of the self as theme in works, 115, 117–18, 119, 120; distancing techniques and silencing of poetic voice, 102, 103, 104, 107, 108, 121, 131, 159–61, 162, 168, 172, 174; eccentric behavior of, 100–1, 103, 110, 130, 131, 155; esoteric tradition and, 12, 104, 118, 121, 149, 153, 172; fusion of art and life, 70, 131; interview, in *Pensamiento*, 123, 124, 132–37, 139–40, 144, 146–47, 153–54; language and, 154–55, 158, 162, 170; light images in works of, 112–13; on madness, 138, 139–42, 144; madness and psychiatric confinement, 101, 102, 103, 104–5, 107, 110, 112, 114, 120, 128–30, 145; madness as theme in works, 13, 104, 105–11, 112, 115–16, 118, 121, 128, 160–61; masks as theme in works, 111, 112; monologue, in *Pensamiento*, 123; Orphic voice of, 9, 124, 152; "other" in works of, 105, 112, 113–15, 117, 129; on other poets, 141–43; outlook/worldview, 171; poetic voice, 7, 121, 123, 130, 146, 147, 149, 155, 159, 162; on poetry, 153; political life, 172; quest for the absolute/knowldege, 125, 130, 138; on reason and unreason, 137–38; on the role of the poet, 150; structure of poems, 117–18, 142; surrealism and, 171, 181n.7.
—Works: "Canto del cisne," 104, 105–6, 107, 109, 112; "Cena," 104, 119–20; "Dos días," 176n.11, 182n.11; *Estrella de mañana*, 102, 105, 115, 121–22, 147, 160; "Feria," 104, 110–11, 112–13, 117; "Fuegos mentales, Los," 131–32; *Hecho de estampas*, 102, 121; *Jacobo Figman: Obra poética*, 104,105; *Molino rojo*, 101–2, 103, 105, 107, 113, 120, 147, 152; "'Otro, El,'" 104, 113–15, 117, 129; Poem XXXVII, 161–62; *San Julián el Pobre*, 104; "Subcristal," 104, 108–9, 112, 117; "Sub-drama," 182n.13; "Vísperas de angustia," 104, 113, 115–17. *See also* Zito Lema, Vicente
Fleurs du mal. See Baudelaire, Charles
Flight to Lucifer, The (Bloom), 22
Foucault, Michel, 95–96, 98, 99, 104, 124, 130; on madness, 132–33, 147–48. Works: *Madness and Civilization*, 95, 124, 130
"Fragmentos para dominar el silencio." *See* Pizarnik, Alejandra
Freud, Sigmund, 11, 87, 88
"Fuegos mentales, Los." *See* Fijman, Jacobo

Gálvez, Manuel, 104
Garments, as symbol, 30–31
Generation of 1922 *(Martinfierristas)*, 100
Generation of 1940, 17, 18; Orozco as member of, 15
Generation of 1950, 71
Generation of 1960, 71
"Génesis." *See* Orozco, Olga
Genet, Jean, 75
"Génie" (Rimbaud), 32
Girondo, Oliviero, 70, 100
Girri, Alberto, 16, 175n.8

Gnosticism, 20–21, 24–25, 153–54; alchemy and, 42; cosmic evil doctrine, 23, 24–25, 30, 40; deceptive versus absolute concept, 28; divine spark image, 46; dualism and, 25, 26, 29, 36; esoteric tradition and, 163; fall from paradise and, 28–29, 33, 36; hermeticism and, 25, 37, 40; human condition as separate from God, 29–30; influence of, on contemporary literary tradition, 22–23; magic and, 55; mythology of, 38; occultism and, 24; pessimism and, 40; pluralism and, 34; symbolism and, 24, 26; worldview, 49
Goethe, Johann Wolfgang von, 22, 43. Works: *Faust*, 43
Gómez de la Serna, Ramón, 17

Hebrew scriptures, 26
Hecho de estampas. See Fijman, Jacobo
Heinrich von Ofterdingen. See Novalis
Hell, descent into, 8
Hermes Trismegistos, 36, 37, 38, 42
Hermetic androgyne, 48
Hermeticism, 21, 137, 163; alchemy and, 42; astrology and, 53; gnosticism and, 25, 37, 40; magic and, 54; mythology of, 38, 39; poetry and, 6–7; principles of, 35–36, 37, 39; romanticism and, 36–37; universal sympathy doctrine, 44, 49; worldview, 37, 53, 151
Hölderlin, Friedrich, 95
Homer, 152
Human nature, 95
"Hymn of the Pearl, The," 31
Hyperconsciousness, 30

Illuminations, Les. See Rimbaud, Arthur
Illuminism, 3, 32
Imagination, 126
Imbert, Enrique Anderson, 23
Incantation, 59, 60, 155
Inclán, Ramón del Valle, 101
"Infierno musical, El." See Pizarnik, Alejandra
Infierno musical, El. See Pizarnik, Alejandra
Inspiration, 96

Interior voice (poetry), 5
Invisible reality, 98
Irrationality, 96–97, 109, 155

Jacobo Fijman: Obra poética. See Fijman, Jacobo
Jiménez, Juan Ramón, 17
Jonah and the whale, 47
Juarroz, Roberto, 71
Judaism, 55
Juegos peligrosos, Los. See Orozco, Olga
Jung, Carl G., 22, 43, 45, 47, 48, 56

Kabbalah and Criticism. See Bloom, Harold
Knowledge: dangerous, 54; forbidden, 12–13, 50; mystic, 23; occult, 10, 13; poetry and, 153; as power, 40; sacred, 95; secret, 44, 94; shared, 133; superhuman, 50

Lange, Norah, 70
Language: absolute, 97, 151, 154; associative, 6; creative function of, 6–7; esoteric tradition and, 156, 158–59; false, 130; impotence of, 163; literary, 142; loss of, after the fall, 97; magic of, 12, 99, 155, 158; oracular power of, 7; original/normal, 12, 98, 99, 151; poetic, 6, 69, 148, 149, 151, 152, 156, 158, 164; power of, 156, 157, 158, 163, 164; rational properties of, 12; sacred origins of, 158, 168; transformational power of, 171; universal, 4, 152, 172, 173
Larrea, Juan, 17
Lautréamont, Comte de (Isadore Ducasse), 71, 79, 86, 93, 125, 167; mental illness of, 142–43
Leopardi, Giacomo, 22
Literary evil, 75
Literary tradition, 10, 40, 97, 171
Literature and Evil. See Bataille, Georges
Logos (poetic word), 3–4, 9, 12, 20, 74, 99, 153, 156–58, 170; of magic, 58–59

Madness, 95, 124, 130, 132–33, 149; criminality and, 130; esoteric tradition and, 95, 124; inspiration of, 96; occult and, 95;

"otherness" as, 98; poetic, 96, 118–19, 140, 141, 147; psychological view of, 95; as punishment for occult knowledge, 13. See also Mental illness
Madness and Civilization. See Foucault, Michel
Magic, 54, 59, 65; black, 55, 62, 65; charms (talismans and amulets), 47, 55, 56–58, 59, 68, 73, 156, 162; as dangerous game, 54; gnosticism and, 55; hermeticism and, 54; of language, 12, 155, 158; poetry and, 3–4, 6, 12, 58–59, 64, 149, 150, 151; religious tradition and, 55, 78; ritual, 56; sacred, 78; spells, 62; verbal, 55. See also Occultism
"Mala suerte, La." See Orozco, Olga
Malinowski, Bronislaw, 56, 59
Mallarmé, Stéphane, 9, 59, 71, 149, 171; belief in poetry as magic, 151; chance as theme in works, 11; poetic language and, 6
Manifestoes of Surrealism. See Breton, André
Marechal, Leopoldo, 100
Masochism, 88
Mediumism, 52
Mental illness, 11, 95, 109, 119, 125–26. See also Madness
Metaphysical poetry, 17, 29
"Miradas que no ven." See Orozco, Olga
Modernism, 173, 175n.1
Molina, Enrique, 16, 18, 70, 71, 104
Molino rojo. See Fijman, Jacobo
Molloy, Silvia, 70
Moreno, César Fernández, 16, 17, 18
Museo salvaje. See Orozco, Olga
Mutaciones de la realidad. See Orozco, Olga
Mystery cults, 2
Mysticism, 10, 23
Mythology, 40

Name/naming, 62–63, 64, 65, 164, 174
Name of God, 55
Name of the Rose, The. See Eco, Umberto
Neo-Platonic thought, 5, 54

Neoromanticism, 16, 17, 71
Neruda, Pablo, 16–17, 159. Works: *Residencia en la tierra*, 16, 18, 159
Nerval, Gérard de, 32, 95, 125, 142
Neuroses, 78
Nietzsche, Friedrich, 95
Noche a la deriva, La. See Orozco, Olga
Nombres y figuras. See Pizarnik, Alejandra
Nostalgia, 62
Novalis (Friedrich von Hardenberg), 4–5, 54, 59, 69, 120, 150, 151. Works: *Heinrich von Ofterdingen*, 4, 9
Numerology, 52

Oblivion, as theme in poetry, 30
Obra poética. See Orozco, Olga
Occultism, 3, 10, 13, 40, 149, 163; aesthetic principles and, 1; astrology and, 53; existence and essence gap and, 10; gnosticism and, 24; madness and, 95; religious tradition and, 7; surrealism and, 14. See also Esoteric tradition; Magic
"Operación nocturna." See Orozco, Olga
Optimism, 37
Oracular function of poetry, 7, 10, 156, 163
Oracular trance, 52
Origins, myth of, 23
Orozco, Olga, 4, 16, 125, 148; alchemy and, 44, 46, 47–48, 49; alienation in works of, 47, 182n.16; antonym as literary tool, 48–49; astrology and, 53; biographical data, 14–16; celestial double as theme in works, 32–33; dangerous games and, 41, 50, 54, 65, 150, 163; divination and, 50, 51–52; elsewhere as theme in works, 28; enigmatic sign as theme in works, 26–27, 50, 52, 65, 158; esoteric tradition and, 12, 14, 15, 18–19, 20, 35, 72, 149, 172; fall from paradise as theme in works, 28–29, 39; feminine orientation, 19; forbidden garden as theme in works, 13; fusion of art and life, 70; gnosticism and, 20–21, 23, 25, 29, 30–31, 35, 41, 73, 165; heart imagery, 56, 57–58; hermeticism and, 21, 35, 37, 47; human statue as theme in works, 38–39, 41; light and dark imagery, 23–24,

Orozco, Olga—*continued*
26, 37, 46, 53; madness as theme in works, 13; magic and, 54–55, 56, 156, 165, 178n.3; metaphor of the text, 37–38, 41, 59; mirror imagery, 37, 41; occultism and, 39, 41, 48, 59–61, 62–64, 65; orphanhood as theme in works, 73; Orphic song and, 9; "other side" as theme in works, 19–20, 25, 27, 32, 41, 65, 98; outlook/worldview, 15, 18–19, 25, 29, 35, 165, 171; paradise lost theme in works of, 33; pessimism in works of, 24, 34–35, 37; Pizarnik and, 67–68, 70, 98, 164, 166, 181n.1, 183n.5; pluralism in works of, 33; poetic voice/language, 7, 15, 59, 65, 71, 149, 150, 155, 158, 162–65, 173–74; prophesy and oracle as theme in works of, 52; repetition in works of, 62; rhetorical devices, 34; on the role of the poet, 150, 156, 165; romanticism and, 176n.2; sacred and profane elements in works of, 20–21; salt as symbol in works, 38, 45, 47–48; on silence, 160; silence and, 168; structure of poems, 33–34, 37, 62–64; surrealism and, 14, 16, 171; symbolism in works of, 38; talismans and amulets as theme in works, 47, 56, 68, 73, 162; transcendental themes in works of, 19–20, 32; on transgression and madness, 98; use of suprarational tropes, 19, 20; wall as symbol in works of, 155–56, 164, 165.
—Works: "Animal que respira," 44; "Anotaciones para un autobiografía," 53; "Atavíos y ceremonial," 29; "Caída, La," 39; *Cantos a Berenice*, 19, 20, 32, 51–52, 163–64; "Cartomancia, La," 52, 53, 155; "Catecismo animal," 32; "Ceremonia nocturna," 179n.3; *Con esta boca, en este mundo*, 20; "Desdoblamiento de Dios en máscara de todos," 34; "En el bosque sonoro," 155; "En el final era el verbo," 164–65; *En el revés del cielo*, 19–20, 25; "En la rueda solar," 46; "Génesis," 45; *Juegos peligrosos, Los*, 18, 20, 52, 57, 59; "Mala suerte, La," 46; "Miradas que no ven," 25–26; *Museo salvaje*, 46; *Mutaciones de la realidad*, 19, 163; *Noche a la deriva, La*, 19, 163; *Obra poética*, 177n.4; "Operación nocturna," 29; "Para destruir a la enemiga," 59–61, 62–64, 65, 155; "Para hacer un talismán," 57–58, 59; "Para ser otra," 48; "Para un balance," 47; "Pavana para una infanta difunta," 67–68, 73; "Pequeños visitantes," 27–28; "Poesía como juego peligroso, La," 54; "Presagio, El," 50, 52; "Presentiments in ritual dress," 50; "Rara sustancia," 34, 45, 155

Orphic myth and modes, 8, 9, 124, 149, 155
"'Otro, El'" (The "other"). *See* Fijman, Jacobo

"Palabra que sana, La." *See* Pizarnik, Alejandra
"Para destruir a la enemiga." *See* Orozco, Olga
Paradise lost theme, 2–3, 20, 73
"Para hacer un talismán." *See* Orozco, Olga
"Para ser otra." *See* Orozco, Olga
"Para un balance." *See* Orozco, Olga
"Pavana para una infanta difunta." *See* Orozco, Olga
Paz, Octavio, 3, 9, 10, 12, 72, 158, 164, 171
Pellegrini, Aldo, 70, 104
Penrose, Valerie, 88. Works: *Erzébet Báthory, la Comtesse Sanglante*, 88, 89–90
Pequeños cantos, Los. *See* Pizarnik, Alejandra
"Pequeños visitantes." *See* Orozco, Olga
Perón, Juan Domingo, 17
Pessimism, 17–18, 24, 34–35, 37, 40
Philosopher's stone, 42
Philosophical tradition, 10, 40, 54, 171
Pico della Mirandola, Giovanni, 151
Pistis Sophia, 55
Pizarnik, Alejandra, 70, 124, 125, 142, 143, 148; alienation in works of, 182n.16; art and life separation and, 70, 158; Bataille and, 76–77, 79, 91, 179n.6; biographical data, 69–70; child figure in works of, 73, 76, 80–82, 83, 84; critical assessment of,

75, 76; dangerous states and, 75, 87, 91, 169; death as presence in works of, 66, 73–74, 75, 76, 80, 81, 83–88, 94, 169–70; eroticism in works of, 80, 87–88; esoteric tradition and, 12, 149, 172; experimental prose forms, 166; forbidden garden as theme in works, 13, 86; influences on, 70, 74; madness as theme in works, 13, 80, 81, 98–100, 104; murder in works of, 84, 89; mysticiam and, 169; neoromanticism and, 71; obscentity in works of, 75, 76, 180n.11; Orozco and, 68, 70, 98, 164, 166, 181n.1, 183n.5; orphanhood as theme in works, 167; Orphic song and, 9; outlook/worldview, 171; paradise lost as theme in works, 73; in Paris, 72, 76; poetic language and, 7, 71, 73, 75, 81, 149, 156, 158, 165–70; on poetry and the role of the poet, 150, 156–58; principle of evil in works of, 74, 75, 76, 79–80, 90, 94; repetition in works of, 89, 90; sexuality as theme in works, 76; silence and, 168–69, 172; social behavior, 166; suicide as theme in works, 76; suicide of, 4, 66, 69, 86, 91, 164; surrealism and, 70, 72, 73, 79, 171; transgressive writing, 75, 76, 93; violence in works of, 76, 80, 81, 88, 89.
—Works: *Árbol de Diana*, 71; *Aventuras perdidas, Las*, 70; "Bucanera de Pernambuco o Hilda la polígrafa, La," 166; "Cantora nocturna," 72; *Condesa sangrienta, La*, 75, 79–80, 88–92, 167; "Deseo de la palabra, El," 157; "Despertar, El," 82; "En contra," 93; *Extracción de la piedra de locura*, 71, 72, 85, 99–100; "Fragmentos para dominar el silencio," 156; "Infierno musical, El," 93–94; *Infierno musical, El*, 71, 79; *Nombres y figuras*, 178: chap. 4 n.2; "Palabra que sana, La," 172; *Pequeños cantos, Los*, 178: chap. 4 n.2; "Sueño de la muerte o el lugar de los cuerpos poética, El," 84; "Tangible ausencia," 167; *Textos de sombra y Últimos poemas*, 175n.4; *Tierra más ajena, La*, 70; "Toda azul," 168; *Trabajos y las noches, Los*, 71;

"Tracíon mística, Una," 168–70; *Última inocencia, La*, 70
Plato, 96, 97, 132, 140, 152
Pluralism, 33, 34
Pneuma (concept), 24, 33, 57, 153–54
Poe, Edgar Allan, 6
Poem XXXVII. *See* Fijman, Jacobo
Poesía Buenos Aires (magazine), 70
"Poesía como juego peligroso, La." *See* Orozco, Olga
Poetic word. *See Logos*
Positivism, 11
Possession, 50, 56, 96, 97
Possession divination, 52
"Presagio, El." *See* Orozco, Olga
"Presentiments in ritual dress." *See* Orozco, Olga
Prophecy, 7, 95, 96, 163
Protochemistry, 43
Psyche, 5, 7, 126, 150
Psyche (Greek concept), 24
Psychology, 50

"Rara sustancia." *See* Orozco, Olga
Rationalism, 43, 54, 97, 126
Reality, 12
Reason/rational thought, 137; rejection of, 11–12
Reintegration, 34–35, 36, 39, 159
Religious tradition, 10, 11, 12, 40, 54; occultism and, 7, 49–50, 55, 78; prohibition against beholding the face of God, 12–13, 19; prohibition against eating of the tree of knowledge, 19
Renaissance, 2–3, 5, 37, 42
Residencia en la tierra. *See* Neruda, Pablo
Rilke, Rainer Maria, 16
Rimbaud, Arthur, 32, 66, 71, 79, 86, 93, 158, 171; alchemy and, 49; belief in poetry as magic, 151; on dark side of the psyche, 7–8; fall from paradise as theme in works, 8; on language, 152; mysticism in works of, 10; on the poet as seer, 7–8, 9, 150; surrealism and, 9–10; transmutation of experience as theme in works, 43. Works: *Les Illuminations*, 8; *Une saison en enfer*, 8, 9, 158

Romanticism, 6, 93, 151, 152, 171; aesthetic principles of, 5, 118; alienation and, 66; English, 173; German, 3, 35, 54, 97, 114–15, 143, 149, 173; hermeticism and, 36; passion for the unknown and, 11

Sade, Marquis de, 74–75, 88, 89, 90
Saison en enfer, Une. See Rimbaud, Arthur
Salvation, 34, 36
San Juan de la Cruz, 4, 159
San Julián el Pobre. See Fijman, Jacobo
Science, 11, 12, 43
Sefamí, Jacobo, 18
Self: disintegration of, 115, 117–18, 119, 120; irrational, 115; loss of, 30; quest for, 44; universe and, 44–45
Seven (number), 63
Shamanism, 7, 59
Shelley, Percy Bysshe, 22
Sleep metaphors, 30
Social structures, 173
Socrates, 96, 132
Song, 72–74
Soul (concept), 24
Spanish Civil War, 17
Speaking in tongues, 52
Spiritualization of matter, 47
"Subcristal." *See* Fijman, Jacobo
"Sub-drama." *See* Fijman, Jacobo
Subversive poetry, 79
"Sueño de la muerte o el lugar de los cuerpos poéticos, El." *See* Pizarnik, Alejandra
Suicide, 66, 98. *See also* Pizarnik, Alejandra
Supervielle, Jules, 101
Surrealism, 93, 137, 144, 149, 173; aesthetic principles of, 11, 12, 16, 70, 102, 127; descent into hell and, 8; foundations of, 10–11; "Generation of 1940" and, 17; influence of, 12; influence of Rimbaud on, 9–10; irrationality and, 97; occultism and, 14; passion for the unknown and, 11; poetics and, 70, 152; quest for the absolute in, 118; rational thought and, 126; rejection of reality, 12; sceptical view of religion and science, 11; techniques of, 99; worldview of, 12
Surrealist Manifesto. See Breton, André
Swedenborg, Emanuel, 5, 97, 151–52, 154, 172, 173
Symbolism: aesthetic principles and, 11; descent into hell and, 8; doctrine of *correspondances*, 37; French, 5, 8, 59; gnosticism and, 24, 26; passion for the unknown and, 11
Sympathetic magic, 54

"Tangible ausencia." *See* Pizarnik, Alejandra
Tarot cards, 52, 53, 57, 163
Tears of Eros, The. See Bataille, Georges
Textos de sombra y Últimos poemas. See Pizarnik, Alejandra
Thénon, Susana, 70
Tierra más ajena, La. See Pizarnik, Alejandra
"Toda azul." *See* Pizarnik, Alejandra
Trabajos y las noches, Los. See Pizarnik, Alejandra
"Tracíon mística, Una." *See* Pizarnik, Alejandra
Transcendence, 34, 71, 147, 149–50, 170
Transcendental consciousness, 30, 31
Transgression/transgressive writing, 75, 76, 98, 124, 147, 155, 166, 167, 168, 170
Transmutation, 42, 46, 48, 49; of the soul, 56; of substances, 43, 44
Truth, 98, 133
Tzara, Tristan, 10

Última inocencia, La. See Pizarnik, Alejandra
Ultimo Reino (magazine), 176n.11
Unconscious, 11, 55, 127
Universal sympathy concept, 44, 49
Unreason, 96, 124, 137–38

Vallejo, César, 17
Van Gogh, Vincent, 98, 162
Visible universe concept, 5
Visions of Excess: Selected Writings, 1927–1939. See Bataille, Georges

"Vísperas de anguistia" (Evensong of anguish). *See* Fijman, Jacobo

Wilcock, Juan Rodolfo, 16
Wisdom divination, 52, 54
World War I, 11, 171
World War II, 17, 77
Wuthering Heights. See Brontë, Emily

Yahni, Roberto, 70

Yeats, William Butler, 43
Yrigoyen, Hipólito, 17

Zen tradition, 133
Zito Lema, Vicente, 102, 103, 123–27, 132–37, 144, 146–47, 153; structure of, 126–27, 146. *See also Pensamiento de Jacobo Fijman, o El viaje la otra realidad*
Zodiac, 178: chap. 3 n.2

Melanie Nicholson is associate professor of Spanish at Bard College in Annandale-on-Hudson, New York. She has published articles and translations in the *Yale Review, Latin American Literary Review, Chasqui,* and *Revista de Estudios Hispánicos.*

OHIO UNIVERSITY LIBRARY
Please return this book as soon as you have finished with it. In order to avoid a fine it must be returned by the latest date stamped below. All books are subject to recall after two weeks or immediately if needed for reserve.

CF